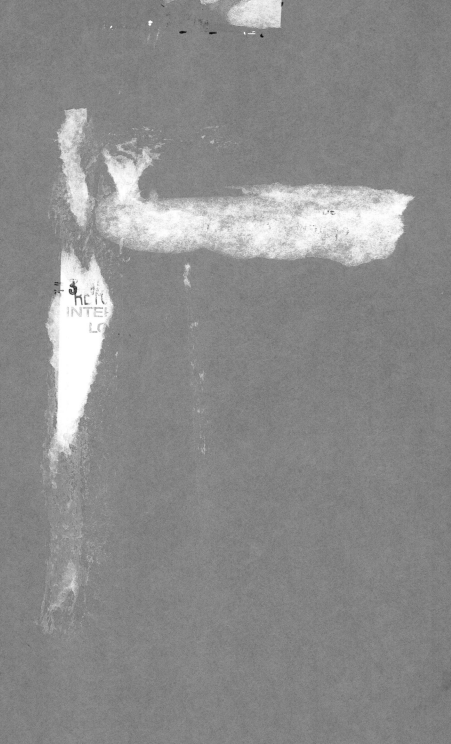

The WIZARD of Oz

THE OFFICIAL 50TH ANNIVERSARY PICTORIAL HISTORY

BY
JOHN FRICKE
JAY SCARFONE
WILLIAM STILLMAN

INTRODUCTION BY JACK HALEY, JR.

Hodder & Stoughton
LONDON SYDNEY AUCKLAND TORONTO

A Book from Puck Productions.
Art direction and interior design by
Michaelis/Carpelis Design Associates, Inc.

British Library Cataloguing in Publication Data

Fricke, John
        The Wizard of Oz: The Pictorial History
        History.
        I. Children's Stories in English. American writers.
        Baum L. Frank. Oz Stories — Critical studies.
        I. Title II. Scarfone, Jay III. Stillman, William
        813'.52
        ISBN 0 340 50848 5

First published in Great Britain 1989

This edition published by arrangement with Warner Books, Inc., New York

Published by Hodder and Stoughton,
a division of Hodder and Stoughton Ltd,
Mill Road, Dunton Green, Sevenoaks, Kent TN13 2YA
Editorial Office: 47 Bedford Square, London WC1B 3DP

CONTENTS

Just fifty years ago, Metro-Goldwyn-Mayer released its three million dollar adaptation of L. Frank Baum's fantasy, *The Wizard of Oz*. The film had taken more than eighteen months to prepare, photograph, and edit, but the final result created a sensation that surprised even MGM.

In the intervening decades, *Oz* has remained both exhilarating and unforgettable to each succeeding generation. Through theatrical engagements and an unprecedented stint as an American television tradition, the film now enjoys a unique, happy hold on the memories and emotions of countless millions of people.

With such fame, the facts surrounding the production of *Oz* have become almost as legendary as the picture itself. Articles, essays, and books have subjected the film and its history to a variety of interpretations, exaggerations, and alterations; the story has been presented by writers whose perspectives have ranged from positive to negative, impassioned to dry, or unimpressed to revisionistic.

It was our original plan to assemble a straightforward picture book rather than repeat again (from any angle) the much-told background saga of the film. There was no previous compilation of that kind, the material could be drawn primarily from our own collections, and many of the most colorful and interesting *Oz* visuals hadn't been seen since 1939. Almost immediately, however, additional research for such a book uncovered literally scores of photographs that had been filed away for years, somehow undiscovered by any other writers or enthusiasts. It was exciting and encouraging for us to suddenly double the number of our prospective illustrations, but putting them in the necessary explanatory context meant once again recounting the tale of *Oz* from its beginnings. That, in turn, became a genuine pleasure when further research led to new information about the film and also pointed out (or cleared up) inaccuracies in famous, accepted "facts" about its inception, development, production, and reception. (Perhaps not surprisingly, MGM's *The Wizard of Oz* evolved in a much more gradual, logical, and chronological manner than implied or stated in some earlier accounts.) Finally, as work continued, we were fortunate to make contact with dozens of collectors, historians, and family members of those principally involved in creating *The Wizard of Oz*. All of them were willing to be part of the growing project.

This book is the result: a complete, concise chronicle of *Oz*, built around hundreds of illustrations and drawn from MGM records and files, the holdings of many institutions and collectors, and the memories of those who actively participated in the film-making process. The emphasis of the history is strictly *Oz*-related; any reader who desires further detail on the workings of the MGM studio system or the cast, staff, and crew of the picture is encouraged to explore the books noted in the bibliography on page 243.

Trying to objectively and honestly trace the definite facts behind *The Wizard of Oz*—fifty years after the fact—has been a labor of love and enthusiasm. But the film itself was produced with love and enthusiasm, and it has been received by more people with love and enthusiasm than any other entertainment. As such, this is a celebration of MGM's *Oz* and a grateful tribute to its continuing power to entrance "the Young in Heart" of all ages.

John Fricke
Jay Scarfone
William Stillman

August 1989

(at left) Jack Haley reads The Wizard of Oz *to his five-year-old son, Jack Haley, Jr., in a 1939 publicity photo.*

Childhood memories can be murky. Like most of us, my memory banks apparently kicked in with a certain clarity somewhere between age seven and eight. The only exception is a particular period during my fifth year on this planet. It was when *The Wizard of Oz* seemed the most important subject in my young life. If a five-year-old could be consumed by an obsession, then Oz was clearly mine.

My father and I enjoyed the time-honored ritual of parent-reading-to-child at bedtime. I knew all about Babar the Elephant and other children's tales. Ironically, I'd listened to and studied the marvelous illustrations of perhaps a half-dozen of the Oz books. And then one day, my Dad announced that he was to play the Tin Man in a movie. What joy! What rapture! From that moment on, I was obsessed with Oz. And probably drove my family crazy.

Soon after Christmas in 1938, my father took me to MGM. I'd been a visitor to movie sets before. I vaguely recall being present at wrap or birthday parties at Fox when Dad appeared in several films with Shirley Temple. But none of that prepared me for my introduction to the *Oz* sound stages.

Munchkinland absolutely stunned me. I had never seen such startling colors or such strangely-shaped dwellings where all these hundreds of curious people lived. For a five-year-old to step into that extraordinary world was mind-boggling. Children today are at least somewhat prepared for their visit to Disneyland. I was definitely not ready for the visual impact of Oz.

Holding tightly to my father's hand, I wandered about the huge set. I was convinced that all those funny little people lived in those funny little cottages. Where else could they live?

Dad introduced me to a very important Munchkin. I could tell by his outfit. They had been friends and probably worked together in vaudeville years before. I shook this person's hand—remember, we were eyeball-to-eyeball—and immediately sensed he was an adult. Despite his strange voice, I got my first clue from the fact he had a luxuriant mustache. Also, he had some breakfast egg stuck in it. A sure sign. Only grown-ups had eggs for breakfast.

While they were reminiscing, I studied this little person's costume. I had never before seen anyone wearing a huge, green-felt, stove-pipe hat. Also, he had a watch and chain. The watch was the size of the biggest alarm clock I had ever seen. That's how I knew this gentleman was a very important Munchkin.

Then my Dad introduced me to Dorothy. Judy was in full makeup and costume. I immediately accepted her as the heroine of the books that had been read to me. Judy Garland *was* Dorothy Gale as far as I was concerned. My father left the set to record a number for the soundtrack. Judy's next set-up was some time away. (Probably the shooting of "Follow The Yellow Brick Road.") To my surprise, she dismissed my governess and announced that she and I would have "tea" in her dressing room.

In retrospect, this was a form of play-acting by a sixteen-year-old who hadn't quite caught up to that phase that ordinary eleven or twelve-year-old girls go through. I barely knew about coffee much less tea. However, the precisely laid-out tea set interested me. The ceremony involved in producing a warm, sweet-tasting drink captured my attention, and Judy took it all very seriously.

Years later—about thirty of them—I produced a television special on which Judy was the guest star. I asked her if she remembered my visit to the *Oz* set. "Yes," she said. "Was I a brat?" I asked. "No," she replied. "You were a doll. A living doll." And so that was all either of us could recall about tea-time with Dorothy.

My brief, but memorable, visit to the *Oz* set is not the only recollection of that intense period of my life. I remember every night climbing up in my father's lap at the end of dinner. Invariably, I would find a tiny particle of silver makeup still on his face and lovingly remove it. These were great moments for me. Evidence that the Tin Man and my Dad were one and the same.

Then came the dark days. They seemed endless to me. My mother tells me it lasted only a week or so. The family's inner sanctum—my parents' bedroom—was sealed off from all light. The only illumination was a low intensity red light bulb—shaded by a towel over the lamp. Here the Tin Man languished while he recovered from an eye infection brought on by his silver makeup.

Dad recovered, finished *Oz*, and went on with his life and career. The movie had no special significance to him for many years. It had been just another assignment. Another job. And a very uncomfortable one at that. When *The Wizard of Oz* was first shown on television, he couldn't have cared less. But as the years passed, he came to realize that this movie would represent the pinnacle of his long and successful career. I suspect he thought there were other efforts more worthy of recognition—but the enduring popularity of *Oz* eventually got to him. He finally joined the other millions who gathered each year to watch the television broadcast of this wonderfully endearing film.

Besides his performance as the Tin Man, he was proudest of a subtle but important quality he contributed to the movie. When the actors reported to a meeting with their new director, Victor Fleming, he asked each of them for their input before shooting began. Dad made a suggestion that Fleming jumped at: the Kansas farm hands should speak in their normal voices but, when they encounter Dorothy in Oz, their intonation should change.

"How? In what way?" asked Fleming.

"Why not have us speak with wonder and awe in our voices?" said Dad.

He then picked up his script and demonstrated what he meant.

Fleming, all smiles now, asked my father, "How did you come up with this idea?"

And Dad replied: "It's the way I read stories to my son every night at bedtime."

Jack Haley, Jr.

This book is dedicated
with admiration and gratitude
to the cast, production staff, crew,
and MGM Studio and Loew's personnel
who—exactly fifty years ago—
gave of their professional best
to make The Wizard of Oz;
and to L. Frank Baum,
who started it all.

The dreams that you dare to dream
really do come true.

The Marvelous Land of Oz

I t began with the bottom drawer of a filing cabinet. Lyman Frank Baum, eight days from his forty-second birthday, sat with his family in their Chicago home on the evening of May 7, 1898. As on many other occasions, he was entertaining neighborhood children with a fairy tale about fantasy characters of his own creation.

Suddenly, the enthusiastic curiosity of one little girl got the best of her. "Oh, please, Mr. Baum," she interrupted. "Where did they live?"

According to Baum family legend, the soft-spoken storyteller glanced around the room until his eyes fell on a filing cabinet. The top drawer was labeled A—N. The bottom drawer was labeled O—Z.

And so was born the marvelous land—a home for Dorothy, the Scarecrow, the Tin Woodman, and the other outlandish, nonsensical inhabitants of Oz invented by L. Frank Baum. Although he couldn't have realized it that night, he had finally (if inauspiciously) discovered the key to the writing career of which he'd dreamed. And he was beginning as well to create a cornerstone in the history of both children's literature and motion pictures. Two years to the day after Baum found the name of his magic kingdom, Chicago presses were printing the first edition of *The Wonderful Wizard of Oz.*

Oz meant the end of Baum's financial struggles. He was born in Chittenango, New York, on May 15, 1856, and grew up in a well-to-do family. But reverses of fortune in the Baum oil concerns and other ill-maintained business ventures left him to his own devices as a young adult. During the final decades of the nineteenth century, Baum was alternately an actor, playwright, poultry expert, purveyor of axle lubricant, store manager, newspaper editor, reporter, and traveling salesman. He sought his careers as far west as Aberdeen, South Dakota, before settling in Chicago with Maud Gage—whom he'd married in 1882—and their four sons. By 1898, he was full-time editor of *The Show Window,* a magazine devoted to the art of deco-

rating store windows and mounting interior displays of merchandise. The preceding year, his first collection of short stories for children had been published as *Mother Goose in Prose;* it was followed in 1899 by a best-selling collection of jingles: *Father Goose, His Book.*

Much of Baum's spare time in 1899 was spent in expanding and writing the story he had told with the "help" of his filing cabinet. When it was finished, he called it *The Emerald City;* it was also known as *From Kansas to Fairyland, The Fairyland of Oz,* and *The Land of Oz* before becoming *The Wonderful Wizard of Oz.* (The adjective was dropped from the title in 1903.)

L. Frank Baum in a portrait circa 1905. (courtesy Peter E. Hanff)

1

If it took until the turn of the century for Baum to get started, his flow of stories then poured forth with seeming grace and speed. Between 1900 and 1919, he authored some thirty books of fairy tales, a like number of "series books" for teenagers, several novels for adults, short stories and verse, scripts and lyrics for several musical shows, and scenarios for silent films. A good proportion of the output centered on Oz, including fourteen full-length children's books.

The Wizard of Oz, as the first and most famous of these, told the story of Dorothy, a little girl whose Kansas home is hit by a tornado. She and her dog, Toto, are transported to a fantasy land and, when the winds deposit their house atop the Wicked Witch of the East, Dorothy is proclaimed a heroine by the tiny Munchkins whom the Witch had enslaved. A Good Witch from the northern section of Oz provides the little girl with the magic silver shoes of the Wicked Witch and advises her to travel to the Emerald City where the Wizard can help her return home. On her trip down the Yellow Brick Road, Dorothy meets a Scarecrow, a Tin Woodman, and a Cowardly Lion, who join her in hopes that the Wizard will grant their requests as well. The Scarecrow wants a brain, the hollow Woodman a heart, and the Lion a measure of courage. The travelers are attacked by the fearsome Kalidahs; the Scarecrow is temporarily stranded in the middle of a river; and Dorothy, Toto, and the Lion fall victim to the potent aroma of a poppy field. The Scarecrow and Tin Man manage to carry the girl and dog to safety, but the Lion is rescued only by the efforts of hundreds of tiny field mice who agree to pull him out of the flowers on a cart built by the Woodman.

When Dorothy and her companions finally reach the Emerald City, each has an individual audience with the Wizard. He appears to Dorothy as a Great Head, to the Scarecrow as a lovely lady, to the Tin Man as a monster beast, and to the Lion as a ball of fire. The Wizard promises to help all of them if they will kill the Wicked Witch of the West.

Despondently, the travelers set out for the Winkie Country at the west of Oz. The Wicked Witch sends wolves, crows, bees, and her Winkie army to conquer them, but only the Winged Monkeys can achieve her goal. The Scarecrow and Tin Woodman are destroyed, the Lion captured, and Dorothy and Toto are taken to the Witch's castle, where the little girl is put to work. The Witch, aware of the power of the silver shoes, steals one of them, and Dorothy throws a bucket of water on her in anger. The Witch melts away, and the girl is free to liberate the Cowardly Lion from his cage in the castle courtyard.

The delighted Winkies help Dorothy to find and re-

pair the Scarecrow and Tin Man, and the quartet and Toto are flown back to Emerald City by the Winged Monkeys. When they enter the throne room of the Wizard, the dog accidentally topples a screen and, behind it, they discover the humbug Wizard, a little man from Omaha. He manages to provide Dorothy's friends with their requested items (although the story all along makes it clear that they already possess what they are seeking), and he agrees to take the Kansas girl home in a hot-air balloon.

But only the Wizard manages to sail away when the balloon is launched, and Dorothy is forced to travel to the Quadling Country to seek help from Glinda, the Good Witch of the South. She and Toto are again accompanied by their three friends and, on this trip, they encounter fighting trees; a land where everything (including the tiny citizenry) is made of china; a giant spider; and a hill populated by odd creatures called Hammerheads. The Winged Monkeys come to their aid once more and carry them to Glinda's castle. The beautiful Good Witch tells Dorothy to tap her heels together three times, and the magic of the silver shoes

David C. Montgomery as the Tin Woodman and Fred A. Stone as the Scarecrow in the record-breaking 1902 musical The Wizard of Oz. *Former vaudevillians, Montgomery and Stone achieved stardom in Oz, ultimately playing in the show for over three years.*

will take her home. Glinda also sends the Scarecrow back to rule the Emerald City, the Tin Woodman to rule the Winkies, and the Lion to a Quadling forest to be King of the Beasts. Dorothy says her final good-byes, clicks her heels, and goes home to her Aunt Em and Uncle Henry in Kansas.

The success of *The Wizard of Oz* encouraged Baum to put the story on the musical stage. Although he wrote a fairly straightforward adaptation of his book, producer Fred Hamlin and (especially) stage director Julian Mitchell reconstructed it from start to finish. Baum's intended extravaganza became instead a wild, gorgeously mounted comic opera, brimming with vaudeville turns and unrelated songs and performers. The show went on to achieve the most noteworthy— if fleeting—fame of any musical at the beginning of the century. After a Chicago opening and tour in 1902, *Oz* moved to Broadway in January 1903 and played in New York for an astounding 293 perfor-mances. It then toured again and was still being pre-sented as late as 1911. Much of the initial success of *The Wizard* was due to the team of David C. Mont-gomery and Fred A. Stone, who appeared as the Tin Woodman and Scarecrow. A vaudeville duo, Mont-gomery and Stone were uproarious and inventive; Stone especially performed amazing acrobatic and physical tricks. He *was* the Scarecrow to tens of thou-sands of theatergoers for the four years he and Mont-gomery stayed in the show, and his performance in *Oz* was remembered for decades afterward.

In addition to his work with *The Wizard* on stage, Baum wrote extensively for children from 1901–1903. But the fame of the musical and continuing sales of the *Wizard* book led to thousands of letters from children who wanted him to tell them more about Oz. His sequel, *The Marvelous Land of Oz,* ap-peared in 1904. (This title, too, would lose its adjec-tive in later printings.) Baum dedicated the book to Montgomery and Stone; its working title had been *The Further Adventures of the Scarecrow and Tin Woodman.*

With the second Oz book, The Reilly & Britton Company became Baum's main publishing outlet and, under that name (and the ensuing Reilly & Lee, begin-ning in 1918), they issued all succeeding Oz books for nearly sixty years. *The Marvelous Land* also saw the first association of Oz and John R. Neill (1877–1943), a Philadelphia artist whose skill, heart, and humor brought genuine beauty and excitement to the people and strange countries he created in pictures. (Two years earlier, Baum had had a falling out with his origi-nal Oz illustrator, W. W. Denslow (1856–1915). Denslow's drawings contributed a great deal to the

(left) John R. Neill illustrated all of Baum's Oz titles but The Wizard, *then went on to picture the titles by Ruth Plumly Thompson. He later wrote and illustrated three Oz books of his own. (below) W. W. (William Wallace) Denslow, illustrator of* The Wonderful Wizard of Oz *and the first person to depict the citizens of the land "over the rainbow."*

success of *The Wizard,* and his highly individual talent was responsible for depicting many of the original Oz characters as they would always be envisioned.*)

Baum's unsuccessful stage adaptation of *The Land of Oz* opened in Chicago in 1905 as *The Woggle Bug.* But its failure did little to inhibit his creative flow, and other books and stories continued to appear. Most of the titles were well crafted and well received; some of

*The original publisher of *The Wonderful Wizard of Oz*, the George M. Hill Company, went out of business in 1902; subsequent editions of that book were produced by the Bobbs Merrill Company.

The first screen version of The Wizard of Oz *was part of Baum's 1908* Fairylogue and Radio-Plays, *but the financial burden of the lavish production forced the author/ producer to close the show after a three-month tour. (courtesy John Van Camp)*

Baum founded the Oz Film Manufacturing Company in Los Angeles in 1914 and produced several "shorts" and at least four full-length features. Three of the latter were fairy tales, and the third of these, His Majesty, the Scarecrow of Oz, *incorporated characters and plot elements from* The Wizard of Oz. *(It was actually released under the title* The New Wizard of Oz *in 1915.) In this still, some old friends are reunited: Dorothy, the Scarecrow, the Wizard, and the Tin Woodman.*

his fantasy writing at that time was clearly the equal of that in *The Wizard of Oz*. Yet whatever notice the books achieved, the children continued to clamor for more about Oz.

So, in 1907, Baum sent Dorothy back for a second visit in *Ozma of Oz*. The next title not only included the little girl but brought back the old humbug himself (*Dorothy and the Wizard in Oz*, 1908), and a fifth book was published in 1909. Finally, in quiet desperation, Baum wrote *The Emerald City of Oz* (1910). An elaborately presented, beautifully produced and illustrated volume, *The Emerald City* was the author's attempt to satisfactorily end the series. Dorothy returned to Oz permanently (with Uncle Henry and Aunt Em) and, after Princess Ozma defeated an attempted invasion by the nefarious Nome King and his villainous associates, Oz was rendered invisible to all outsiders—even its "Royal Historian"—through the sorcery of Glinda the Good.

Baum was finally free to write other fantasies. His major efforts for the next two years were excellent books, but neither *The Sea Fairies* nor *Sky Island* attained the mass acceptance or sales of the Oz stories. About the same time, the author had a new raft of financial difficulties, largely due to debts from an elaborate and expansive stage production he had created in 1908. *The Fairylogue and Radio-Plays* was a combination of hand-colored silent films, slides, live orchestral accompaniment, and narration by Baum himself. The show brought Oz to the screen for the first time, but the undertaking was too costly to return its investment.*

By 1912, Baum's need for assured income (coupled with the ceaseless flow of mail from Oz enthusiasts) led the author to accept the advice of one of his correspondents. A little girl wrote to suggest that, in spite of Glinda's "barrier of invisibility," Baum might reach Oz via "the wireless," the radio/telegraph receivers then coming into common use. In his introduction to *The Patchwork Girl of Oz* (1913), Baum acknowledged that idea and how it had enabled him to reestablish communication with the Emerald City and hear the latest Oz news for publication in a new book.

From then on, he added a title to the Oz series every year through 1920. His other writing continued as well, and he even created another mildly successful Oz stage show, *The Tik-Tok Man of Oz* (1913). Baum also did some additional dabbling in silent film production via his own Oz Film Company in 1914, but distribution problems and difficulties in placing what was rather arbitrarily dismissed as "kids' entertainment" meant an early demise for the organization.

Baum's last two Oz titles were published posthumously. After several years of ill health, the Royal Historian died quietly at his Hollywood home on May 6, 1919. (He and Maud had moved to California in 1910.) Reilly & Lee, however, had no intention of letting the successful Oz series come to an end, and vice-president William Lee approached Ruth Plumly Thompson to continue the tradition of an annual Oz book. She was delighted with the opportunity, as it would ensure a regular income from which to support an ailing younger sister and, eventually, her mother as well. The publishers assured Maud Baum of a royalty for herself or Baum's heirs on any future Reilly & Lee Oz books, and Baum's widow agreed to Miss Thompson's appointment.

Ruth Plumly Thompson (1891–1976) began writing professionally when barely out of her teens, and by 1914 she was contributing a weekly page of children's prose, poetry, and activities to the *Public Ledger* in her native Philadelphia. Her first book, *The Perhappsy Chaps,* was published in 1918; she also contributed to such magazines as *St. Nicholas.* Her first effort for

*William Selig, who produced the *Radio-Plays* film footage, was briefly given the screen rights to the early Oz stories in lieu of reimbursement for his work. In 1910, he released a series of Oz one-reelers: *The Wonderful Wizard of Oz, Dorothy and the Scarecrow in Oz,* and *The Land of Oz.*

Ruth Plumly Thompson was only a teenager when this picture was taken, but she had already begun her writing career. She would eventually pen more Oz books than any other author. (courtesy Dorothy Curtiss Maryott)

Reilly & Lee, *The Royal Book of Oz* (1921), was credited to Baum but "enlarged and edited by Ruth Plumly Thompson." The volume was, in fact, entirely "RPT"'s creation, but the publisher's division of authorship provided an effective transition. Miss Thompson continued adding an annual Oz title to the list for eighteen years. Her final Reilly & Lee book was titled *Ozoplaning with the Wizard of Oz,* an obvious effort to tie in with MGM's *Wizard of Oz* film, released the same year. Miss Thompson authored several other children's books in the 1920s and 1930s and continued to write for magazines through the 1960s. She also answered mail from Oz fans that all but swamped her for the rest of her life.

From 1940 to 1942, the new Oz books were both illustrated and written by John R. Neill, who had been providing the pictures for the series since 1904. His own three titles were rambunctious, wildly plotted, and lavishly illustrated contributions; when he died in 1943, he left the partial manuscript of a fourth volume, *A Runaway in Oz.*

World War II then interrupted the Oz series, and it

A production still from the 1925 Wizard of Oz film; the end product was a wildly original story with little relation to Baum's book. Comic Larry Semon directed the picture and played the Scarecrow. His wife, Dorothy Dwan was a vampish Dorothy, and—a year before the beginning of his celebrated partnership with Stan Laurel—Oliver Hardy was the Tin Man.

wasn't until 1947 that Baum/Oz aficionado Jack Snow contributed *The Magical Mimics in Oz*. Snow (1907–1956) was a radio writer and long-time Baum collector and historian. His second Oz book appeared in 1949, but Reilly & Lee accepted the first effort of a new author, Rachel Cosgrove, for the subsequent *Hidden Valley of Oz* (1951). (Snow's books were illustrated by Frank Kramer [1909–   ], Miss Cosgrove's by "Dirk" Gringhuis [1918–1974].) In 1954, Snow contributed an encyclopedic *Who's Who in Oz* that provided biographies of the characters in all thirty-nine of the Oz books to date.

For the rest of the decade, Reilly & Lee allowed the Oz series to languish. As noted in *The Oz Scrapbook* (1977), the entire series was still officially in print, although several titles were "out of stock." But a major new campaign for the books sprang up after the Henry Regnery Company bought Reilly & Lee in 1959. All the Oz books were reprinted, picture-book abridgments of the first four Baum titles were published, and Jean Kellogg (who adapted the picture books) ghost-rewrote segments of a 1904–1905 Baum newspaper comic page for a new, oversize volume, *The Visitors from Oz*. The five new books were illustrated by Chicago artist Dick Martin (1927–   ), a major force in latter-day Oz bibliography and enthusiasm. Reilly & Lee also published the first book-length biography of L. Frank Baum in 1961. *To Please a Child* was co-authored by Baum's eldest son, Colonel Frank Joslyn

Baum, and Russell P. MacFall, then night editor of the *Chicago Tribune*.

All this Oz activity culminated in *Merry Go Round in Oz* (1963), the first official addition to the series in twelve years. Written by the gifted Eloise Jarvis McGraw (1915–   ) with her daughter, Lauren McGraw Wagner (1944–   ), the fortieth Oz book was also illustrated by Dick Martin.

By the mid-1960s, the publishers' enthusiasm once again began to wane. All but the Baum titles were allowed to go slowly out of print, and eventually those were available only in oversize paperback editions and increasingly difficult to find.* It was left to the International Wizard of Oz Club to provide the next continuations of Ozian history. Founded in 1957 by teenager Justin G. Schiller of Brooklyn, New York, the Oz Club began with sixteen members and a four-page mimeographed newsletter, *The Baum Bugle*. By its thirtieth anniversary, the club had grown to a worldwide membership of twenty-five hundred, and the *Bugle* was a professionally printed "journal of Oz," rich in biography, bibliography, and illustration. The club's vital Special Publications Program led to the appearance of *Yankee in Oz* (1972) and *The Enchanted Island of Oz*

*Fueled by the enthusiasm of Judy-Lynn del Rey, Ballantine/Del Rey paperbacks reissued the fourteen Baum Oz books between 1979 and 1981 and followed those with the first fifteen Thompson titles during 1985 and 1986. The untimely death of Mrs. del Rey in 1986 meant the halt of the Oz project, and the Thompson books were once again out of print by 1988. But Del Rey kept the Baum stories available.

(top left) An oil portrait of L. Frank Baum by Ouilvey, 1908. (courtesy Justin G. Schiller) (top right) This folio was issued circa 1904 and collected some of the Songs Sung in Hamlin and Mitchell's Musical Extravaganza The Wizard of Oz. *The cover shows Fred A. Stone, Anna Laughlin, and David C. Montgomery as the Scarecrow, Dorothy, and the Tin*

Woodman. (above) A poster for the 1902 musical. In addition to Dorothy, the Lion, Tin Man, and Scarecrow, several unique stage characters are also shown: Pastoria, rightful King of Oz, is propped up on the Lion, and Tryxie Tryfle, a Kansas waitress, rests on Imogene the Cow. (The latter served as the musical's substitute for Toto.) (courtesy Barbara S. Koelle)

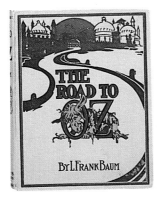

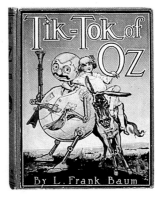

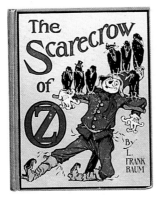

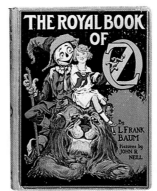
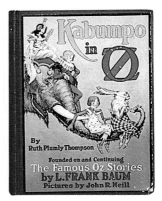

The famous series of Oz books: (first row) 1900, 1904, 1907, 1908; (second row) 1909, 1910, 1913, 1914; (third row) 1915, 1916, 1917, 1918; (fourth row) 1919, 1920, 1921, 1922.

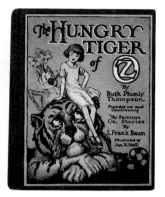

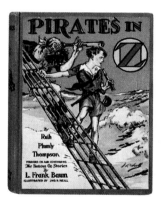

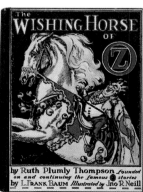

The Oz books from (first row) 1923, 1924, 1925, 1926; (second row) 1927, 1928, 1929, 1930; (third row) 1931, 1932, 1933, 1934; (fourth row) 1935, 1936, 1937, 1938.

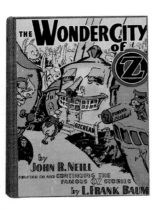

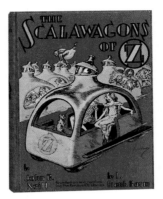

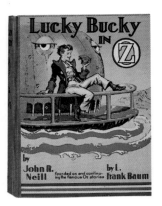

The Oz books from (first row) 1939, 1940, 1941, 1942; (second row) 1946, 1949, 1951, 1963; (third row) the encyclopedia of Oz, Who's Who in Oz *(1954); an adaptation of early Baum newspaper stories,* The Visitors from Oz *(1960); and the books published by the International Wizard of Oz Club: 1972, 1976; (fourth row) 1980, 1986.*

Oz was one of the comparatively early Technicolor features, and all aspects of the production were subject to on-camera testing. This page, and pages 12, 13, 14, and 87, reproduce actual frames taken from the original 35mm film shot during such test moments. (top left) Judy Garland, in her number 3 Dorothy dress and blond wig, in a wardrobe test with Munchkins Nona Cooper, Karl Kosiczky, and Nita Krebs, August 1938. (top right)

Costume and makeup test for a Winged Monkey. (middle left) Frank Morgan tested an ultimately rejected concept for the Wizard on November 16, 1938, along with (middle right) his soldier hat, cloak, and mustache. (bottom) Tests for four Emerald City costumes were made on the Lion's Forest set (probably late November 1938).

In Munchkinland, December 1938: *(top left) The Lollipop Guild (from left: Jackie Gerlich, Jerry Maren, Harry Doll). (top right) Dorothy stands with Coroner Meinhardt Raabe and Mayor Charley Becker. (middle left) The camera prepares for a long shot of cast and set. (middle right) The Munchkins are arranged* *for the finale of their welcome to Dorothy. Victor Fleming stands at extreme left, in profile; choreographer Bobby Connolly, in slouch hat, is just left of center. (bottom left) A colorful grouping of "little people." (bottom right) Billie Burke as Glinda.*

Scenes That Were Never Seen: *(top left) Bert Lahr, Buddy Ebsen, and Ray Bolger in disguise as Guards, October 1938. (top right) A close-up of the Witch near the apple orchard. (middle left) This model was tested as the head of the Great Oz. It proved unmanageable; front-projection photography of an actor's head was utilized instead. Stand-ins of Oz: (middle right)*

Stafford Campbell as the Scarecrow and Bobbie Koshay as Dorothy. (bottom left) Betty Danko as the Wicked Witch. (bottom right) Lahr's stand-in did the athletic first appearance of the Lion, bounding onto the Yellow Brick Road in November 1938.

Making the movie: *(top left) Garland and Haley in the Haunted Forest, January 1939. (top right) A test of the Winged Monkeys in flight. (middle left) A rehearsal of the sequence in which the Scarecrow will be set afire and the Witch will melt. (middle right) Obscuring a technician behind her, Garland* views the footage of Margaret Hamilton in the Witch's crystal. *Some memorable images: (bottom left) The exterior of the Witch's tower was a miniature set. (bottom right) Some of the Witch's most important magical tools: her pestle and mortar and hourglass.*

(1976), both by Ruth Plumly Thompson. Mrs. McGraw and her daughter (writing then as Lauren Lynn McGraw) collaborated on *The Forbidden Fountain of Oz* in 1980 and, finally, Dick Martin—who illustrated all three Oz Club books—wrote and pictured his own *The Ozmapolitan of Oz* in 1986.*

Reilly & Lee did much to promote the Oz books in the 1920s and 1930s, but it was Baum's son, the aforementioned Colonel Frank Joslyn Baum, who expended the most effort to exploit other rights to the stories and characters after his father's death. Colonel Baum had originally hoped to become the second "Royal Historian of Oz" but was in military service overseas when Ruth Plumly Thompson was contracted for the post. His alternate pursuits were not always successful; the first, a series of Oz dolls, failed in 1924. His fantasy, *The Laughing Dragon of Oz,* was issued by Whitman as a "Big Little Book" in 1935 but, when Reilly & Lee sued, Whitman agreed not to reprint the volume and abandoned plans to publish the remainder of the manuscript (already in preparation as *The Enchanted Princess of Oz*).

Many of Colonel Baum's endeavors involved dramatic treatments of the Oz material. As early as 1924, he approached MGM for a possible film deal, but the proposal scarcely reached the negotiation stage. In

*There have also been dozens of other original Oz novels, written by the fans themselves and privately published in everything from typescript/photocopy format to professionally set and illustrated volumes like Onyx Madden's colorful and moving *The Mysterious Chronicles of Oz*.

The Wizard of Oz *served as the basis for a short cartoon in 1933 although, once again, the story drifted from Baum's original.*

1925, he received screen credit—as "L. Frank Baum, Jr."—for his work on the scenario of a silent motion picture version of *The Wizard of Oz*. The film was vastly different from the book on which it was purportedly based. Dorothy appeared as a combination Kansas flapper and lost princess, and the Scarecrow, Tin Woodman, and Lion were seen only briefly as incidental characters in a plot line about court intrigue and romance. The picture was a quick failure, despite the presence and guiding hand of popular Larry Semon as both Scarecrow and director. Like the earlier Oz films, the 1925 Chadwick release virtually ignored the fact that the strong original story and spirit of the first Oz book were major factors in its popularity.

Colonel Baum next licensed the rights for a series of short Oz films, only one of which was actually completed. The unsuccessful *Scarecrow of Oz* (1931) featured a California children's performance group called The Meglin Kiddies.* The following year, Baum sanctioned an Oz cartoon, to be produced by animator Ted Eshbaugh but, when it was finished, legal complications with the Technicolor Corporation precluded its exhibition. (The only fruitful Oz production during the early 1930s was an NBC radio series of fifteen-minute programs for which Maud Gage Baum handled negotiations. The shows were sponsored by Jell-O, incorporated adventures from the first six Oz books, and ran three afternoons a week from September 25, 1933, through March 23, 1934.)

MGM again entered the picture in 1933 when they briefly considered producing an Oz cartoon series, but Colonel Baum begged out of the deal in order to pursue an agreement with Samuel Goldwyn for the specific sale of *The Wizard of Oz* as a musical comedy film. Goldwyn planned to star Eddie Cantor as the Scarecrow, and columnist Louella O. Parsons noted in the *Los Angeles Examiner* (September 27, 1933) that Goldwyn's other casting ideas included W. C. Fields as the Wizard and either Helen Hayes or Mary Pickford as Dorothy. (Miss Hayes was thirty-three years old in 1933. Miss Pickford was forty.) Three months later, the British magazine *Picturegoer* stated that Goldwyn would use the new "three-strip Technicolor" process for his version of *Oz*.

It took Colonel Baum several months to prove to Goldwyn that he had cleared all rights to the *Wizard of Oz* property, and it wasn't until January 26, 1934, that a final contract was established between them.

*Earlier that year, The Gumm Sisters had ended a three-year association with the Meglin School, after appearing in a number of their stage shows and a 1929 film short. Frances, the youngest of the three Gumms, would—by 1935—change her name to Judy Garland.

The cast of NBC's 1933–34 Oz radio program posed for publicity stills although, for the show itself, they were not required to appear in costume. (from left) Nancy Kelly as Dorothy, Bill Adams as the Scarecrow, Jack Smart as the Cowardly Lion, and Parker Fennelly as the Tin Woodman. (Kelly went on to extensive stage and film work; Fennelly's later roles included Titus Moody on the warmly-remembered Fred Allen programs and a long stint as commercial spokesman for Pepperidge Farm products.)

Goldwyn paid forty thousand dollars for screen rights to the first Oz book.

But Eddie Cantor's film career was beginning to wind down by 1934, and the project lay fallow for several seasons. It enjoyed a brief resurgence in 1936 when, after her success in Goldwyn's *These Three,* child actress Marcia Mae Jones was cited as a possible Dorothy. Around the same time, the Fanchon and Marco School of the Theatre announced plans to use the other Oz stories ("23 Frank Baum fables") as vehicles for their own first film releases. The films never materialized but, in April 1937, the "other" Oz books were also considered—this time by MGM—for a possible new cartoon series. An intercorporate proposal suggested that Metro could "rewrite the stories and use the Oz characters to conform with cartoon treatments, injecting the necessary elements to make these cartoons as appealing to the adult trade as to the juvenile trade." Howard Dietz was then in the midst of his thirty-five-year stint as director of advertising and publicity for Loew's, Inc., the New York-based MGM parent company. He researched the idea with "librarians, booksellers, and [our] theatre department" and found much opposition to the idea of Oz cartoons as "they would not appeal to adults."

But later that year the decade-plus of motion picture interest in Oz finally coalesced with several other noteworthy corporate situations in the Hollywood film community. Given the force of the combined events, a motion picture of *The Wizard of Oz,* reasonably true to L. Frank Baum's original story, would finally be brought to the screen.

(on facing page) The "triumphal return" procession was one of MGM's major Oz production numbers. (For the details behind its fate, see pages 118 and 120–122.)

PART ONE
The Oz Diary: Creating a Classic

CHAPTER 1

Acquisition and Casting

In 1937, Arthur Freed was an MGM songwriter. His successes included "Singing in the Rain," "Broadway Rhythm," "You Are My Lucky Star," "Temptation," "Pagan Love Song," "I Cried for You," and "Broadway Melody." But his goal was to produce films, and he specifically sought to start that new career with a picture for fifteen-year-old Judy Garland. The starlet had come to MGM in October 1935 and, after a couple of minor film assignments, had just made a substantial hit in the autumn 1937 release, *Broadway Melody of 1938.*

Ambition at the ready, Freed approached Louis B. Mayer, legendary head of the studio and officially MGM's vice-president in charge of production. Mayer gave a conditional blessing for Freed to pursue an appropriate vehicle for Garland, and the fledgling producer arranged a meeting with agent Frank Orsatti to discuss possible properties. Orsatti not only represented some of Mayer's interests but had served as representative for Colonel Frank J. Baum as well. When Freed mentioned the Oz stories as his own childhood favorites, Orsatti knew that Samuel Goldwyn held the screen rights to *The Wizard.* Freed told the agent to approach Goldwyn for a deal.

An equally important element of the Oz equation came with Mervyn LeRoy's arrival at MGM. After months of negotiation, Mayer had personally hired the director away from Warner Bros. in hopes that he could effectively replace Metro executive producer Irving Thalberg, who had died in 1936. LeRoy's contract with MGM officially began on February 3, 1938, but during their preliminary discussions the preceding autumn, Mayer had asked him what he wanted to produce. One of LeRoy's first suggestions was *The Wizard of Oz;* he had loved the book and stage show as a boy and had dreamed of one day filming the story.

The aspirations of both Freed and LeRoy were suddenly and brightly underscored by the success of Walt Disney's *Snow White and the Seven Dwarfs.* Premiered on December 21, 1937, it was the first full-length animated feature and not only established

Disney and his studios but, virtually overnight, made fantasy and children's stories more palatable to producers than they had ever been before. *The Wizard of Oz*—a hit for thirty-eight years as a book, and a more-than-fondly-remembered stage extravaganza—was a prime follow-up candidate.

Mayer, however, recognized the film as a major gamble and a spectacular, inordinately expensive project. As a result, he felt it would be too enormous an undertaking for Freed's first effort as a producer. Depending on which Hollywood legend is to be believed, Mayer either bought the property for LeRoy and asked him to take Freed on as an assistant, or Mayer authorized purchase of *Oz* for Freed and then suggested he learn production technique under the more experienced LeRoy.

Whatever the exact progression of events, MGM vice-president Eddie Mannix closed for purchase of *Oz* with Sam Goldwyn on February 18, 1938. The deal was not publicized until the following week; on February 19, the *New York Times* noted that the success of *Snow White* had led five film studios to approach Goldwyn to sell *The Wizard of Oz.* Twentieth Century-Fox hoped to use the story as a vehicle for their Shirley Temple, the number-one box office attraction in the nation. But MGM's bid was higher than that of Fox and, on February 24, *Daily Variety* headlined the official announcement: "LeRoy Will Produce 'Wizard of Oz.'" (The day before, the same paper carried an item that heralded Arthur Freed's new position as "production assistant" to "the Mervyn LeRoy Unit at Metro.") MGM paid Goldwyn seventy-five thousand dollars for *The Wizard of Oz,* although it took until June 2 to confirm his legal right to the property; on June 8, Goldwyn got his check.

Even before the initial deal was set, tentative plans for *Oz* had begun at MGM, and by February 1938 the project was growing in scope and in corresponding challenge and conflict. The original hopes of beginning the picture on April 19, April 22, or May 9 came and went, although the studio planned to use *Oz* as a

DAILY **VARIETY** DAILY

FOUNDED BY SIME SILVERMAN
News of the Show World
Published Daily, excepting Sundays
and Holidays
By Daily Variety, Ltd.
Sid Silverman, President
1708-10 North Vine Street,
Hollywood, Calif.
Phone HOllywood 1141

Vol. 18 February 24, 1938 No. 68

Copyright 1938, by Daily Variety, Ltd.
Annual, $10 - - Foreign, $12
Single Copies, 5 Cents
Entered as second class matter Septem_er
5, 1933, at the post office at Los Angeles,
California, under Act of March 3, 1879.

**LeRoy Will Produce
'Wizard of Oz'—**

Metro has acquired the screen
rights for 'The Wizard of Oz' from
Samuel Goldwyn and has assigned
Judy Garland to the role of Dorothy.
Mervyn LeRoy will produce the
Frank Baum childhood fantasy.

The first public notice of MGM's plans for Oz *appeared on page 3 of* Daily Variety, *Thursday, February 24, 1938.*

gala holiday release at the end of the year. LeRoy and Freed encountered delays or time-consuming revision in virtually every major area of preproduction all through late winter, spring, and summer 1938. As a result, it took more than seven months to cast, script, score, staff, and physically create the characters and Land of Oz in Culver City. But if the producer and his associate didn't always thrive on the obstacles, they at least persevered.

As early as January 31, Freed prepared a tentative outline of principal *Oz* players—the first step in what would be a long casting procedure. He forwarded a copy of his memo for LeRoy's consideration on February 10 and, in addition to suggestions for the roles of Dorothy, the Tin Woodman, the Scarecrow, the Wizard, and two witches, Freed also listed two original characters not in the Baum stories: "The Princess of Oz, who sings opera" and "The Prince," to be played by Betty Jaynes and Kenny Baker. That portion of the proposal indicated that Freed and LeRoy were already working together. Baker was a LeRoy protégé, and the producer was also interested in providing a screen vehicle for Jaynes.

Freed's other casting suggestions were drawn from the awesome roster of MGM contract performers. At the top of his list, of course, was Judy Garland, with whom he'd been associated since her first MGM auditions. LeRoy, meanwhile, had been a fan since

Garland's initial feature *Pigskin Parade* (1936) and claimed he felt then that she would be a perfect Dorothy in a screen version of *The Wizard of Oz*.

The teenager was unquestionably right for the role as Freed described it: "An Orphan in Kansas who sings jazz." Her early features often capitalized on her "hot" swing-singing abilities, and her success in *Broadway Melody of 1938* had led to even greater opportunities in a series of rabidly well received radio shows and personal appearances. In February 1938, she was away from MGM on a series of cross-country singing engagements to promote a new film, *Everybody Sing*. Response to Garland "in person" was such that her tour was extended by several weeks and, at Loew's State on Broadway, she brought in business ten thousand dollars above the average weekly gross for that time.

So her star was well in the ascendant, and *Oz* was envisioned from the start as her showcase. When Louella Parsons broke the news of the deal between Goldwyn and MGM in the *Examiner* on February 24, the column headline read "Judy Garland to Play Dorothy in Metro's 'Wizard of Oz' Film." A problem quickly arose, however, in that the New York–based president of Loew's Inc., Nicholas Schenck, was op-

> Sylvan Lake,
> Alberta.
> April 3d, 1938.
>
> Mr. Mervyn LeRoy,
> Producer,
> Hollywood, Cal.
>
> Dear Sir:—
> I am much interested in your proposed production of "The Wizard of Oz." As a child I revelled in the story. As schoolteacher and mother I have read the book often to children and still find it decidedly fascinating.
> I should like to suggest that the characters follow the original illustrations (by W. W. Denslow) as far as possible, in appearance. I think that Toto should be a Scottie and that he should not talk as do the lion, the scarecrow and the tin woodman.
> Sincerely yours,
> Mary H. Hedemark.

Mervyn LeRoy passed this letter along to his associate producer Arthur Freed: a Canadian Oz fan had heard of the proposed production and wanted to offer her suggestions on how the property should be handled.

THE WIZARD OF OZ

The first pictures of Dorothy, Toto, and their Ozian friends were drawn by W. W. Denslow.

posed to the expensive *Oz* project. With no intended slight to Garland, he felt that if the picture was to be made, it would need a completely proven box-office star. Schenck was probably the man responsible for the continual push to borrow Shirley Temple from Fox so that she could play Dorothy.*

Louis B. Mayer understood Schenck's motives and approached Darryl F. Zanuck at Fox about using Temple. Freed—in an at best halfhearted gesture of compliance—even sent arranger/composer Roger Edens over to the rival lot to listen to the ten-year-old sing. She was a charmer, and much closer in age to Dorothy than was Garland—but she was not a prime vocalist. Finally, and not unexpectedly, Fox unequivocally refused to loan their prize attraction to MGM.

According to legend, Schenck next wanted MGM to borrow Deanna Durbin from Universal for the part. (Then there was supposedly talk of using Warner Bros.' Bonita Granville, who had never made a musical.) Perhaps all the furor over "alternate Dorothys" occurred in mid-March, as *Daily Variety* on March 15 did a story on upcoming Metro films and noted that *Oz* would feature "Ray Bolger and an all-star cast." It was the only time the name of Judy Garland did not appear in a press report about the cast of the picture. On the other hand, in spite of years of conjecture,

*There is a popular but probably apocryphal Hollywood legend that Louis B. Mayer offered the loan of Metro's Jean Harlow and Clark Gable to Fox for *In Old Chicago* with the understanding that Fox would reciprocate by loaning Shirley Temple to MGM for *Oz*. If there is any truth in the story, the envisioned *Oz* was a different production than the LeRoy/Freed package. Harlow died on June 7, 1937, several months before LeRoy began negotiations to join Metro.

there was never at any time in 1938 any mention of Shirley Temple or anyone *other* than Judy in the role of Dorothy in either of the trade papers or in any of the daily Hollywood columns of Hedda Hopper, Louella Parsons, or Sidney Skolsky. The LeRoy/Freed battle to assign and assure Judy the role was fought very much behind closed corporate doors.

Freed's January 31 memo next listed Ray Bolger as the Tin Woodman and Buddy Ebsen as the Scarecrow. Both dancers were signed by MGM in the mid-1930s after individual Broadway successes. In 1938, the tall, lanky, thirty-year-old Ebsen had appeared in seven films (compared to Bolger's three), had been tentatively scheduled to work with Judy Garland in a couple of early pictures, and then finally partnered her in the dance finale of *Broadway Melody of 1938*. His assignment to the somewhat larger role of the Scarecrow was thus not surprising. (Some columnists expressed disappointment that Fred Stone was not considered to re-create his Scarecrow, but Stone was sixty-five in 1938.)

The thirty-four-year-old Bolger had loved the Oz stories since he was four and had been drawn to a performing career after seeing Fred Stone in *Jack O'Lantern* (1917). He was delighted to have a part in *The Wizard of Oz* but was "really upset and angry" to be cast as the Tin Woodman. He remembered that, when he signed his MGM contract, there had been a discussion of the kind of roles he would play, and he recalled a "verbal agreement" with the studio that he would portray the Scarecrow if an Oz film was produced. Bolger felt the role would afford him the

When Ray Bolger taped a guest spot for "The Judy Garland Show" TV series in October 1963, he and his hostess reminisced about Oz. Bolger specifically recalled how Bert Lahr initially "fought with the studio. They wanted to give him a five-week guarantee, and he insisted on a six. [They said] five; he said six. They said five; he said six. They settled for six . . . and the picture ran seven months!" ("Every day!" Judy Garland laughed in agreement. "He must have made a lot of money on that! We've got to call him about that!") Item number 6 of Lahr's contract gives actual illustration of the "battle."

METRO-GOLDWYN-MAYER PICTURES
CULVER-CITY
CALIFORNIA

Screen Actors Guild Minimum Contract for Free Lance Players

CONTINUOUS EMPLOYMENT—WEEKLY BASIS—WEEKLY SALARY
ONE WEEK MINIMUM EMPLOYMENT

THIS AGREEMENT, made this **9th** day of **September** , 193 **8** , between LOEW'S INCORPORATED (hereinafter called "Producer"), and **BERT LAHR** (hereinafter called "Artist").

WITNESSETH:

1. ROLE AND SALARY: The Producer hereby engages the Artist to render services as such in the role of **"COWARDLY LION"** , in a photoplay, the working title of which is now " **"WIZARD OF OZ" – #1060** ", at a salary of **TWENTY-FIVE HUNDRED – – – – – – –** Dollars ($ **2500.00**) per week. The Artist accepts said engagement upon the terms herein specified. Wherever in this agreement provision is made for payment to the Artist of an additional day's compensation, such compensation shall be one-sixth (1/6) of the weekly rate.

6. MINIMUM GUARANTEE: The Producer guarantees that it will furnish the Artist not less than **~~SEVEN~~ SIX** (**~~7~~ 6**), week's employment hereunder; and if the foregoing blank is not filled in, then the Producer shall be deemed to have agreed to guarantee to the Artist that it will furnish the Artist not less than one (1) week's employment hereunder. The guarantee in this paragraph set forth shall be subject, of course, to the rights of suspension and termination granted to the Producer in paragraphs 28 and 29 hereof.

In Witness Whereof, the parties hereto have executed this agreement the day and year first above written.

LOEW'S INCORPORATED
(Producer)

Starting on Salary *9/12/38*

By *F. L. Oatis*

Casting Director O. K.

Bert Lahr
(Artist)

---

chance to do in films the kind of dancing he'd done on stage. In 1983, he offered, "I had nothing against Mr. Ebsen at all. I admired him very much; he had a great, wonderful way with his hands, flopping up and down . . . and he danced and he did wonderful, wonderful things. But I thought of the Scarecrow as a man without a brain . . . and it so fitted me . . . [It meant] I could do anything that I wanted to do, all the kinds of steps that I wanted to do."

Until summer 1938, Ebsen was slotted to play the Scarecrow. But Bolger contested the situation: "My wife and I went up to Mr. Mayer's office and Mr.

LeRoy's office and fought and fought and fought." LeRoy finally agreed to switch roles for the two actors, and Ebsen's reaction was, if anything, laconic. When Hedda Hopper asked him in mid-September what he was going to do in *The Wizard of Oz,* the actor drawled, "Suffer, mostly." He'd had a first fitting for the Tin Man's costume a few days before.

There was no mention of a Cowardly Lion in Freed's January memo as there was some doubt as to whether that character could be effectively created for the screen. An early concept of the part saw the animal as only an enchanted version of the Prince of Oz.

By early May, LeRoy was (according to Hedda Hopper) pondering two possibilities: Should the role be played by MGM's Leo the Lion, the roaring trademark animal seen at the beginning of every Metro picture? (If so, his dialogue would be dubbed in.) Or should the Cowardly Lion be played by a man in a costume, as in prior Oz stage and silent-film productions?

Actually, the image of "a man in a costume" had prevailed. An Oz draft script in April had included allusions to a Bert Lahr-esque Cowardly Lion—"Put 'em up! Put 'em up!" That casting possibility was endorsed by the enthusiasm of E. Y. "Yip" Harburg, at that time under consideration for the job of lyricist for the picture. Harburg had worked with Lahr on Broadway and rhapsodized over the kind of material he and partner Harold Arlen could write for the comic. A May 20 Freed-to-LeRoy memo mentions Lahr as if he were set for the picture and, on July 25, Sidney Skolsky announced Lahr's casting in his Hollywood Citizen-News column. (Though the forty-three-year-old actor appeared at Metro for his first costume test on August 29, he didn't sign a contract for Oz until the second week in September.)

Frank Morgan was Freed's January recommendation for the title role of the film. LeRoy's choice, however, was Ed Wynn, then starring on Broadway in Hooray for What! and Harburg, who had written the lyrics for that musical, supported the selection. But when the Wynn show closed in late spring, the Oz script had not been finalized and was missing the "multi-role" format that would enable the same actor to play the Wizard, Professor Marvel, the doorman, the cabby, and the soldier in the Emerald City. The part of the Wizard was augmented only by a five-line appearance as a Kansas doctor in the final scene, and Wynn felt it all too brief and turned it down. (He later, according to LeRoy, expressed much regret at missing out on the picture.)

Although MGM's Wallace Beery put himself forward for the part, LeRoy next went after W. C. Fields, perhaps remembering Goldwyn's prospective casting of 1933. Louella Parsons stated on August 4 that Fields wanted one hundred fifty thousand dollars for the job. Six days later, however, the Hollywood Reporter declared that Fields's commitment to Universal for You Can't Cheat an Honest Man would prevent him from appearing in Oz.

From then on, the role seemed at least momentarily in the grasp of every Hollywood character actor even remotely right for the part. The Reporter piece listed others under consideration, and Morgan was again mentioned, as were Hugh Herbert and Victor Moore. On August 20, Sidney Skolsky wrote that LeRoy had approached Robert Benchley, but Parsons plugged Morgan again on August 29. The Hollywood Reporter confirmed the latter had "the inside track" on September 3, but three days later announced LeRoy was testing Charles Winninger. The situation became almost farcical on September 9 with the report that negotiations had again begun with Fields and that MGM was prepared to pay him the requested one hundred fifty thousand dollars. Louella Parsons added that Fields would actually sign for the film on September 9 or 10.

That contract never materialized. By September 17—and depending upon which column one read— Metro either reneged on the salary or the Universal shooting schedule indeed came up in conflict with that for The Wizard. This time, however, no alternative name other than Frank Morgan was broached. Through all of the rumored casting, he maintained great interest in the film and was apparently always in the running; he was the only actor mentioned in a July script memo that first put forth the concept of "multi-roles" for the Wizard performer.

With the field finally cleared, Daily Variety reported on September 21 that Morgan was doing a screen test for the part. (Oz adapter/scenarist Noel Langley later remembered it as "one of the funniest things I ever saw.") On September 22, the role of the Wizard was assigned to forty-eight-year-old Frank Morgan.

There were two listings for witches in the January 31 memo, and the first of these (simply "A Witch" in Freed parlance) was obviously Baum's Good Witch of the North, whom Dorothy meets in Munchkinland. Freed's suggestion for the part, Fanny Brice, was a contract comedienne at Metro and had just completed Everybody Sing with Judy Garland. Both LeRoy and his assistant producer had in mind at this point a comic opera approach to Oz, more in keeping with the stage musical than with the original book. The celebrated Brice comedy would work well with such a plan.

When Noel Langley came on as a screenwriter several weeks later, he offered another idea. Beatrice Lillie was an equally original Broadway comic presence, and Langley's description of the "North Witch" was at least a nod in her direction: "a . . . kindly, cheerful little woman who chatters very brightly and quickly and puts in a high trill of a giggle when she can find room for it." Some of Langley's dialogue was also a fine approximation of the outrageous Lillie personality: "Nobody could be more pleased than I am that somebody's killed the Wicked Witch of the East at last. I tried hard enough, goodness knows: who hasn't?" and "I'm afraid you've made rather a bad enemy of the Wicked Witch of the West. How I loathe

Denslow's Wicked Witch; Glinda; the Good Witch of the North; the Munchkins and the Wizard.

that woman!" But Lillie was involved in the London musical revue *Happy Returns* so, on September 12, Louella Parsons announced that Billie Burke, another Metro character comedienne, would play the Good Witch. The role had by then been amalgamated with Baum's Glinda, the beautiful Good Witch of the South, and Burke was an ideal choice for the MGM combination of characters. She had been a famous stage beauty two decades earlier and now, at fifty-three, was known for her slightly daffy screen characterizations. That image would also dovetail well with a portion of the Langley dialogue.

Edna Mae Oliver was the name Freed penciled in as "Another Witch" on his January 31 listing but, by May 20, another Freed memo indicated that the decision on her casting had still not been made. Over the next few months, at least two other actresses were considered for the role of the Wicked Witch, and one of them actually tested for the part. Margaret Hamilton had come to Hollywood in 1933 when she was

thirty-one; her first film, coincidentally at MGM, saw her in a reprise of her Broadway role in *Another Language.* In the next five years, she did supporting roles in twenty-five pictures. While only three of these were for Metro, she was on the Culver City lot making *Stablemates* in summer 1938 and was asked to test for the role of the Witch. In 1983, with wry warmth and self-awareness, Miss Hamilton recalled the events leading up to her audition. She had always

adored *The Wizard of Oz.* I'd had it read to me when I was four years old; my mother bought it for me. But it never occurred to me I'd ever be the Witch . . . (*Dorothy,* maybe! . . .) But one day [my agent, Jess Smith] said, "They're sort of interested in you for a part in *The Wizard of Oz.*"

I said, "Oh, gosh! Think of that! I've loved that story from the time I was four years old! What part is it?"

And he said, "Well . . . the Witch."

And I said, "The *Witch*?!"

And he said—the final thing—"Yes . . . what else?"

Well, I thought, "That's kind of an exciting part but, gee . . . " I had my eyes on something else. (I don't know what it *was* exactly, but I didn't think about the Witch! However, I *ought* to have, because I'd had my nose quite a long while!)

And so I went in one day, and I was interviewed by the man who was second in line. I had usually gone to the third or fourth [casting assistant for interviews] and, to my amazement, it was the second. I thought, "Things are looking up!"

And he said, "How do you feel about playing the Witch?"

And I said, "I feel *great* . . . if I get it."

And he said, "Well, we're thinking about it . . . we'll get in touch with your agent."

And that's the final line sometimes. They never get in touch with your agent or anyone else.

But the necessary arrangements were made for a test. Margaret Hamilton had already played the Wicked Witch in community theater productions of *The Wizard of Oz* and, for her MGM audition, commandeered some raggedy costume pieces from wardrobe and a prop broom. Then she waited—until Saturday, August 20 when she read in the trades that the role had gone to Gale Sondergaard.

The year before, Sondergaard had been presented with the first Academy Award ever given in the Supporting Actress category. She was honored for her performance in *Anthony Adverse* and, as that film had been directed by Mervyn LeRoy, it wasn't surprising that he thought of her for *The Wizard of Oz*. Hamilton reacted with customary quiet acceptance: "I really did feel good for her. I thought it would be great . . . except I just couldn't see her as the Witch. She was—still is—a perfectly beautiful person."

What Margaret Hamilton didn't know was that the early script concepts of the Wicked Witch had drifted from that of a nasty but near-comical woman to one who was decidedly evil and sinister—but frighteningly beautiful. LeRoy was undoubtedly influenced by the success of *Snow White's* evil queen, whose high-style, high-cheekboned appearance was effectively contrasted by her hateful machinations. The thirty-nine-year-old Sondergaard was ideal for the newly glamorous but still Wicked Witch of the West.

The remaining names on Freed's January 31 memo were the aforementioned Kenny Baker and Betty Jaynes. Baker was further noted as one of the *Oz* leads in a *Hollywood Reporter* item on March 1. But his role, rewritten first from that of a prince to a grand duke then back to a prince, was finally written out of the script altogether. By June he was en route to London to film *The Mikado* for Universal. Jaynes's part in *Oz* was subject to the same fate, although the proposed vocal contrast between her opera and Judy Garland's "jazz" was merely tabled until the two girls shared a duet in the 1939 film *Babes in Arms*. (LeRoy also planned to team Garland and Jaynes in a screen version of *Topsy and Eva*, but the production was abandoned while still in development.)

It was February when Freed noted that Leo Singer was to be MGM's liaison for the many midgets required to play the Munchkins. Singer headed up a successful vaudeville troupe of little people, and he was both entrepreneur and occasional opportunist. He initially agreed to supply his own group of thirty midgets as a nucleus for the Munchkins and then supplement them with seventy others. In July, LeRoy also interviewed as many little people from the Los Angeles area as he and Singer could find. Those appropriate for the picture began fittings for Munchkin costumes late that month. Hedda Hopper reported in the *Los Angeles Times* on August 5: "The midgets . . . frightened the life out of the desk girl. She heard voices but saw no one—until she got up and leaned over the desk and, looking down, found three midgets."

Singer's deal with Metro was legally briefed on October 1. By that time, he had promised to supply a total

September 30, 1938

Following is a resume of the deal with Leo Singer for "The Wizard of Oz":

(1) He to furnish 124 midgets, salary $100.00 apiece, per week.

(2) Starting date of the midgets is on or about November 11th. In the event unforeseen circumstances prevent starting November 11th, the midgets will receive half-salary until not later than November 22nd, when they will start full salary.

(3) Singer leaves this week to pick up midgets, for which we are to pay his railroad transportation and, in New York and Chicago, provide him with a car.

(4) Singer's deal with us at present is $100.00 per week until the picture starts, $200.00 thereafter. I suggest that, in lieu of expenses for Singer while he is on the road picking up midgets, that we start him at $200.00 per week, this salary to start upon his leaving town.

(5) We to provide Singer with a block season ticket, in other words, a floater. He pays for all side trips and renders us an account.

Vaudeville manager Leo Singer agreed to contract the Munchkins for MGM; his deal was summarized in this letter.

A Denslow Winged Monkey.

dant. Walshe was a veteran vaudeville animal impersonator.

The final member of the *Oz* principal cast was the subject of a search that also lasted until nearly October. On September 1, Alta Durant gave notice in her *Daily Variety* column that LeRoy was still looking for "a Scottie, a well-educated one, a dog intelligent enough to follow Judy Garland through several sequences of *The Wizard of Oz*." The producer had at that point seen "every other known brand of canine with really remarkable IQs . . . but thus far no Scottie with sufficient education." Enter Terry! Trainer Carl Spitz had a female Cairn terrier in his stable of "movie dogs," and she had already performed on screen. When he took Terry over to MGM, they were overjoyed.

At long last Toto.

of 124 midgets, and the studio agreed to pay his transportation expenses in the cross-country search for the little people. Singer's salary was one hundred dollars per week from September 1 to October 4. (After that, he was to be paid two hundred dollars per week until the completion of the Munchkin portion of the picture.) Metro also stipulated that the manager would "assist us in handling & directing [the] midgets . . . "

The little people were due in Culver City by November 11. Singer was allotted fifty dollars salary per week for each midget during their initial work in Hollywood on wardrobe and makeup tests. The salary would jump to one hundred dollars per week when actual rehearsals began for the Munchkinland segment, and the little people were guaranteed three weeks' work. Singer set off in early October to finalize arrangements with as many midgets as he could locate and interest.

For the roles of Dorothy's Aunt Em and Uncle Henry, Freed first slated May Robson and Charles Grapewin. The latter was actually announced for his part on August 12. Shortly thereafter he decided to retire from the screen, and the producers tabled final decision on the assignments until late autumn. The Kansas sequences were planned for the final stages of the shooting schedule and, given all the other production delays, there was no rush.

Metro contract player Mitchell Lewis was selected in late summer to serve as Captain of the Winkie Guard, adjunct to the Wicked Witch and overseer of her soldiers. On October 4, the studio announced it had imported Pat Walshe to play Nikko, commandant of the Winged Monkeys and the Witch's confi-

CORNWALL COLLEGE
L R C

25

CHAPTER 2

Scripts, Songs, and Staff

Though there was manifest enthusiasm for *The Wizard of Oz* in every creative department, MGM had great difficulty in deciding just how to approach the story for the screen. A multitude of theories, treatments, scenes, and scripts were presented to the producers between February and October 1938. It's hard now to determine whether the film was delayed by the efforts to achieve a workable screenplay, or whether complications in other areas of the production provided the time to work and rework the scenario. The first versions of MGM's *Oz* were crammed with extraneous new characters and situations; fortunately, the longer the writing went on, the more excess was trimmed away. The simplicity of the original story and its themes was gradually brought to the fore, but getting "back to Baum" was a long and sometimes arduous task.

Despite the success of *Snow White,* Metro was concerned that movie audiences would reject the idea of human beings as nonhuman fantasy characters. William Cannon, Mervyn LeRoy's assistant, was put to work to somehow eliminate that problem and, on February 26, he submitted a four-page precis on *The Wizard of Oz* and the creation of "a fairyland of 1938 and not 1900." Cannon envisioned Oz as a country possessing modern conveniences and contrivances, with backgrounds and scenery "modernized . . . to appeal to the modern person's idea of a fairyland." Cannon also felt that fantasy magic, used many times in the book, should be displayed only sparingly in the film, "especially when . . . used with human beings."

Finally, he wanted to eliminate the entire concept of a living Scarecrow and Tin Woodman and went through a lengthy explanation of how that could be accomplished: "The Scarecrow Man will [instead] be a human being dressed like a Scarecrow . . . a man so dumb that any job they tried to give him, he couldn't do. So [the people of Oz] finally decided that, if he couldn't think, he must not have a brain. The only thing they could find for him to do . . . that didn't require any thinking, and that a person without a

brain could do, was to stand in the middle of a field and be a scarecrow." Cannon's Tin Man, too, would be "a human being in the tin suit . . . a man who was always getting into fights—telling people what to do and doing nothing himself . . . thinking only of himself." The people of Oz decide that such a man must not have a heart, so they "put him in a suit of tin . . . and let him spend the rest of his days cutting down trees all by himself."

In Cannon's version, the Wizard is revered as the greatest man in the country, and everything he says is right. Both the Scarecrow and Tin Man agree that, if the Wizard would only say they have brains and a heart, "everyone in the Land of Oz would believe it."

Cannon's rationale was quickly rejected by LeRoy and Arthur Freed. Their film would have to be a fantasy and as faithful to the Oz story as possible. A rumor went around Hollywood in early March that the producers even approached Walt Disney to come briefly to MGM on an outside deal to supervise the *Oz* script. Disney's participation never materialized; instead, a steady procession of writers began to work on the project. (Cannon would be the first of fourteen.) If Freed and LeRoy couldn't write the screenplay themselves, they could—once provided with written pages—creatively edit the material. Freed was especially good at this.

The first week of March, LeRoy gave Irving Brecher the job of scripting *Oz.* He was pulled off almost immediately and assigned instead to do a treatment of the producer's *At the Circus* for the Marx Brothers. By March 7, Herman Mankiewicz was on the picture and, during three weeks of work, contributed a rough summary and an incomplete script of the first portion of the film.

The Mankiewicz version was a somewhat uneasy amalgam of the Oz book and comic-opera stylistics. He painted a picture of Kansas very much influenced by Baum. Mankiewicz's prairie is a vast, gray expanse of land, and Aunt Em and Uncle Henry are "worn by toil" and laugh and smile only in connection with

The Princess Betty, surrounded by a half
dozen beautiful young women of her court, is
standing there with the Grand Duke Alan. I
don't think that these people can dare look
like Munchkins. They should be American in
appearance, like Dorothy.

Betty

Here she comes, Alan -- the ~~magnificent~~ little girl
who has made it possible for me to be with you
again.

Alan

For me to be with you again, you mean.

Betty

Isn't that the same thing?

Alan

Oh, no. It can't be a particular treat at all for
you to be with me -- but for me to be with you --
I really can't believe we are together again.

Betty

We're never going to be apart again.

Betty and Alan sing a simple love song.

At its conclusion, the coach pulls up.

Alan rushes forward and hands Dorothy out
of the carriage.

Dorothy

I've only been with the Munchkins a little while,
and I know everything is very peculiar here, but
you're not the Princess Betty, are you?

A page from the Herman Mankiewicz Oz script, dated March 1938. Part of the premise of his original Ozian subplot called for a musical contrast between jazz as sung by Dorothy and opera as sung by a new character, Princess Betty of Oz. (Jazz was then the all-encompassing descriptive word given to popular "hot" music; the same "Opera vs. Jazz" idea had been utilized for Garland and Deanna Durbin in 1936 in both an exhibitor's short and in the MGM one-reeler, Every Sunday.*) In the Mankiewicz version, Dorothy's house fell on the Wicked Witch of the East and not only freed the Munchkins but liberated the captive Princess as well.*

Dorothy. The heroine is first seen crossing the plain and singing "a happy song full of homely allusions to the simple properties and concerns of her simple daily life." The subsequent family dinner is interrupted by the arrival of a lost limousine, and its passengers—a haughty woman, her equally haughty daughter, and a Pekinese—spend several pages of dialogue at the farm to little purpose other than the revelation that Dorothy is an orphan. (When the limousine pulls away, Dorothy seriously confides in Aunt Em, "I wish you'd seen that little girl just now . . . I felt so sorry for her. She hasn't got an aunt at all; only a mother.")

The cyclone strikes, and Aunt Em and Uncle Henry enter the cellar through a trapdoor in the kitchen

floor; Dorothy chases Toto (who has run under the bed), and they are left in the house when it is picked up by the storm. As in Baum's book, the dog falls through the open trapdoor, but the wind keeps him aloft until Dorothy can pull him safely into the room. When the house crashes into Munchkinland, Mankiewicz cues in a celebratory musical production number, and Dorothy receives the silver shoes of the Wicked Witch of the East from the Good Witch of the North. The scene is also interlarded with moments created for "Princess Betty" Jaynes and her musical amour, the Grand Duke Alan (Kenny Baker). They are eventually dispatched to the lair of the Wicked Witch and end up singing to each other from separate cages in her courtyard.

The Mankiewicz Witch of the West does not appear in Munchkinland but is shown behind an office-like door in her own castle. She keeps twenty ferocious wolves as pets but is as much a comic villain as an evil one, and her manner seems occasionally more offhand than vehement or vindictive. When she

A DOOR,
like an office door, with an upper half of
frosted glass. On it is painted, like the
name of a law firm:

"WICKED WITCH OF THE WEST

Cruelties, Tortures
and all kinds of
Devilments

Decent People Keep Out !

This Means You !"

DISSOLVE TO:

INTERIOR OF THE ROOM.

The Wicked Witch of the West is seated
behind an enormous desk, like an American
businessman's desk, which is the only article
of furniture in this very large and dismal
room. A trembling little man -- a Munchkin,
but not one of the three in the previous scene
with Dorothy -- is standing in front of the
desk. The Wicked Witch has only one eye.

Wicked Witch

What do you mean, a house fell on the Wicked Witch
of the East?

Munchkin

(in tiny voice)

But a house did fall on her.

Mankiewicz treats the Wicked Witch of the West as more comic and cantankerous than threatening and evil, perhaps in keeping with the original idea of casting character actress Edna Mae Oliver in the part. That popular veteran was suggested as the Witch by Arthur Freed as early as January 1938—and he was still suggesting her four months later.

hears about the fate of the Witch of the East, she rhetorically asks her evil Munchkin assistant, "What was she doing standing around where a house could fall on her? It's things like this that sometimes make me feel like giving up the witch business completely." When the Munchkin spy displeases her, the West Witch threatens to destroy him "utterly . . . I'm going to sneeze you and your whole family right off the face of the earth."

Mankiewicz uses much of Baum's dialogue to send Dorothy off to see the Wizard and in her subsequent meetings with the Scarecrow, Tin Woodman, and Lion. There is also an indication of the quiet, pointed humor that would be a solid part of the film's success. When Dorothy is confronted by the Scarecrow and his request, she comments to Toto, "You see the difference between Kansas and here, Toto? Here, if you've got no brains, they stuff you and make you a scarecrow—but back home, Uncle Henry used to say that if you had no brains, you could always go to work for the Government." The Scarecrow and Tin Man both indulge in some light terpsichore at their initial meetings with the girl from Kansas, which leads Dorothy to ask, "Does everybody in this country dance when he's happy?"

The trio and Toto meet the Cowardly Lion, who talks (but not like Bert Lahr) and walks on all fours. He gives the dog a ride on his back and carries all the travelers over a gulf that intersects the Yellow Brick Road.

Even while Mankiewicz was writing, LeRoy had Ogden Nash and Noel Langley at work as well. (It was common practice in Hollywood for several writers to simultaneously and sometimes unknowingly work on the same project.) Mankiewicz was dismissed at the end of March, and Nash contributed nothing usable during his stint on the picture. But Langley ultimately received screen credit for his adaptation of *The Wizard of Oz* and co-credit for the screenplay. He warranted the billing; between March and June, he authored four scripts derived from his first treatment.

It was Langley who convinced Freed and LeRoy that some of the Oz characters should first be established as Dorothy's acquaintances in Kansas (an idea he might have, at least in part, lifted from the 1925 *Wizard* movie, wherein Larry Semon and Oliver Hardy appeared as farmworkers before donning their disguises in Oz). Langley thus created Hunk and Hickory, the farmhands who become the Scarecrow and Tin Woodman, and Mrs. Gulch, who comes to take Dorothy's dog to the sheriff and turns up in Oz as the Wicked Witch.

The writer went on to develop the montage of airborne travelers who passed by Dorothy's window up inside the cyclone; a Cowardly Lion who spoke in best Bert Lahr parlance; a grove of fighting apple trees, similar to some in the Baum book; and a deadly poppy field from which Dorothy and her companions were saved by the Good Witch. (In Langley's earliest treatment of the scene, the Good Witch summoned Jack Frost to snow down the flowers, much as the Good Witch "Locasta" summoned the Frost King for the same purpose in the 1902 musical.)

He also contributed scenes involving a talking Horse-of-a-Different-Color: an animal with "red zebra stripes, purple and green skin." (In a later draft, the writer gave the horse a cabby to take over the dialogue.) It was Langley who provided Toto with the opportunity to reveal the Wizard hiding in the throne room; who then let the humbug magician attempt a return to the United States in a balloon; and who finally brought in the Good Witch to explain to Dorothy the magic of her slippers, sending her back to Kansas with the phrase, "There's no place like home." He also wrote Dorothy's wondrously affecting good-byes to her three companions and, in the last scene, gave the Wizard a Kansas counterpart as a doctor called in to treat the dreaming girl. (It was apparently Langley who encapsulated the Oz portion of the picture as Dorothy's dream, perhaps in a conscientious effort to pave the way for fantasy a 1938 audience could find believable. He was responsible as well for the dedication at the beginning of the movie and for changing the magic footwear of Baum's book from silver shoes to ruby slippers. The latter would better show off the Technicolor photography.)

Many elements of Langley's adaptation and early scripts provided a solid framework for the film. But some of his other ideas were unusable, whether he was contributing original material or trying to make the best of a situation presented to him (i.e., the necessity of roles for Jaynes and Baker). He gave bizarre twists to some aspects of the story and characters; in one version, he manufactured a budding romance between Dorothy and Hickory, the farmhand who was originally to become the Scarecrow (as played by Buddy Ebsen). At the very end of the script, Hickory is sent off to agricultural college, and Dorothy has an awkward but poignant farewell with him at a Kansas train depot. Langley also had Hickory search for Dorothy during the cyclone and lift her gently onto her bed when she was knocked unconscious. In another draft, Langley's Tin Woodman was something of a womanizer and even gaped lovingly at the Good Witch of the North; he also carried his oil can as one would a hip flask. Finally, the writer limited the travelers to one

```
432        FULL SHOT - TRUCK SHOT - STATION PLATFORM

           Dorothy, Hickory and Hunk marching towards
           CAMERA singing Kansas song. Hickory is dressed
           in his Sunday best and carries a carpet bag.
                                              WIPE TO:

433        FULL SHOT - STATION PLATFORM

           Bell rings as train comes into siding.
                                              WIPE TO:

434        CLOSE SHOT - INT. COMPARTMENT

           Hickory and Dorothy are taking luggage handed
           in through window by Hunk.
                        Hunk
           There's one more bag up by the ticket-office -
           hold the train while I get it!
                    (he runs off)

                      Dorothy (proudly)
           Gee, I'm so proud of you going to college, Hickory!
           You will write every week, won't you?

                      Hickory
           You know I will, Dorothy.  Guess I'm going to
           kind of miss you.

                      Dorothy (diffidently)
           I'm going to miss you too, Hickory.

                      Hickory (diffidently)
           Well, I...I'll write every week.

                      Dorothy
                    (with a sudden burst of confidence)
           Hickory, I've been meaning to tell you.  When
           I was up in Oz....
                    (she stops self-consciously)

                      Hickory
           Up in where?

                      Dorothy
           I guess it doesn't matter.  There'll be plenty
           of other times when I can tell you.  But that
           was where I found out how much I'm going to
           miss you.
```

```
434        CONTINUED (2)

           Sylvia and Kenny come to window.

                      Kenny
           Hi, Hickory - have you got room in there for us?
                    (holding up Sylvia's hand)
           See the ring?

                      Dorothy
           You mean old Gulch's given in at last?

                      Kenny
           No! - We're eloping!

           They hurry from window.

                      Dorothy
                    (half shame-facedly, after a pause)
           Mushy.

                      Hickory (awkwardly)
           Yeah.
                    (the train gives a lurch)
           Say, you'll have to be getting off!

                      Dorothy
           Yes.
                    (suddenly and very gravely she puts
                    her arms round Hickory and hugs him)

435        CLOSEUP - HICKORY AND DOROTHY

                      Hickory
           I guess I'll miss you most.
                                              WIPE TO:

436        LONG SHOT - ROAD OUTSIDE STATION

           Mrs. Gulch and Walter come peddling down
           the street as Dr. Pink goes up it in his
           buggy.

437        CLOSE SHOT - MRS. GULCH, WALTER

                      Mrs. Gulch (furiously)
           Faster, faster, Walter!
```

```
438        LONG SHOT

           They hit Dr. Pink's buggy and the bicycle
           turns over; hits a water-trough, and in
           go Mrs. Gulch and Walter.

439        FULL SHOT - PLATFORM

           Train is pulling out.  Hickory and Sylvia
           and Kenny wave from windows to Hunk and
           Dorothy on platform.

440        CLOSEUP - DOROTHY HUGGING TOTO

           There is a smile on her face and tears in
           her eyes as she sings the last two lines
           of the Kansas song.


                      THE END
```

visit to the Emerald City, where the Wizard immediately granted their requests. Then, as Dorothy waited to be taken back to Kansas in his balloon, she was captured by the Winged Monkeys. The Scarecrow, Tin Man, Lion, and Wizard took off with the Horse-of-a-Different-Color to rescue her from the Wicked Witch (and, en route, passed Baum's Dainty China Country from the Oz book).

Langley wrote in as well extrinsic suggestions for several musical numbers: a song about Oz for the farmhands to sing to Dorothy; a rebuttal song from Dorothy about the superiority of Kansas; and an interlude for the Scarecrow and Tin Woodman to sing and dance in the poppy field.

Above all, the scripts were padded by the activities of nonessential characters. These included:

- Mrs. Gulch's niece, Sylvia, and her beau, Kenny. In Oz they became Princess Sylvia and Prince Florizel, though Langley later renamed the hero Kenelm or Kenelin. Under any name, the prince was turned into the Cowardly Lion by the Wicked Witch. He managed to break the spell by performing a brave deed, and then he (not Dorothy) killed the Wicked Witch.

- Mrs. Gulch's son, Walter. He became the

In one of Noel Langley's early script treatments (April 1938), he kept the film plot going after Dorothy's return to Kansas. Farmhand Hickory is off to agricultural college, and there are slight intimations of a brewing romance between him and the teenage Kansas girl. Meanwhile, Mrs. Gulch's niece is running away with a beau and, when the bicycle-pedaling woman (and her son Walter) give chase, they collide unexpectedly with the carny wagon of Dr. Pink (an early incarnation of Professor Marvel). Dorothy bids farewell to Hickory from the train station platform and sings a reprise of her Kansas song (at that point, Roger Edens's "Mid Pleasures and Palaces").

Wicked Witch's son, Bulbo, and much of Langley's action was devoted to the Witch's attempts to conquer Emerald City and make Bulbo the King of Oz. (Bulbo would then marry Princess Sylvia.) At first Bulbo's Kansas incarnation was to be Uncle Henry.

● Lizzie Smithers, a Kansas farm helper. She provided love interest for farmhand Hunk/the Tin Woodman (at this point still to be played by Ray Bolger). In Oz she also served as assistant to the Wizard.

● a dragon (who in later drafts became a gorilla, then a lion). This was the beast the Cowardly Lion had to fight to prove his courage and again become the Prince of Oz.

Aiding Langley in the needed revisions from script to script was the gentle but insistent prodding of Arthur Freed. On April 25, when Langley was deep into rewrites of his first draft, Freed dictated a long memo that clearly demonstrated his understanding of the components necessary to make the film a popular success:

The main objective above everything else is to remember that we are telling a real story. In Kansas, it is our problem to set up the story of Dorothy, who finds herself with a heart full of love, eager to give it but, through circumstances and personalities, can apparently find none in return . . . She finds escape in her dream of Oz. There she is motivated by her generosity to help everyone first before her little orphan heart cries out for what she wants most of all (the love of Aunt Em) . . . Too much stress cannot be placed on the soundness of the sentimental and emotional foundation of this story, because it is only against such a canvas the novelty and comedy and music of our venture can ever mean anything. When we get to Oz, there must be a solid and dramatic drive of Dorothy's adventures and purposes that will keep the audience rooting for her.

None of our treatments have conveyed this and, once this is done, I feel we have licked our biggest problem. Music can be a big help properly used as an adjunct and accent to the emotional side of the story . . . The whole love story in *Snow White* is motivated by the song "Some Day My Prince Will Come" as Snow White is looking into the well. Dialogue could not have accomplished this half as well. I make this illustration for the purpose that we plant our *Wizard of Oz* script in a similar way through a musical sequence on the farm. Doing it musically takes all of the triteness out of a straight plot scene . . .

I think, also, that the Wicked Witch must be more of an antagonist to Dorothy's problem and, to a far greater extent, the Wizard's problem with the Wicked Witch should be secondary to Dorothy's. We must remember at all times that Dorothy is only motivated by one object in Oz; that is, how to get back home to her Aunt Em, and every situation should be related to this main drive . . .

I would like to repeat again the urgent necessity of getting a real emotional and dramatic quality through the Oz sequences. I would like to see Dorothy in some spot in Oz with her companions utterly crestfallen and lost with a complete feeling of despair. Therefore, I believe at this time, we should go into this phase of the story very fully so that, when the picture is over, besides our laughs and our novelty, we have had a real assault upon our hearts.

The memo also queried the necessity for the dragon in the Witch's castle, the logistics of creating the Winged Monkeys, and the value of Sylvia and Kenny ("their story should in some way affect Dorothy's life and the fulfillment of her desires in order to give it any dramatic interest").

Freed's contributions were invaluable; virtually all of his suggestions were eventually followed, either by Langley, subsequent scenarists, or the songwriters.

By Langley's final, June 4 script, Sylvia, Kenny, and Lizzie Smithers were all gone. Dorothy and her friends made two trips to the Emerald City (as in the Oz book) and in between they traveled to the Witch's castle, where the Kansas girl melted the Witch (who had hit Toto with her broom).

But there were still flaws as well. The plot to conquer the Emerald City remained intact, and both the Wicked Witch and Mrs. Gulch were saddled with a peevish son. Dorothy and her companions were forced to form a slapstick human pyramid to sneak into a rear palace window in their first attempt to see the Wizard and, at the end, a woodpecker destroyed the Wizard's balloon before he and Dorothy could depart for Kansas.

Langley thought the June 4 script had been accepted as the final screenplay. But LeRoy and Freed were still dissatisfied and, that same first week of June, brought in two more writers. Florence Ryerson and Edgar Allan Woolf remained on the picture for two

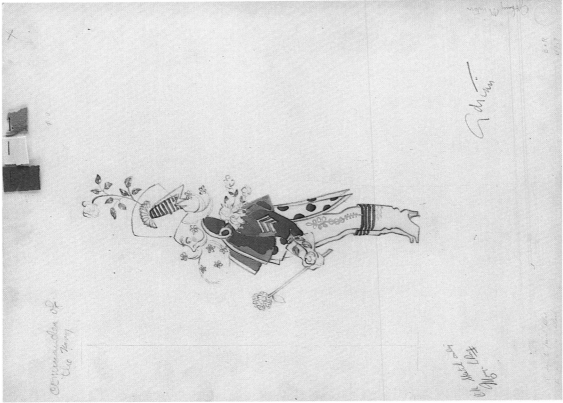

(above and below) Four of the original watercolor costume designs for Oz Munchkins, drawn by Adrian in 1938. The signature of Mervyn LeRoy "okayed" the sketches for execution; also apparent in a couple of cases are the attached samples of the colored felt that was to be used in costume construction. (From the collection of Joseph Simms)

(following spread) "There's Emerald City! Oh, we're almost there, at last! At last!" A publicity Kodachrome; note the path of the camera track through the center of the photograph.

(left) A publicity Kodachrome taken on the Witch's castle set. Notice the string being used to tie Bert Lahr's tail into the appropriate angle for a photograph. (below) A posed publicity Kodachrome, December 1938. In the film itself, Dorothy was never seen crossing the Munchkinland bridge. (On facing page) Bolger, Garland, and Haley in a publicity Kodachrome taken on the Tin Woodman set (November 1938). A slightly different pose would be used by Life for their famous Oz feature the following July.

(top) Bert Lahr and Frank Morgan sat for Kodachrome portraits of their Oz characters in early 1939. The promotional still (below) shows Lahr, Haley, and Bolger in disguise as Winkies, following two legitimate Guards into the castle of the Wicked Witch. (Courtesy the Kobal Collection, SuperStock International, Inc.)

months, revamped the screenplay from top to bottom, added several important sequences, and rewrote much of Langley's dialogue.

It was Ryerson and Woolf who created Professor Marvel, thus establishing the Wizard as a character in Kansas from the very beginning. They then suggested that the actor who played the Wizard and the Professor also appear as the Emerald City gatekeeper, cabby, and soldier, giving the assignment greater dimension and length. (He was even tentatively scheduled to play most of the staff of the Wash & Brush Up Co., including a blackface bootblack.) Ryerson and Woolf named the Good Witch of the North after Baum's Glinda (the Good Witch of the South), and they made Mrs. Gulch a Miss by eliminating her son, Walter. That, in turn, cut out the Witch's son, Bulbo, and the subplot about attacking the Emerald City. They also deleted a sequence wherein the Witch sacrificed one of her guards to her pet lion, and they appropriated some of Mankiewicz's dialogue from his March screenplay.

But Ryerson and Woolf made their own errors in adding characters and creating inappropriate situations. Professor Marvel traveled with a dwarf companion and a mangy, caged old lion, obvious Kansas allusions to the Munchkins and Bert Lahr. The writers hoped to eliminate the Horse-of-a-Different-Color from the Emerald City scenes (and suggested instead that he be used in Munchkinland). They wanted to soften the death of the Wicked Witch of the East by having her transformed rather than killed when the farmhouse fell on her, and they planned a collapsible rainbow bridge, designed by the Witch of the West as a trap for Dorothy. Their new finale in Oz was especially manic: the citizens of the Emerald City turned on the Wizard, and he and all the principals were forced to flee in his balloon. Once aloft, the balloon was burst by a woodpecker, and Glinda and the Munchkin Fire Department had to come to the rescue.

Langley was furious when he discovered his script had been altered. He found the Ryerson/Woolf work

> so cutesy and oozy that I could have vomited. I said, "The hell with it. Forget the whole thing. Take my name off it."
>
> They had the characters going over a rainbow bridge. Halfway up, they were to fall through the bridge. I told [Freed] that to build that bridge would cost at least $64,000. When Louis B. Mayer heard about it, he promptly declared there would be no rainbow bridge to Oz or anywhere else on the MGM lot.

Langley's reaction was further vindicated when, as a courtesy to the producers, director George Cukor read the new script and told LeRoy, "It simply will not work cinematically." Ultimately, Freed and Harburg made peace with Langley, and the writer and lyricist reworked portions of the scenario yet again. Harburg had already spent time with Ryerson and Woolf, creating dialogue segues into his songs; he had also written part of the presentation scene for the Wizard to grant the requests of Dorothy's companions. (The segment had originally been conceived as the Wizard's musical number.)

There were other writers who contributed to *Oz* between April and September—Herbert Fields and Samuel Hoffenstein in the spring, Jack Mintz during the summer. Little if any of their work made it into the "final" shooting script of early October, which was basically a composite of Langley, Ryerson, Woolf, and Harburg. Even that script was subject to last-minute changes and possessed awkward little quirks and some rather heavy-handed treatment. Dorothy often bemoaned the lack of love and care she received at the farm. Aunt Em was written as an oddly snappish woman (although the producers deleted a charming scene just prior to the cyclone wherein she abruptly decides to rescue Toto herself "if I have to massacre the sheriff and th' whole Gulch family to do it!"). Professor Marvel's dwarf and lion were replaced by an assistant named Goliath, who is frightened even by Toto; there was still no farmhand role to be played by Bert Lahr. The Wicked Witch was described as Gale Sondergaard had been hired to play her, with "a dangerously quiet and silky voice" and wearing "a slinky black robe with flying sleeves." (She even gained a name, Gulcheria, in one quickly discarded draft.)

The final events that would shape *The Wizard of Oz*—and the writer responsible for the final polish of the script—were still in the future. What the October script did possess were lyrics to the songs that had been written between May and August by Harburg and Harold Arlen. The score was a major consideration for Langley, Ryerson, and Woolf in anything they wrote or rewrote during that time. The songs were being built into the plot situations and thus influenced (or were influenced by) the screenplay.

When the picture was first announced, the idea of new *Oz* songs baffled and irritated several entertainment reporters who expected the old Broadway score to be utilized. "Why," whined Louella Parsons on March 8, "do the film companies buy old musical favorites and then disregard the songs that have already proved popular with the public . . . The old-time songs are new to the rising generation, and those who loved

212   CONTINUED (2)

            Lion (spasmodically)
        Trapped like mice -
                (correcting himself)
        - rats!

            Witch
        With only yourselves to blame! But now you're
        here, I'll use you!
                (sharply to guards)
        Bring them after me!
                (she turns and goes along passage
                and the guards prod the three along
                behind her)

213   CLOSE SHOT - DOROTHY

        at the other side of the door.

            Dorothy (in distress)
        Scarecrow! Tin Man! Lion! Are you there?
        What's happened?
                (silence greets her and she turns
                and sees the hour-glass)

214   CLOSEUP - HOUR GLASS

        Only a thin trickle of sand remains in the
        upper half.

215   MED. SHOT - TOWER

        The Witch comes to the wall of the tower and
        gazes across the courtyard at the other tower
        opposite. The Winkies push the Tin Man,
        Scarecrow and Lion into a line behind her.

            Witch (looking up)
        Yes... the moon is just right, and the hour-glass
        has just a few seconds to go --

            Scarecrow
        You let Dorothy -

            Witch
                (turning on him with a snarl)
        Silence, you!

                            CONTINUED:

220   LONGER SHOT -

        as he falls through the center of the rainbow.

221   WITCH'S TOWER

        The Witch is looking down into the courtyard
        with an expression of fiendish delight.

            Witch
        Aha! Aha! It works! It works!
                (she grins at the horrified Scarecrow)
        Now call Dorothy over. Go on! Call her!

            Scarecrow
        No I won't! You can't make me!
                (the Witch points her broomstick at
                him. He chokes, struggles to fin-
                ish his words)
        I w-won't...
                (in spite of himself he calls Dorothy)

222   INT. DOROTHY'S ROOM

        Dorothy is standing, wearily leaning against
        the door. Suddenly she hears the call, looks
        surprised, and runs to the window. She
        looks out, sees the beautiful rainbow bridge lead-
        ing to the window of the Witch's tower room.
        All of her friends are visible beyond. With
        a glad cry, she starts up the side of the
        rainbow bridge.

223   LONG SHOT (TRICK SHOT)

        showing the little figure running up the
        curve of the rainbow bridge.

224   INT. WITCH'S TOWER ROOM

        as her friends realize Dorothy's peril.
        They tear themselves away from the spell of
        the Witch.

            Scarecrow
        Stop! Stop! Go back!

            Tin Man
        Go back!

            Witch (savagely)

215   CONTINUED (2)

        The guards prod him with their spears. The
        Witch turns back and stretches out her hands.
        They are reflected against a far tower on
        the other side of the courtyard.

216   LONG SHOT - CASTLE - MINIATURE - TRICK SHOT

        Flashes of glorious, blinding color start
        swirling. A rainbow has formed a bridge
        between the two towers. This is very long
        and passes across the whole courtyard which is
        a great distance below. It is a beautiful
        sight but, like most rainbows, it grows thinner
        and thinner as it curves upward. The general
        effect is like one of the lovely curved bridges
        in Venice.

217   WITCH'S TOWER - RAINBOW IN BACKGROUND

            Witch
                (gloatingly)
        Aha! My old hand hasn't lost its cunning!
                (turning to the guards)
        Here, you!
                (the most hideous of the Winkie guards
                steps forward. She speaks to him)
        Dorothy is across there in that tower room. Bring
        her to me.
                (sharply, as he salutes and turns back
                toward the stairs)
        Not that way, you fool! Use the new bridge.

        Without any change of expression, the
        Winkie goes to the wall.

218   LONG SHOT - BRIDGE

        As the guard marches up, with his eyes
        straight ahead in a military fashion. He
        reaches the center of the bridge.

219   CLOSE ON GUARD

        as he realizes he is falling through. An
        expression of mingled surprise and horror
        comes over his hideous countenance. He
        clutches for support, but there is nothing
        to hold him.

225   CLOSE ON DOROTHY -

        who has almost reached the top of the curve.
        She sees her friends motioning her to go back.
        Suddenly she looks down.

226   LONG SHOT - FROM DOROTHY'S ANGLE PAST HER FEET
        This shows the thinness of the rainbow, with
        the courtyard a great distance below.

227   CLOSE ON DOROTHY -
        as she realizes her peril. Her face expresses
        terror. For one moment she is appalled, then
        suddenly pulls herself together, throws back
        her head.

            Dorothy
        I'm not afraid.

228   LONG SHOT - DOROTHY
        as her little ruby slippers seem to come to life
        with an irridescent glow. They run across the
        perilous center of the bridge as though carrying
        her with them.

229   WITCH'S TOWER
        as Dorothy runs down the descending side of the
        bridge and falls into the arms of her friends.

            Witch (screaming and beating the
                floor with her broomstick)
        It's those slippers! You couldn't have done it with-
        out those slippers!

230   LONGER ON SCENE -
        The Witch, in a perfect frenzy of rage, is
        screaming for her guards. A number of Winkies
        rush in through the door - also Winged Monkeys.

            Witch (pointing to the others)
        Seize them! Kill them! Throw them out the window!

        The guards start toward the three who try to
        stand them off and protect Dorothy. The Lion
        strikes out at a guard. The Tin Man and Scare-
        crow also join in. It develops into a regular
        fracas.
        The room is lit by torches in the wall. Furiously
        the Witch strikes her broom in the fire. The end
        blazes up. She advances on them, screaming. She
        strikes at the Scarecrow. The Scarecrow's voice
        rises above the din.

Ryerson and Woolf devised an elaborate "Rainbow Bridge" sequence, deleted from the Oz screenplay after a couple of drafts. (Another of their abandoned ideas saw Dorothy, Toto, and their three companions return to the Emerald City from the Witch's castle by flying through the air on her magically lengthened broomstick.)

them in the old days enjoy hearing them again." But few, if any, of the eclectic songs from the original musical had anything to do with the *Oz* story, and Arthur Freed pushed from the beginning for an integrated film score, with each song designed to develop a character or advance the plot. It was a fairly innovative approach for that time; only a handful of stage and screen musicals had been so integrated (although the procedure would become de rigueur a few years later).

Among Freed's first choices to do the music for *Oz* was Jerome Kern, possibly in partnership with lyricist Dorothy Fields or Ira Gershwin. Freed idolized Kern, whose 1927 *Show Boat* (written with Oscar Hammerstein II) was regarded as one of the first examples of an integrated musical. But Kern was recovering from a heart attack and mild stroke in early 1938 and, though working again, he apparently didn't feel strong enough to consider an assignment as complex as *Oz*.

On March 17, the press was notified that the *Oz*

An outline for a series of "Munchkinland" songs, written for Oz by Roger Edens (undated but circa March/April 1938). Edens was already a musical mainstay at Metro, having arrived there in 1934 to do vocal arrangements and adaptations; he was Judy Garland's champion from the day of her first audition in 1935. He composed and wrote for her, provided coaching and accompaniment, and routined her radio and stage appearances. It was Edens who created "Dear Mr. Gable," which the fourteen-year-old sang on February 1, 1937, at MGM's birthday party for its leading male star. (Edens continued to write and arrange for Garland into the 1960s.)

songs would be written by Mack Gordon and Harry Revel, borrowed by MGM from Fox where they had done three scores for Shirley Temple pictures. Nothing came of the announcement; the duo instead wrote three numbers for Judy Garland to sing that spring in *Love Finds Andy Hardy. Daily Variety* for April 18 reported that Nacio Herb Brown (Freed's songwriting partner) would team up for the first time with Warner Bros.' Al Dubin to work at MGM on *Oz*. Their assignment didn't progress beyond the announcement itself. Meanwhile, Roger Edens was drafting several *Oz* songs of his own, whether as an audition or as a helpful guideline for whomever got the job. His "prologue" number for Dorothy was called "Mid Pleasures and Palaces," and he followed that with an extended Munchkinland sequence, wherein Dorothy would be musically welcomed to Oz in a multipart production routine.

By May 3, MGM interoffice communication noted that Arlen and Harburg had finally been signed for *Oz*. The two were also among Freed's favored choices for, though they didn't at that time have the track record of some of the others, he much admired their sprightly and whimsical Broadway songs of several preceding seasons. (When Arlen brought the news of their assignment to his good friend Jerome Kern, the latter reportedly responded with an appreciative but mildly incredulous, "You got it?") Harburg and Arlen were hired on a fourteen-week deal for twenty-five thousand dollars, one-third of which was an advance on royalties. The duo reported to Metro on Monday, May 9, and the script from which they first worked was one of Langley's early drafts. Many song spots were already cued in, although Harburg's talent as a librettist enabled him to more tightly focus or advantageously revamp some of the specific situations.

The writers' first number was tailored to the description of Dorothy as a "jazz" singer. They titled the song "The Jitterbug," even though the word *jitterbug* was already in use as slang for any hep-dancing teenager of the time. The Arlen/Harburg "Jitterbug" was a unique, pink-and-blue, mosquitolike insect whose bite gave one "the jitters" and, as such, caused a wild dance. (The idea was probably derived from the swarm of bees sent by the Wicked Witch to attack Dorothy and her friends during their trip through the Winkie Country in the *Oz* book.)

By early June, they finished the triumverate theme, "If I Only Had a Brain/a Heart/the Nerve," for which Harburg simply wrote new lyrics to one of their old songs, dropped from *Hooray for What!* the year before. By the end of the month, the job was virtually completed, including their own Munchkinland sequence. Arlen and Harburg's number was formatted in much the same fashion as Roger Edens's earlier sample and consisted of eight parts:

a) Come Out, Come Out Wherever You Are— Glinda and the Munchkins
b) It Really Was No Miracle—Dorothy and the Munchkins
c) patter/general greeting and tribute—the Munchkins and Glinda
d) Ding! Dong! The Witch Is Dead— Munchkins
e) patter/Munchkin Mayor, City Fathers, and Coroner
f) reprise: Ding! Dong! The Witch Is Dead— Munchkins
g) The Lullaby League/The Lollipop Guild/The .Mother Goose Club*—Munchkins
h) We Welcome You to Munchkinland— Munchkins

From start to finish, the sequence was more than six minutes of song, dance, and rhymed dialogue.

Finding a ballad melody for what would become "Over the Rainbow" gave Arlen more trouble than anything else in the score. He had read Freed's April 25 memo and realized the necessity for a song that could bridge the transition between Kansas and Oz. Finally, during an evening trip to the movies with his wife, Arlen suddenly ordered her to pull their car to the side of Sunset Boulevard, and he jotted down the long-sought-after musical phrases that had just come to mind. He finished the music over the next few days; Harburg later claimed the bridge (or middle) section was based on a whistle the composer always used to summon his dog (although the astounded Arlen dryly denied this).

The lyricist's initial response to the music was not one of joy. Arlen played it for him in a grandiose, bravura manner, and Harburg thought it almost symphonic, better suited to the style of a legitimate baritone like Nelson Eddy than a little girl in Kansas. But Ira Gershwin heard the melody shortly thereafter and praised it. That compliment—and Arlen's much subdued piano rendition for Gershwin—changed Harburg's opinion, and he wrote a lyric built around his reaction to the "grayness" of Kansas (heavily emphasized by Baum in the first few pages of the Oz book). Harburg felt that the only color in Dorothy's life would have been a rainbow.

*The last of these stanzas was dropped from the routine prior to prerecording.

On June 29, Bill Cannon prepared a list of the songs Arlen and Harburg had completed to date, along with other numbers suggested in the script that the team had yet to produce. The former category included the aforementioned titles, plus Lahr's "If I Were King of the Forest," and a frequently-reprised but as-of-then untitled "Marching Song" (which was undoubtedly "We're Off to See the Wizard"; it was Arthur Freed's suggestion to precede the chorus with a directive verse, "Follow the Yellow Brick Road"). The Cannon rundown noted that the picture was also to give Dorothy a double reprise of "Over the Rainbow." She would sing a couple of lines on her arrival in Munchkinland and another brief excerpt when locked in the Witch's castle. A reprise of "Ding! Dong! The Witch Is Dead" was slated after the melting of the Witch, to be begun by the Winkie Guards in the Witch's tower and continued by a huge ensemble in the Emerald City. One of the reprises of the "Marching Song"—in the poppy field—would later be replaced by an additional Arlen/Harburg/Herbert Stothart song, "Optimistic Voices" ("You're out of the woods, you're out of the dark, you're out of the night . . . ").

The remaining three feature numbers on the list had either not been completed by June 29 or were dropped from the script before the songwriters could work on them. "Death to the Wizard of Oz," a funereal march for the Winkie Guard, disappeared from the screenplay along with the Witch's plot to conquer Emerald City. The "Wizard's Song," as noted above, became a Harburg dialogue scene rather than a song. "The Horse-of-a-Different-Color" was to be a production number in Emerald City Square; its slot was filled instead by "The Merry Old Land of Oz" (initially known under its working title, "Laugh a Day Away").

Arlen and Harburg finished their work and continued to polish and refine the score during July, while Ryerson and Woolf wrestled with their contributions to Langley's script. Meanwhile the other creative elements of the film were being aligned in the studio's efforts to visually produce the Land of Oz as imagined by millions of readers. From the onset, the picture was recognized as perhaps Metro's most ambitious project to date, and it made for virtually unprecedented demands on the personnel in every department.

The keynote of the work, as expressed by studio craftsmen at the time, was to get away from any precedents, to create Oz, its characters, and events like "nothing in existence." For research purposes, they had the Oz books, photographs of the stage show, and their own technical skills and knowledge. What mattered more was creative imagination, corporate enthusiasm, and financial support. They had those, too.

It was decided early on that *The Wizard of Oz* would be shot entirely on sound stages, with no exterior or location work. By reading even an early/ temporary *Oz* script, the art department was able to estimate that it would have to design over sixty sets for the picture, including miniatures and mock-ups. Their list of necessary creations for *The Wizard of Oz* included a Kansas farm; an acre-large poppy field; a Munchkin village; a couple of forests; a cornfield; a Yellow Brick Road; a grove of talking trees; an Emerald City; a menacing castle; and such set pieces as the Witch's hourglass and the Horse-of-a-Different-Color.

The sets were first envisioned by art director William Horning, who passed along his ideas to sketch artist Jack Martin Smith. (Both Horning and Smith were overseen in their work by Cedric Gibbons, head of the art department.) Once the sketches were approved, blueprints were made and the construction department took over. The sets were to be built in conjunction with the filming of the picture, always one or two steps ahead of principal photography.

It was also decided that some of the incredible scenic effects of Oz would not be built but created instead by the use of matte paintings. In this procedure, the sets were drawn in crayon on large boards, the drawings were filmed, and the film was then processed with the footage of the rest of the scene. Matte shots in *The Wizard of Oz* included the view of the Emerald City across the poppy field, the interior towers and arches of the city, some of the Kansas backgrounds, and the overview of the battlements and towers of the Witch's castle.

The special-effects department under A. Arnold (Buddy) Gillespie was equally challenged. They viewed the script as a project that required a tornado; a house picked up, carried, and dropped by a tornado; a number of people inside a tornado who flew past a window; a melting witch; a flying witch; a flying and skywriting witch; a troupe of flying monkeys; a fireball; a floating bubble that dissolved into a Good Witch; and a Great Head on a throne, surrounded by fire and smoke. Much of the special effects work would be done in miniature and with process photography; Gillespie began his experiments and tests in late summer 1938. As with set construction, however, many of the effects were planned to coincide with principal photography, and many others would be done in post-production work.

It became the job of cinematographer Harold Rosson and his crew to photograph these sets, effects, scenes, and songs. Rosson was assigned as "first cameraman" for *Oz*; he had worked in color before, and his past experience was regarded as essential to the production. The process of Technicolor photography was still relatively new in 1938, and its capabilities would be stretched beyond known limits by the demands of the picture. Rosson realized early on that *Oz* would be best served by a camera continually on the move. Perched on a boom, its constant "float" could then enhance the views of the gigantic sets and keep the colors of the massed costumes (like those in Munchkinland) from becoming a muddy blur.

Another of Rosson's considerations was the amount of lighting required to photograph in Technicolor at that time. Though arguably the best equipped studio in Hollywood, MGM was forced to borrow additional powerful arcs from other film companies in order to adequately illuminate the Ozian vistas. Rosson then had to make sure the lights didn't reflect off the ruby slippers, or the Tin Woodman's costume, or Glinda's crown. The cameras themselves were highly sensitive and required testing every morning and cleaning every evening. In addition, there weren't many of them in existence in 1938, and a studio had to reserve them months in advance when planning a color picture. When they wanted to capture a big scene from several angles at the same time, Rosson and his crew had to resort to occasional night shooting. It was the only time the majority of the cameras were available to them.

From conception, the film was planned to feature the fantasy of Oz in color and the reality of Kansas in black and white. The original release prints in 1939 would further heighten the effect by processing the Kansas segments in sepia-tone; it gave those scenes a warm amber-and-brown sheen and helped to intensify the contrast between the monochromic interior of the farmhouse and the multi-hued Munchkinland plaza.

As Arlen and Harburg finished their score, Freed and LeRoy planned the routing of the musical numbers. The songs would be prerecorded, and orchestrations for several of them were begun as soon as decisions were made on their staging. Herbert Stothart of the MGM music department was set to score the picture; for additional composition, arranging, and orchestration, he would use the talents of George Bassman, Murray Cutter, Paul Marquardt, and Ken Darby. (Roger Edens handled much of the vocal arranging for the principals.) The prerecording sessions were conducted by Stothart and his associate, George Stoll, and they would perform the same duty during post-production underscoring of the film.

With all departments at work in summer 1938, there were still two major decisions to be made attendant to *The Wizard of Oz*. The film was deep into preproduction but had no director or choreographer.

In his May 20 casting memo to LeRoy, Freed concluded, "I presume that you are following through on your idea of getting Buzz Berkeley to direct the musical sequences." Busby Berkeley was synonymous with the most elaborate, complex song-and-dance numbers in 1930s motion pictures. Additionally, he had worked with LeRoy at Warner Bros., so it was natural that he be considered for *Oz*. Louella Parsons noted on June 20 that Berkeley's *Oz* assignment was assured "if he finishes *Comet Over Broadway* in time." But the next month Warners rushed the director into another of their own pictures, *They Made Me a Criminal,* so LeRoy instead brought Bobby Connolly to MGM as dance director for *Oz*. They had also worked together (if briefly) at Warners, where Connolly spent most of his film career. The choreographer was signed in August, and it was immediately announced he was "devising new explorative routines" to accommodate "the necessary short strides" for the Munchkin dances. He also helped plan the prerecording of the principals' numbers.

LeRoy himself wanted to direct *The Wizard of Oz* but was already overloaded with the multitude of production details. A logical choice for the job then materialized when Norman Taurog signed a long-term contract with MGM on May 13. His preceding decade of directorial credits had won Taurog a reputation for guiding young performers to superlative achievement (Jackie Cooper in *Skippy,* Deanna Durbin in *Mad About Music,* and Tommy Kelly in *The Adventures of Tom Sawyer*); the director had himself been a child actor. On May 14, MGM announced his first vehicles for the studio as *Boys' Town* and, following that, *The Wizard of Oz*.

When Taurog was interviewed in 1976 for *The Making of The Wizard of Oz*, Aljean Harmetz said the director "remembered the summer of 1938 very clearly . . . [but] he never even heard a rumor that he was being considered" for the Mervyn LeRoy musical. Taurog's memory was somewhat (if understandably) faulty after thirty-eight years; his assignment was much more than mere rumor. Both trades announced it again on July 16, and *Daily Variety* reprinted the news ("Taurog Directs 'Oz' ") on its front page for August 12. On August 26, Horace Hough was named as Taurog's assistant for the picture, and MGM's legal files confirm that Taurog worked on (and was paid for) three days of *Wizard of Oz* direction (possibly overseeing early test footage in July and August).

Then, without warning, a general production list in the September 1 *Hollywood Reporter* named Richard Thorpe as director of the picture. The official studio confirmation of this news came six days later; *Daily Variety* offered that the "switch was made to permit Taurog to start preparations for *Huckleberry Finn...*" (He had done an earlier film of the Mark Twain classic in 1931.) Thorpe had been at MGM for three years, directing a variety of movies. He had a reputation for bringing in pictures on budget and on schedule, which must have been a real attraction as the studio watched preproduction costs mount on *The Wizard of Oz*. Thorpe immediately started preliminary work on the picture; at that point, *Oz* was scheduled to start filming in mid-September.*

	LOEW'S INCORPORATED	
Copy to:	**TENTATIVE**	
Publishers		
Home Office	**PRODUCTION MUSIC**	MUSIC DEPARTMENT
Publicity & Adv.		
Music Dept.		

Production _____#1060_____   Date _____OCTOBER 10, 1938_____

Title of Number:	Title of Picture:
OVER THE RAINBOW	WIZARD OF OZ
Music by:	**Star or Stars:**
Harold Arlen	
Words by:	**Featured Artists:**
E. Y. Harburg	Judy Garland, Buddy Ebsen, Ray Bolger, Bert Lahr.
Words and Music by:	**Director:**
	RICHARD THORPE

Style of Number: Fox Trot **X** , Waltz_____   First Shown at:

'Waltz with F. T. Version_____, Ballad.**X**   Town_____

Theatre_____

Comedy_____

Remarks: A - Sung by Judy Garland to Bolger & Ebsen (two farm hands) with an optimistic outlook into the future.

Signed: _____GEORGE G. SCHNEIDER_____   OFFICE OF NAT W. FINSTON
                                                       Department Head.

A music department directive, describing an early concept for the staging of "Over the Rainbow." At this point in script development—a few days prior to the start of principal photography under Richard Thorpe—Dorothy was to have sung the song to the two Kansas farmhands, Bolger and Ebsen. (There was, at that time, no third farmhand role for Bert Lahr.)

*Once production actually began (in mid-October), Thorpe requested that writer Sid Silvers work with him on-set, revising the script as needed. That made Silvers thirteenth on MGM's "official" list of those who had contributed or been assigned to *The Wizard of Oz*: Cannon, Brecher, Mankiewicz, Nash, Langley, Freed, Fields, Hoffenstein, Ryerson, Woolf, Harburg, Mintz, Silvers.

CHAPTER 3

Wardrobe and Makeup

If the special-effects work and set construction for *The Wizard of Oz* were planned to either just precede, coincide with, or follow principal photography, there were two behind-the-scenes departments whose Oz magic was, by necessity, demanded "up front." It would be their responsibility to design, create, and enhance the inhabitants of Oz, making them at the same time unreal and believable.

Gilbert Adrian and Jack Dawn were, respectively, the heads of the wardrobe and makeup departments at MGM in 1938. It was late winter when they were given the challenge of bringing to the screen the denizens of a fantasy land. The work would prove to be both memorable and groundbreaking.

The two men first "conceptualized" the possible different and appropriate appearances of the various Ozians and then sketched their ideas for LeRoy. (The drawings of the costumes were watercolored in accordance with the requirements of the new, temperamental Technicolor cameras, which did not always accurately reproduce hues. It was a procedure that was followed as well for the settings of the picture.) If and when LeRoy approved, Adrian and wardrobe moved on to fittings with the cast, and Dawn and his department applied, rejected, revised, and reapplied the complex character makeups. Neither creative division was limited to a single approach; whether imagining a dress for Dorothy or viable garb for a Scarecrow or Tin Woodman, Adrian sketched a variety of ideas for each of the major players. Dawn and his faction matched this dedication in their attempts to simulate the famous characters while simultaneously maintaining the personalities and recognizable facial characteristics of the *Oz* stars. In this makeup technique, MGM was clearly making a conscious effort to avoid the disastrous situation of Paramount's "live actor" version of *Alice in Wonderland* five years earlier. That film boasted an all-star cast but failed both with critics and at the box office. Its lack of success was due at least in part to the fact that few stars were discernible under the heavy character masks and makeup.

William Tuttle worked under Dawn in 1938 and ultimately became head of the MGM makeup department himself. When looking back at his *Oz* association forty-five years later, Tuttle remembered, "We enjoyed a luxury that we seldom get today, and that is preparation time . . .We had several months to prepare, and so [Jack Dawn] got the most skilled people in the various areas of makeup . . . those who were skilled in prosthetic work, those who were skilled in beards and wigs . . . " As early as August, a special makeup annex was prepared at MGM for the vast number of department trainees who would be required for *Oz* work in the months ahead. Tuttle recalled that Dawn

> got some of the people from the messenger service and the mail room . . . and had them over there. And they're the ones who are in the makeup business today, they became so interested in it.
>
> It was really a monumental task from a makeup standpoint. And I think that all of the techniques that were involved in [*Oz* and its] various creative aspects . . . have never really been duplicated. And there's really nothing new that's come along since then. The entire field of makeup was encompassed in that picture.

Adrian's designs for MGM leading ladies had already gone beyond film fame to influence the entire fashion world. When assigned to *Oz*, he reveled in the expansive demands it posed. Hedda Hopper quoted him as "having more fun over *Oz* than a trip to Europe," and the Oz books were announced as "favorite stories of his youth." The designer supposedly sent home to Naugatuck, Connecticut, for his old schoolbooks; he had sketched Oz characters and wardrobe in their margins twenty years earlier.

Adrian developed at least four designs for Judy Garland's single costume and at least one design for the ruby slippers prior to the start of principal photogra-

On August 27, Judy Garland modeled three potential Dorothy dresses and two different wigs. Blond "Wig 1" is shown in the top row of photographs and the photo at left in the bottom row. "Wig #2 Red" is shown in the middle photo of the bottom row. None of these dresses met with the approval of the production staff, but by October 13 a variation on the first outfit had been decided upon (as had the initial blond wig and style). During the two weeks of footage shot by director Richard Thorpe, Dorothy Gale appeared as she does in the photo at right in the bottom row.

phy. To flatten her bosom, Garland was also bound into a snug-fitting brassiere which she wore under her costume throughout the filming; her sixteen-year-old figure was considerably more mature than that of a supposedly younger child.

Oddly, Garland's initial wardrobe and especially her makeup seemed to remove her as far as possible from her natural appearance. It's uncertain whether the idea was to make her look younger, more like a storybook heroine, or more like Shirley Temple. The rationale behind the approach is difficult to understand as *Oz*, of course, was conceived to highlight Judy Garland. Tests were done to determine whether Dorothy should be a blond (as in all but the first Oz book) or a redhead. When shooting finally began, the star had a cascade of tousled blond hair and a rouged, baby-doll visage.

More than twenty years later, Garland would laughingly say of her first weeks in *Oz*, "I looked like a male Mary Pickford by the time they got through with the alterations." Screenwriter Moss Hart even provided her with the opportunity to do a takeoff on the original Dorothy makeup in the screen test sequence of Warner Bros.' *A Star is Born* (1954): band singer "Esther Blodgett" is made over in much the same fashion with a golden wig, puttied nose, and an exces-

sive cosmetic appearance. When Garland informally introduced a showing of *Star* at London's National Film Theatre in 1969, an audience member recalled Esther's test in the film and asked if MGM had ever tried to tamper with Judy's face in the same fashion. The star shot back, "They certainly did! . . . They gave me a blond wig—and they thought my nose 'went in' too much. So they put a piece of rubber here" (indicating the bridge of her nose). "I looked like I could pick locks with that nose. And this was all because I was *perfect* for *The Wizard of Oz*. And I kept thinking . . . well . . . if I'm so *perfect* for this part . . . why are they putting rubber on my nose?" (The concept of a redesigned Garland nose was abandoned before shooting began.)

Although Ray Bolger modeled several variations of the Scarecrow costume before LeRoy was satisfied, it was his makeup that caused the most difficulty. He was subjected to weeks of tests before a final treatment was adopted: a light mask of baked rubber, no more than a facial coating but designed to simulate burlap. Once applied to Bolger's face, the mask could be painted with makeup and, though the masks were reusable, they seldom lasted more than a couple of days. The dancer went through over forty of them during the course of the production.

On September 22, Ray Bolger tested an initial Scarecrow costume and two different, fairly light makeups.

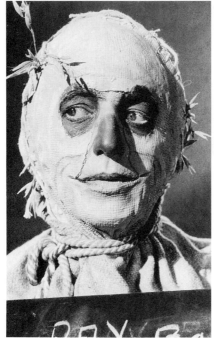

(top row) Bolger tried an altered costume with different trousers on October 3, along with three other makeups. Here, for the first time, the Scarecrow's head was covered with a burlap-like sack, and a portion of his face was made-up to match. At top left, Bolger's facial makeup is similar to Fred Stone's in the 1902 Wizard stage show. For the top center photograph, some of the facial lines were removed; for the top right photo, further modification was made—and "straw" eyebrows were added. October 8 brought a couple more experiments (bottom) and, when Thorpe began making the film the next week, this conception was (with minor adjustments) the one used for the Scarecrow.

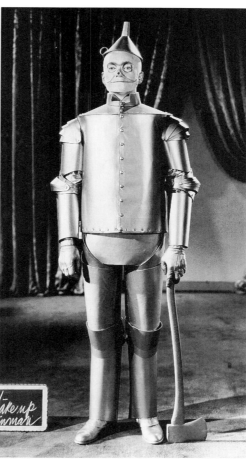

Buddy Ebsen first tried out the Tin Woodman costume on September 22 (extreme left). His makeup was virtually nonexistent in keeping with the department theory that the stars of Oz had to remain recognizable. That look was deemed unacceptable, however, and Ebsen posed in a complete Tin Woodman makeup on October 3 (at left and below). For that test, Ebsen also sported gloves and a different pair of pants and shoes. Additional changes would be made in makeup, tin collar, and gloves before Thorpe began shooting. (See page 71 for the "finished" Ebsen Tin Man.)

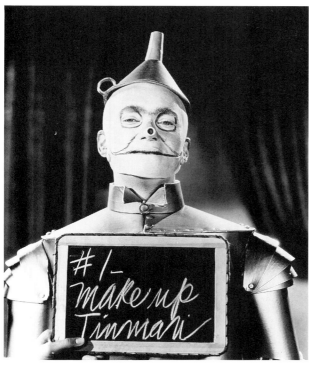

Buddy Ebsen's Tin Woodman costume also enjoyed several incarnations, including a first attempt that encased the actor in sheet aluminum. When this proved unwieldy, the studio came up with an outfit of buckram, covered with metallic cloth and painted silver. Ebsen underwent the same makeup experimentation as Bolger and was finally fitted with a skullcap and rubber nose and chin. These pieces and his face were covered with white "clown" makeup (mixed with household bluing) and then dusted with silver aluminum powder so that the Tin Man would have the proper shine.

Bert Lahr was draped in fifty pounds of genuine lion skins, lined with heavy padding to fill out the costume. Jack Dawn's makeup for the already leonine Lahr was, according to the star, "made of rubber, paper, and several other ingredients that only its creator knows, [and then] fitted over my head and most of my face. It was made to pull up my nose, giving it that retroussé effect that makes the Lion look so silly, and to drop down over my cheeks for jowls." The face piece was inserted with individual whiskers and then surrounded by a fur wig and beard. Paw-mittens covered Lahr's

Bert Lahr appeared in a test of his lion suit on August 27. The sketchy lines on his face were intended either as an example of the aforementioned desire to enhance but not obscure the actor's own characteristics or as an indication of possible directions a heavier makeup could take. (Before filming began, Lahr's mane was restyled, and ears were positioned on either side of his head.)

hands, and his wildly gesticulating tail was controlled from the catwalks above the set by a wire and fish-pole-like attachment. (Harry Edwards was assigned the job as Lahr's tail manipulator.)

A glamorous 1930s makeup was applied to Gale Sondergaard: sweeping false lashes, arched penciled eyebrows, and a glossy lipstick. Her Wicked Witch dress, hat, and cowl headdress were completely covered with sewn-on black sequins, and the final costume was, in its way, as uncomfortably heavy as Lahr's lion outfit.

Billie Burke's fairy princess ensemble was a less complicated affair. At the time, her own smiling comment was, "I look like a fugitive from German opera . . . but, in a way, I'm supposed to. Glinda's a heroic figure. She has only to wave her wand, and the world is changed, much as [Queen] Victoria did in real life." Miss Burke's famous red hair was covered by a matching wig and then topped by a towering ornate crown. A star-tipped staff and butterfly choker completed the picture.

Frank Morgan had five completely different costumes and makeups for his roles in *The Wizard of Oz*

On September 22, Gale Sondergaard appeared in sequined costume and hat as the unique, "slinky" Wicked Witch, a concept that drew heavily on the Evil Queen of Disney's Snow White—*even to the elaborate cowl covering her head. (Sondergaard's name is misspelled on the test notation.)*

(above) Frank Morgan and Mervyn LeRoy confer over costume sketches for the actor's various roles. The producer holds one of the Adrian watercolors; another is visible on the chair between them. (At left is assistant director Al Shenberg.) (below) "I'm Glinda... the Witch of the North." Mrs. Florenz Ziegfeld could have been no more glorified by her late husband than she was by Adrian and the MGM makeup department. (This is probably a portrait taken during the course of filming as opposed to a costume test shot.)

Frank Morgan played five roles in The Wizard of Oz. His first costume and makeup tests on November 16 encompassed the four guises he would employ for the Emerald City sequences. He is seen above as the doorkeeper. (The character's cap would ultimately be dropped in favor of an ornate hairstyle; see page 53, bottom right photograph.)

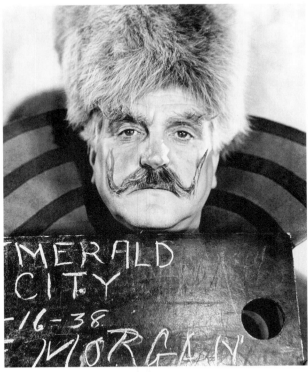

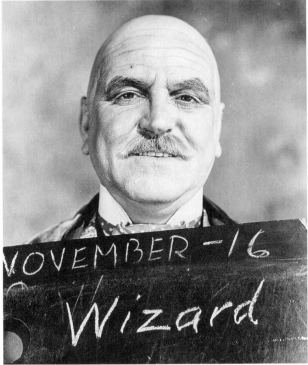

November 16 continued: Frank Morgan (top left) as the cabby who drove the Horse-of-a-Different-Color; (top right) as the soldier/guard at the entrance to the Wizard's palace; and (bottom left) as the Great and Powerful Oz himself. The costumes for the cabby and soldier remained basically the same, but the makeups were changed and most of the ideas for the

Wizard (here derived from the original Denslow drawings of 1900) were also abandoned. (bottom right) Morgan appeared on the Oz Tin Woodman set on November 17 in a test wig and makeup for his Kansas counterpart, Professor Marvel. He wore the same costume he'd utilized for the Wizard test the day before.

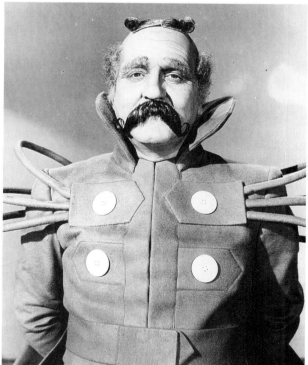

(top left) On November 23, another hairstyle, jacket, and tie were considered for Professor Marvel. (top right) January 7 brought Morgan back to model the final beard makeup for the cabby, albeit minus the coachman's hat. (bottom left) He also posed that day in the final choice for the Wizard's costume, although the makeup and hairstyle were much different when he began filming the part. (bottom right) Changes were made in his doorkeeper makeup on January 7; this was, again, modified further for the actual filming.

but wasn't called upon to test any of them until after the changes were completed on all the other principal characters. The delay, however, didn't spare him from extensive alterations of his own: each of his five characters went through some adjustment after the preliminary tests were made, and in some cases the initial designs were forsaken and Morgan withstood an entirely new approach.

The supporting cast required similar tolerance. Adrian designed a simple little jacket for the Winged Monkeys, and the undersized men who played the parts wore them over their simian suits. The monkey makeup was composed of built-up rubber prosthetic pieces, topped by a wig. The studio then developed several shapes and sizes of wings for the creatures, until it was finally decided to use the smallest of these; they were easiest to manipulate. But the combination of wig, mask, wings, and full-length costume was uncomfortable at best. The oversized men hired as the Winkie Army of the Wicked Witch were equally encumbered in their ornate layered-and-trimmed coats.

Some of the costume tests for the Wicked Witch's Winged Monkeys centered around the shape and size of their wings. The "small wing" concept was demonstrated on September 14 (top left). On September 22, a small cap was added to the costume; the hand makeup for the monkey was changed on that day as well and, in addition to the small wings (above, top), test monkey Sid Dawson also modeled a large pair (above).

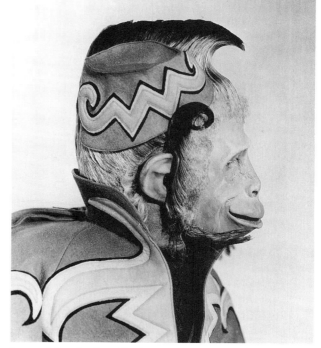

(top) For October 3, a "bat wing" effect was created for the Winged Monkey; note the electrical cord leading to a motor on the actor's back that activated the wings. (When actual filming began, the wings were moved by individual battery packs.)

(bottom) On October 15, close-ups were made of the monkey makeup. It was a forerunner of that used nearly thirty years later in Planet of the Apes.

and buckles, buttons and bows, tassels and pompons. Beyond these decorations, he further accessorized their wardrobe with flowers and flowerpots, birds and bird cages, high hats and vests. The Munchkin make-up would require layers of effects: prosthetic pieces, skullcaps, and wigs. It was in expectation of working with more than one hundred midgets that Jack Dawn established the aforementioned makeup annex. Even with the advent of the Munchkins three months away, Dawn was preparing an assembly line to deal with them.

Metro contract player Mitchell Lewis posed on August 27 as the Captain of the Winkie Guard. The makeup department later restructured his nose to be more like that of the Wicked Witch.

(Adrian contemplated adopting the design of the Winkie wear for a line of women's winter clothing in 1939!) Their makeup would be a conscious echo of that eventually worn by the Wicked Witch.

For the men of the Emerald City, Adrian and Dawn aligned on a "wooden soldier" look: varnished, lacquered hair and facial characteristics, all as if painted on. The Emerald City women were doll-like in their "dress up" garb—robes, shawls, scarves, snoods—and had similarly painted-on cheek rouge and eyelashes. Hundreds of costumes were required for the Emerald City sequences and, following the guidelines established by Adrian's sketches, the wardrobe department spent the better part of three weeks dying material to supplement the green fabric they'd already acquired. All the shoes had to be dyed as well.

The Munchkins were also conceived as somewhat toylike, but they were—in the Adrian/Dawn version—mischievous baby dolls and kewpie dolls. Their costumes were stylized so that the little people would look even smaller, engulfed in Adrian's oversize belts

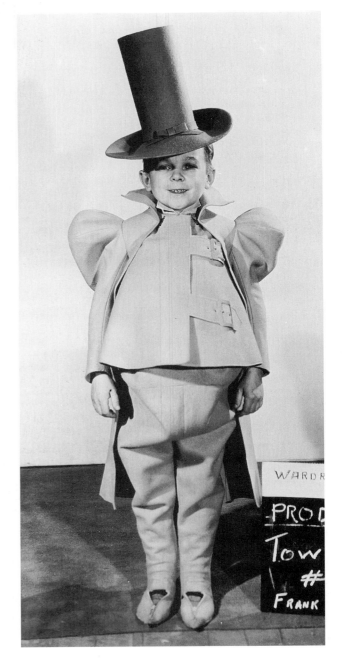

The majority of "Munchkins" arrived at MGM in mid-November. The costume tests on these and the next two pages were made on December 13. Names were, in some cases, misspelled or out-of-sequence on the test boards. (on facing page) "Townsman #2" Frank Cucksey; (above and center) "City Father" Matthew Raia; (above right) "Mayor" Charley Becker; (right; from left) "3 Little Tough Boys" Harry Doll, Jerry Maren, Jackie Gerlich; their real names were Kurt Schneider, Gerard Marenghi, and Jakob Gerlich.

(above, from left)
"Musician Fiddler"
Freddy Ritter, "Herald"
Karl Kosiczky,
"Bearded Man"
Tommy Cottonaro; (at
right and on facing
page) "Townsmen"
Lajos Matina, Joe
Koziel, Tommy
Cottonaro.

(above left) "Comander [sic] Navy" Johnny Winters; (above) "Soldiers" Jakob Hofbauer, "Willi" Koestner.

Final costume and makeup tests were done on December 20 for the ten Munchkins pictured here.

The center Munchkins at left are Coroner Meinhardt Raabe and Mayor Charley Becker. (By coincidence, the date given for the death of the Wicked Witch of the East on the Coroner's certificate was May 6, 1938— nineteen years to the day after the death of L. Frank Baum.)

CHAPTER 4

The Thorpe "Era"

It was September when the basic elements of *Oz* began to come together. The cast, virtually complete, was in the midst of final costume, makeup, and Technicolor tests under Richard Thorpe. The script was slowly being polished, and the score was finished. Bobby Connolly started dance rehearsals with the principals, and Herbert Stothart and Georgie Stoll prepared for the musical prerecording sessions. On Stage 26, the scenic art department was working on the backdrop for the first set while their parent construction department created the accompanying yellow-brick crossroads and cornfield.

Yet there were still delays. A start-date of September 15 was pushed back to the 20, then to the 23. Even that was optimistic: Judy Garland was still shooting *Listen, Darling* and, according to the trades, performed "Zing! Went the Strings of My Heart" for that picture on the 22. Finally, on September 26, *Oz* was scheduled for principal photography beginning October 10.

Between September 30 and October 11, Garland, Bolger, Ebsen, and Lahr reported to Stothart and Stoll to prerecord their solos and group numbers. Even "Snow White" became involved on September 30 when Adriana Caselotti was paid one hundred dollars to sing one line—"Wherefore art thou, Romeo?"—in Ebsen's "If I Only Had a Heart." Disney had used Caselotti as the voice of his cartoon leading lady in 1937.

Meanwhile, another major snag developed the first week in October. Gale Sondergaard's tests as a glamorous evil witch had been done on September 22. Although enormously effective, they seemed to emphasize the fact that this was not the accepted image of the Wicked Witch of Oz. So, Sondergaard retested on October 3—minus the sequins and sweeping eyelashes but with the addition of a horrific wig and bulbous nose. When she and LeRoy saw the stills of the second test, both agreed that this was not how the actress should be represented on the screen. By mutual agreement, she was released from the film, leaving an important role in *The Wizard of Oz* to be filled—and quickly.

Gale Sondergaard retested as a typical ugly Witch, complete with fright wig and restructured nose. She happily bid the Oz assignment good-bye within days of the revisions. (The next year, Sondergaard appeared in The Blue Bird *as a reasonably attractive fantasy character, Tylette the Cat. The film was Darryl F. Zanuck's expensive Technicolor answer to Oz, but its failure marked the end of Shirley Temple's stellar prominence at Twentieth Century-Fox.)*

The following weekend, Margaret Hamilton, a date, and her agent Jess Smith and his wife attended a football game. In 1983, with typical self-deprecating humor, Miss Hamilton recalled that afternoon.

> Who should come in but Mr. Mayer and his family and [Mr. LeRoy. They] sat down about two rows in front of us . . . [Mr. Mayer] turned around and waved to us, and I said, "Who's that?" And Jess said, "Oh, *honestly,* Maggie . . . that's Mr. *Mayer.*"

One of Margaret Hamilton's early test stills was later issued as an Oz publicity photo although, after the first two weeks of shooting, this "look" for the Witch was abandoned and never seen in the finished film.

And I said, "Of what town?"

And Jess said, "He is the *head* of MGM!"

[So] I had a good look at him, [having only] seen him once, quite a few years before that.

And Mr. Mayer said, "Glad you're going to be with us." And I didn't know what he was talking about.

And Jess said, "Not yet . . . they're not decided yet."

And Mr. Mayer said, "What are you talking about?"

And Jess said, "We haven't talked money yet."

And Mr. Mayer said, "Meet me out at the half time."

So, as I remember, they went out and had a little discussion . . . Jess came [back] with a look like a cat that caught the mouse, and he said, "Guess what? You're *in*!"

And I said, "I'm in *what*?"

And he said, "*Maggie* . . . you are in *The Wizard of Oz.*"

And I said, "Oh, I'm *not*! . . . I'm just flabbergasted!" Well, I didn't know what happened the rest of the ballgame, I can tell you that!

The official announcement was made exactly a week after Sondergaard's "ugly" tests. Howard Strickling was MGM's West Coast director of publicity, and in his MGM-news-of-the-day teletype on October 10, he notified Howard Dietz, "Margaret Hamilton replaces Gale Sondergaard in the role of The Wicked Witch of the West." Louella Parsons carried the item in her column two days later and noted that "Gale turned out to be 'too pretty' for the part." (By October 28, Sondergaard was over at Warner Bros., playing the Empress Eugenie in *Juarez.*) Hamilton's makeup and hairstyle were rather hastily devised, and William Tuttle remembers, "At that time, I don't believe there was such a thing as false fingernails that were made commercially . . . we used a film negative and cut out pieces that were glued onto her fingers for long nails."

The October 10 start-date came and went. But on-set tests were done on October 12, and the following day the *Oz* unit—at last—settled into principal photography. *Daily Variety* for October 14 observed the kick-off on its front page: "LeRoy Starts 'Wizard'—Mervyn LeRoy got 'Wizard of Oz' off yesterday at Metro with Ray Bolger and Judy Garland in first song and dance number, 'Scarecrow Song.' " During the week of October 17, Thorpe moved the company onto the set of the Wicked Witch's castle and, when Hedda Hopper came to visit, she got enough copy for half her column in the *Los Angeles Times*:

> Never expected to live long enough to see a zipper on a lion. Imagine my surprise when I viewed Bert Lahr . . . His suffering from the lion's face, which fits on over his upper lip and nose and ties to his ears, he likened to the agony of the Christian Martyrs in their hair shirts. He takes his soup through a straw. He tried a bit of steak for luncheon and was forced to spend so much time working to remove hunk that had anchored between his teeth, he hadn't made it when I left the set.
>
> Ray Bolger as the Scarecrow has an easier time. They gave him an India rubber face to match his body. His face is glued on over his own, leaving nose, mouth, and eyes out. Spent last weekend in seclusion rubbing lemon verbena soothing cream into his pores. He hadn't quite got the knack of pulling off his new face, so considerable of his own came with it . . .

But Buddy Ebsen as the Tin Man really had the miseries. His hair was completely covered with a silver cap. Then over his face is a layer of soft wax, sprinkled with a half a pound of silver dust, and he has a stationary chin strap from ear to ear. He relaxes against a huge ironing board with rests for his arms—supposed to ease the burden of cumbersome pants, which flare up in front like hoops of steel and prevent him from sitting.

They've all got a mad on at Judy Garland. She only suffers a blond wig.

Oz is in Technicolor, which makes the mechanical end three times as hard, but Director Dick Thorpe takes everything in stride. A nervous man would be in a psychopathic ward now . . .

It was an overzealous cameraman, with a love for spotlights, that took the job of the witch away from Gale Sondergaard and gave it to Margaret Hamilton. He made Gale so beautiful that Mervyn LeRoy was certain she couldn't be wicked.

Hopper's column appeared on October 25, several days after her trip to MGM. By then, events on the *Oz* set had gone seriously awry. On October 21, Thorpe had completed a segment that took place in the entrance hall of the Witch's castle. *Daily Variety* commented the next day,

Special camera boom 80 feet in length, with compressed air-operated mounting for Technicolor cameras, yesterday was used at Metro . . . Sequence took place on a long stairway, down which Judy Garland, Bert Lahr, Ray Bolger, and Buddy Ebsen seek escape . . . Camera followed them diagonally at distance of 150 feet for the take, said to be the longest boom shot ever made in color.

Successful or not, the scene would prove to be one of the last Buddy Ebsen did for *The Wizard of Oz*. The actor later recalled, "Production had been under way for ten days when, one night after dinner, I took a deep breath—and nothing happened! It felt like no air had reached my lungs . . . An ambulance took me to a hospital. My lungs felt as though someone had coated them with glue, and my breathing was excruciatingly labored. I wondered if I was dying."

In a series of emergency tests, doctors discovered that Ebsen was suffering from a form of allergic reaction. His lungs were indeed coated—by the alumi-num powder that had been dusted onto his tin makeup. As a result, he was placed in an oxygen tent, spent two weeks at Good Samaritan Hospital and then another month recuperating at home.

Naturally, panic reigned on the *Oz* set when Ebsen didn't appear for his next morning call. Within hours, however, that problem would be superseded by an even greater upheaval. Producer LeRoy was dissatisfied with the majority of the film's rushes to that point, and he decided on October 24 that Richard Thorpe had to be fired. The next day, the press was notified of Thorpe's dismissal and told the director was "seriously ill."

The "Thorpe Stills"

More than two dozen stills were made during Thorpe's two weeks of filming, and many of these have remained virtually uncirculated. A number of others were reproduced and reprinted in newspaper and magazine stories over the years, even though the makeup, costume, and staging concepts portrayed were often at odds with those seen in the finished movie. (Among other diverse elements, the pictures show the blond Judy Garland in a different Dorothy dress [above]; Ray Bolger in different makeup and trousers; Margaret Hamilton in a different makeup and hairstyle; and Buddy Ebsen as the Tin Woodman.) The next eight pages feature the "Thorpe stills."

Thorpe's first footage was shot on the Yellow Brick Road, where Dorothy met and rescued the Scarecrow from the cornfield.

The film unit next moved on to extensive work in the castle of the Wicked Witch. Surviving stills indicate that the following scenes were among those taken: (top left) the Witch as she watched Dorothy and her friends in the crystal ball; (top right and bottom left) the Witch as she sent her Winged Monkeys off to the Haunted Forest to "bring me that girl and her dog!" (Nikko stands near his mistress; the Monkey on the ledge is supposedly Metro stunt man George Noisom); (bottom right and facing page at top) the Witch, poised on her broom, as she prepared her own departure for Emerald City.

(left) The Witch pictured here is probably Hamilton's stand-in, Betty Danko. Much later in Oz filming, Danko would be hospitalized with an injured leg when the Witch's broom exploded during a stunt shot in which she was "flying in" for the star. (below) Thorpe also photographed the blond Dorothy as she was welcomed by the Wicked Witch: "It's so kind of you to visit me in my loneliness!"

Other Thorpe footage: (top left) Dorothy being threatened by the Witch; (remaining photos on this page) Nikko, the Witch's monkey commandant, on his way to "throw that basket in the river and drown" Toto.

(left) Toto in his escape from the Witch's castle. (The still indicates that Thorpe had different staging in mind for this sequence. In the finished film, the dog runs the length of the drawbridge and jumps the widening chasm as the bridge is raised, but the Winkie Guards follow *him*; they are not waiting on the other side of the gap.)

(above) "He got away! He got away!" Dorothy's exultant relief as she witnesses Toto's escape is not shared by the Witch. (above right) "Drat you and your dog! You've been more trouble to me than you're worth, one way and another, but it'll soon be over now!" (right) "I'll give you Auntie Em, my pretty!"

More Thorpe scenes: (left) Lahr, Ebsen, and Bolger, in disguise as Winkie Guards in their efforts to rescue Dorothy; (below) The reunion of the famous quartet—and Toto; Ebsen is on the right. (Another staging change is indicated here. Thorpe keeps the Lion, Scarecrow, and Tin Man in the Guard costumes throughout this sequence and in the escape attempt that follows, where the travelers are cornered at the inner door to the castle; see two bottom photos.)

In the finished film, the wrought-iron chandelier was replaced by a simpler wooden one. The original chandelier—slightly modified—is still visible in the movie as it was rehung outside the inner door of the Witch's castle.

(left) "My little party is just beginning!" The Witch has hurled her hourglass, and the distracting explosion gives the Scarecrow and Tin Man a chance to cut the rope and drop the chandelier on the Winkies. (below) The ensuing chase through the castle eventually leads the cast back past the fallen chandelier and (bottom) once again up the stairs to the Witch's chamber. (This is one of the final stills taken prior to Ebsen's illness and Thorpe's dismissal.)

CHAPTER 5

There'll Be Some Changes Made

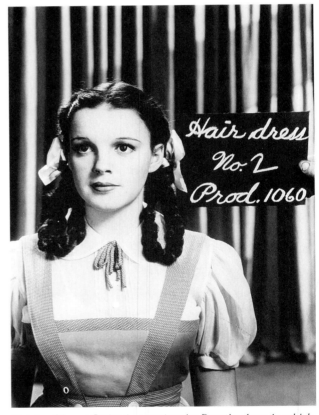

Production didn't stop for long, however. At the same time the press was informed of Thorpe's "illness," George Cukor was announced as the new director of *The Wizard of Oz*. In truth, Cukor was no more than a stopgap and only remained with the project until October 31. But during his brief stay he managed to effect several changes that ultimately contributed immeasurably to the success of the picture.

Cukor was at that time "on hold" while David O. Selznick organized his production of *Gone With the Wind*. When Mervyn LeRoy initially arranged to borrow the director, it was with the understanding that Cukor would be able to complete *Oz* by the first of the year; Selznick had scheduled *Wind* to begin its own complex shooting schedule in January 1939, and Cukor had been set to direct that picture since late 1936.

What became immediately apparent, however, was the fact that *Oz* could never be filmed in the eight or nine weeks left in 1938. *Daily Variety,* in its front-page notice about the director's assignment, offered that Cukor would do a "couple days reshooting . . . before picking up regular schedule." But the changes Cukor hoped to achieve for *Oz* actually meant that all of Thorpe's scenes would have to be scrapped and the entire picture begun from scratch. To compound the situation, Cukor had no interest in directing *The Wizard of Oz*, which he did not particularly admire as a book. He simply agreed to aid in what the production staff now felt were essential renovations.

On Wednesday, October 26, Cukor began new tests of Judy Garland. He was appalled by her appearance in the Thorpe footage and was determined to simplify her makeup and hairstyle. He also brought the young star to the realization that her characterization would be much more effective if she played the part straight amidst all the bizarre Ozians. Thorpe had evidently conceived the role as more that of a fancy,

October 26 saw Garland—wearing the Dorothy dress in which she had been filming—test a simple, more natural makeup and several new hairstyles and hairpieces. For the first time (above) her own hair was utilized, augmented by rather elaborate braids. (Garland never forgot the help she received from Cukor during the days of her Oz make over. When she and husband Sid Luft produced a remake of A Star is Born [1954], Cukor was her first choice for director of the project.)

(above and above right) Several variations of the original blond wig were also attempted on October 26.

(left) On October 31, Garland returned to test her own hair once again, with the addition of a long fall in different arrangements.

(above left) Garland tested two different ruby slippers on October 31. The one on her left foot came from the pair used during the two weeks of Thorpe footage; it is plainer than that ultimately seen in the finished picture. The shoe on her right foot was half of an ornate "Arabian Nights" or "elf" pair, rejected after this test as too elaborate. (The latter shoe was similar to the silver shoe drawn by Denslow for the first Oz book.) (above center and above) October 31 also saw the star test a simpler jumper dress. (left) By the time a new director was assigned to Oz, the new Dorothy was ready to film. These photographs were taken on November 3.

fairy-tale ingenue and had directed Garland accordingly. Instead, Cukor convinced her she had only to be herself—and no ersatz glamourine—to be believable. It was advice that would prove instrumental in the subsequent sincerity of her performance.

During the remainder of Cukor's week, he oversaw production of a couple of new styles of costume, hair arrangement, makeup, and ruby slippers for Dorothy. Ray Bolger's facial makeup was also softened somewhat during that time and, on Monday, October 31, he and Garland appeared for stills and Technicolor tests of the new images. (It was probably Cukor who recommended a new hairstyle and profile for the Wicked Witch as well although, with the switch in directors, Margaret Hamilton did not actually film again until mid-November, two weeks after Cukor's departure from the picture.)

The Wizard of Oz was, in effect, vamping during these days of experimentation and tests. With Cukor obviously only an interim director, Mervyn LeRoy pleaded with the studio for the chance to return to direction himself and take over the foundering production. But Louis B. Mayer once again demurred, feeling that producing the film was still task enough. .

Finally, on October 31, while Cukor was putting the finishing touches on the revised Dorothy and Scarecrow, the studio teletype from Strickling to Dietz carried the news: "Victor Fleming will direct *The Wizard of Oz*."

While Cukor was revamping Judy Garland, Ray Bolger's facial makeup was softened as well. October 31 found him in a couple of different changes and with a visible "ear." Though the ear would be minimized when the picture was begun again the following week, the Scarecrow—as he came to be remembered—was finally ready to go.

Bolger also tried on another pair of trousers on October 31.

George Cukor saw to it that Margaret Hamilton's hair was restyled and pulled back severely to better expose the hateful visage of the Wicked Witch. (As such, it was also closer to the style that would be worn by Miss Gulch.) Her nose and chin were also restructured for maximum effectiveness. There is a (possibly apocryphal) story that the Oz film unit, suitably horrified by Hamilton's appearance, saw to it that the actress's behind-the-scenes "director's chair" bore the legend "Mag the Hag." (If the story is true, there's little doubt that Hamilton took the situation well.)

CHAPTER 6

The Wizard Comes to Life

It was not as strange a choice as it has since seemed to some for, by 1938, Victor Fleming had already developed a reputation as a "savior" of troubled pictures. Still, he was better known—personally and professionally—for his rough-and-ready, "man's man" style. His films were energetic and driving dramas or adventures with (when called for) a wry, contemporary humor. He'd begun his movie career as a cameraman, and then quickly become a director of silent features in the 1920s. By the 1930s, he was responsible for such popular Metro successes as *Red Dust, Treasure Island, Captains Courageous,* and *Test Pilot.* None of these was a fantasy.

So it took the prodding of both LeRoy and Mayer to convince Fleming to accept the *Oz* assignment. LeRoy felt that *The Wizard of Oz* required the touch of a man who had the heart, emotions, and mind of a child, someone who could provide the film with the proper fantasy atmosphere. These elements weren't apparent to the producer in Richard Thorpe or his guidance of the picture, and LeRoy's instincts told him the right qualities would be found in Victor Fleming.

Screenwriter John Lee Mahin had been for several years Fleming's frequent associate, working with him on-set to polish a shooting script as filming went along. When Fleming came to *Oz,* Mahin came with him, and the writer always thought the director finally agreed to take on the project because of his love for his two little daughters, Victoria (then four years old) and Sarah (a year-old baby). Fleming told Mahin, "I did it because I wanted them to see such a picture . . . [about] a search for beauty and decency."

The front page of both trade papers for November 1 carried the news that Fleming was succeeding Thorpe and Cukor. ("1 Week—3 Meggers" was the rather dry headline in the *Hollywood Reporter.*) On November 4, after four days spent in initial script revisions with Mahin, Fleming began shooting the picture all over again. Garland and Bolger were called to redo their introductory sequence at the yellow brick crossroads. In addition to costume and makeup adjust-

ments, the changeover in directors resulted as well in a different look for that set; the road was curbed, and the artificial-looking oval bricks were replaced with more standard rectangular ones.

The new beginnings for *Oz* were immediately fraught with the same odd trials that had plagued the preceding regime. Wallace Worsley, an assistant director on the film, had worked at MGM for more than five years by autumn 1938. (He would continue at the studio until 1949, diversify into television and movie work in New York and abroad, and cap his career with assignments on such successes as *Deliverance* and *Coal Miner's Daughter.*) Almost fifty years later, Worsley remembered November 4, 1938, on Stage 26. The planned segment that day included the services of Jim (billed as "the world's only trained raven") and assistant electrician Chris Bergswich, known at MGM as "the animal man" because of his ability to deal with skittish or recalcitrant movie animals:

> The first day that we shot with Fleming was Judy and Toto coming down the Yellow Brick Road to the Scarecrow . . . and [at one point] he had on his shoulder a raven. We finally got ready for our first shot, sometime between ten and eleven in the morning . . . probably closer to eleven. Chris was hiding in the cornstalks . . . He had a piece of thread on the raven's foot so that, if the raven would start to fly away, he could catch him. Well, on the very first take, the raven flew away and broke the thread. [Stage 26] was one of the new stages, and the beams were about sixty feet above the stage. [Chris] had to climb up there—talking all the time to his raven—and we sat and watched him. Well, we decided to go to lunch. We came back from lunch—he was still up there. Finally, at four o'clock, he still hadn't caught the raven . . . so we all went home. Everybody was in hysterics.
>
> I think he got him about two A.M.

THE WIZARD OF OZ

INTER-OFFICE COMMUNICATION

To____ Messrs. Thau, Mayfack, LeRoy, Chic

Subject____ JACK HALEY

From____ I. H. Prinzmetal ____Date____ 11/19/38

Dr. C. Lewis Gaulden, chief physician for our insurance carriers, examined Mr. Haley on the set this afternoon and advises that Haley is not ill, and that there is no danger of any illness from the present make-up. He advises that Mr. Haley is convinced of this fact.

I. H. Prinzmetal

An MGM memo details the studio's efforts to spare Jack Haley the makeup problems that beset Buddy Ebsen.

Elsewhere at MGM on November 4, a letter of agreement was directed to Loew's, Inc. from Twentieth Century-Fox in which the latter agreed "to lend you the services of Jack Haley . . . for the role of 'Hickory Twicker.'" With Buddy Ebsen far from recovered, LeRoy had no choice but to look elsewhere for a Tin Woodman. He found him in Haley, a thirty-nine-year-old vaudevillian who'd alternated Broadway and Hollywood stardom for the preceding decade. The actor already knew the other *Oz* principals and had worked with Lahr in burlesque and with Garland in *Pigskin Parade*. He immediately reported to MGM for refittings of Ebsen's costume and tests of a new makeup; the former aluminum powder had become aluminum paste, thus eliminating any danger of inhalation.

The press was told of Haley's new role on November 7, and the "official" diagnosis of Ebsen's illness was given as pneumonia. Over the next few months, columnists would also cite pleurisy and the actual allergic reaction as reasons for the actor's replacement. Ebsen finally returned to MGM on December 13 for a part in *Four Girls in White*.

By the second week of November, Mahin was tinkering with the script for Jack Haley's initial scenes while Fleming shot the apple orchard sequence. MGM publicity proclaimed that the studio "rented" three hundred birds from the financially strapped Zoo Park in Los Angeles so that the director could select an appropriate few for background atmosphere amidst the trees. Among others, the birds included golden pheasants, a South American toucan, and an African crane. Much to Garland's delight, a Saurus crane went after Ray Bolger's straw stuffing on the set, and the dancer had to retreat to his dressing room until the bird could be restrained.

Oddity in Oz: *Victor Fleming faced a directorial challenge in offering performance guidance to an apple tree; the tree, at least, appears to be considering the suggestions. (Voices for the Oz apple trees were provided by Abe Dinovitch.)*

78

(right) The rust-free Jack Haley is pictured during his initial days in Oz. Garland is using a different oil can than would be seen in the finished picture, suggesting this, too, was changed when Haley was taken out and tarnished for retakes.

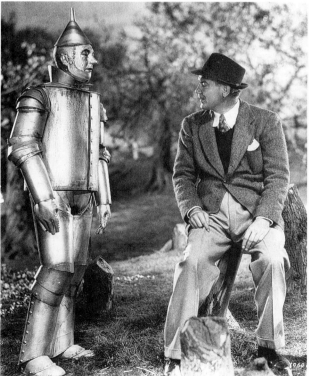

(above) Jack Haley first posed in his rusted costume and makeup on November 15. (right) Victor Fleming has a quiet conversation with the new-to-Oz Jack Haley.

Several more agreeable fowl segued with Fleming to the first Tin Woodman segment by the end of the week. "For three days," Jack Haley recalled shortly thereafter, "I worked in a shiny suit of tin, with a sparkling tin nose, a bright tin strap around my head, a glistening tin pot on my head, and a coat of brilliant tin paint on my face. I glittered no end—for three days." Then it occurred to Fleming and Mahin that the Tin Woodman, at that point in the story, was supposed to have been "standing over there rusting for the longest time." Thorpe's scenes, a month earlier, had been shot out of story sequence, and Ebsen's costume was designed for those later moments in the plot, *after* his character had visited the Emerald City for the first time and been detarnished and polished by the Wash & Brush Up Co.

Thus all three days of filming with the shiny Haley were unacceptable and scrapped, at an estimated cost of more than sixty thousand dollars. The Tin Man's suit was taken out and speckled with red chemical "rust," his makeup was adjusted yet again, and, on November 15, Haley tested his new look. Fleming then began the Tin Woodman scenes once more and, by November 19, Haley, Bolger, and Garland were shooting their chorus of "We're Off to See the Wizard."*

Elsewhere at MGM, another series of Oz adventures was beginning. Leo Singer had done his recruitment work well, and what he hadn't accomplished, MGM publicity had: dozens of midgets were arriving in Culver City to augment Singer's own troupe and the other little people already in the Los Angeles area. An All American Bus Lines coach left New York on November 5, and carried—per studio records— twenty-eight midgets and two "adults"; an additional midget and "adult" were picked up in Pittsburgh, and

*Haley had rerecorded the Tin Woodman's "If I Only Had a Heart" eleven days earlier, and he would later rerecord a couple of solo lines in the introduction to "The Jitterbug" and at the end of "If I Only Had the Nerve." But it was deemed unnecessary to rerecord his group singing with the other principals, so the voice of Buddy Ebsen can still be heard on the *Oz* soundtrack during either chorus of "We're Off to See the Wizard" after the Tin Man joins the travelers.

The Scarecrow and Dorothy invite the Tin Man to join them on their trip to see the Wizard, while the Wicked Witch hovers on the cottage roof to interrupt their conversation. In the right foreground, producer LeRoy leans over to discuss the scene with Victor Fleming, seated in the director's chair. (November 1938)

the bus arrived in Hollywood on November 10.* Other little people hit town via train, bus, and trailer around the same time.

Meinhardt Raabe had worked with midget troupes all around the country during school vacations and after his 1936 graduation from the University of Wisconsin. By 1938, he was twenty-three years old, forty-eight inches tall, and "Little Oscar—the world's smallest chef," working in a promotional capacity for the Oscar Mayer Meat Packing Company. Raabe heard about *Oz* through

what we called the "midget grapevine." Word came through the channels that MGM was going to make a picture; they wanted all the little people. I asked my employer for a leave of absence, and I headed for California. Every little person who walked through the front gate out at MGM got a job as a Munchkin if they were physically able.

There were many of us who came in as independents, who had never had any contact with Singer. [But he] had the master contract to supply the Munchkins so, to go to work, I had to sign up with Singer.

The studio arranged accommodations for all the out-of-town midgets; many stayed at the Culver City Hotel. But, as Raabe remembers, "That little hotel didn't have room for 130 Munchkins, so we were 'farmed out' among the private homes in Culver City. Fortunately, I happened to be in the home of a family who were bit players, so they were able to give me a lot of background information as to the workings of the movies."

The majority of the little people were massed for publicity pictures as they entered the Metro gates on November 11, and the *Oz* staff spent the next few days casting the specific Munchkin performing parts. Meinhardt Raabe was selected "through process of elimination" to play the Munchkin Coroner who would, in the words of E. Y. Harburg, aver that the Wicked Witch of the East "was really, most sincerely dead." Then, according to Raabe, "Adrian and his staff measured each individual Munchkin, asking what lines they had, what their part was." Everyone then got a unique, specially designed costume, made of heavy felt. "It couldn't be flimsy material; it had to stand up" under heavy lights, through days of filming.

*All MGM files regarding the midgets refer to any of the average-size people traveling with them as "adults," the inaccurate implication being that the midgets were not!

This form letter of agreement was signed by all the Munchkins brought to work on Oz *by Leo Singer. They agreed to "look solely to" the manager for their compensation, although he paid some of them considerably less than the one hundred dollars per week per person he was receiving from the studio.*

By November 22, the little people were working on the Munchkinland song-and-dance routines with choreographer Bobby Connolly and his assistants, Arthur "Cowboy" Appell and Dona Massin. A number of the midgets had, of course, done stage work, pictures, vaudeville, and carnival tours. But the majority were not "show business," and Connolly later felt that teaching them to dance was "the toughest job" of his *Oz* work. "We laid out chalk lines on the stage floor to guide them in getting into position for formation. We trained them for days in a lockstep to practice keeping in time to music. Then we went into individual steps."

The little people practiced day after day for several weeks. Meinhardt Raabe proudly acknowledges the *Oz* staff as "very adamant about detail . . . they were perfectionists. We had to be on a certain yellow brick on a certain note in a certain position."

In addition to his work with the Munchkins, Connolly devoted a couple of days in late November to staging the drill formation of the Wicked Witch's Winkie Guards, the ominous coterie who would march to the chant "O—Ee—Yah! Eoh—Ah!" The routine called for more than twenty strong men, all over six feet tall; each Winkie costume of coat, headdress, and armor weighed fifty pounds. (One guard, Ambrose Schindler, was recruited from the University of Southern California where he'd been a star football player.)

The *Oz* participants got a brief respite from rehearsals on November 25 when a small ceremony was held to celebrate Judy Garland's studio-promoted ascendancy from "featured player" to "star" on the MGM roster. As members of the crew and cast looked on, she was presented with her own trailer dressing room.

By that time, Fleming was at work on the Lion's Forest set, filming the first scenes with Bert Lahr. Garland's abundant sense of humor was fast brought to the fore by Lahr's performance and, in their initial film encounter, she was unable—take after take—to keep from breaking into laughter. Her joy was real; Mary Astor, who'd worked with Garland only weeks before, later wrote that the young star "got the giggles regularly. You just couldn't get annoyed, because she couldn't help it—it was no act. Something would strike her funny, and her face would get red, and 'there goes Judy!' would be the cry. And we just had to wait until she got over it." Garland herself admitted to friends in 1966, "Once I've started laughing, I can't stop. At MGM, they all knew that and, if I broke up on

the set at something, the director would yell, 'Take ten!,' giving me time to laugh it out of my system." John Lee Mahin was present for the incident with Lahr and Garland and, in 1983, remembered the way Fleming dealt with the situation:

> Vic was a wonderful man, and this proves it. When Dorothy first met the Cowardly Lion, and he was growling at her and rushing at her, she slapped him. And she was supposed to keep on after him . . . "How dare you growl at people?" Instead, of course, the Cowardly Lion twitched his tail up and started to cry. Well, Dorothy burst out laughing . . . and they couldn't get her to stop laughing. [Finally,] Vic took her behind the set, behind one of the trees: "Now, darling . . . this is serious" . . . and he slapped her face, hard. And he said, "Go in there and work." [They] did it: one take of the scene. He said, "Cut! Marvelous!" Then he turned to me—he was a big, tough-looking guy with a broken nose—he turned to me and said, "I wish you'd hit me in the nose and break it again." I said, "Why?" "Because of what I did to her."

Garland evidently came up to Fleming and overheard him say again to Mahin, "I wish you'd hit me in the

Even in a posed still, Judy Garland seems to be stifling a smile as she pretends to slap Bert Lahr.

This view of Oz "Set No. 11/Lion Forest" was taken on November 21, 1938. (courtesy Bill Chapman)

nose" for, according to the writer, "she said, 'I won't do that . . . but I'll kiss your nose.' And she kissed him, right on the nose."

The star's relationship with the director continued on that happy plane. He affectionately nicknamed her "Judalein" and kept careful watch over the playful treatment she sometimes received from her three ex-vaudevillian costars. Garland herself warmly remembered this as long afterward as 1962. In a television appearance with Jack Paar, the host led her into some merry reminiscences about *Oz* and asked her to tell the audience "how those clowns tried to crowd you out . . ." She kiddingly responded that Lahr, Bolger, and Haley "are my friends *now,* but then . . ."—the implication being that, as a young girl, she was understandably not part of their circle.

> Well, whenever we'd do that little dance up the Yellow Brick Road, I was supposed to be with them . . . and they'd shut me out! They would close in—the three of them—and I would be in back of them, dancing. And I wasn't good enough to say, "Wait a minute, now . . . !" So the director, Victor Fleming—who was a darling man; he was always up on a boom—would say, "HOLD it! . . . You three *dirty* HAMS, let that little girl in there! *Let her in there!*"

The narrow road and overwhelming bulk of the men's costumes did make it virtually impossible for the four to stride comfortably abreast out of the Lion's Forest. And, although Garland's anecdote is best regarded as an example of her lifelong penchant for embellishing a situation to entertain her listeners, it also gives an indication of the kind of kidding, humor, and morale-boosting that pervaded the *Oz* set—necessary measures in coping with the mounting difficulties of the production. Ray Bolger later stated, "We joked a lot because that was the only way we could survive."

For Bolger, Lahr, and Haley, *Oz* was—from the beginning—an ordeal. The men got up at 4:30 A.M., six days a week, to be at MGM in time for what could be up to two hours of makeup and costuming. In spite of the change from aluminum powder to paste for the Tin Man's face, Haley suffered a severe eye infection that kept him off the picture for several days; he had to stay at home in a darkened room until the ailment cleared. Additionally, his forty-pound costume made it impossible for him to sit down and, between takes, his only recourse was to recline on a slant board.

Bolger suddenly developed tiny lines in his face, the residual effect of gluing on and peeling off the Scarecrow mask for four months. Margaret Hamilton had a slight green tint to her skin even weeks after playing the Wicked Witch. But Bert Lahr suffered most of all.

When stripped out of the lion skins after a take, Lahr and his costume had to be blasted with air from blow dryers, both to cool him down and to make the perspiration-drenched wardrobe bearable for the next shot. His discomfort was acute and, as such, everything seemed to conspire against him. When he saw Haley relaxing between takes on his slant board, insomniac Lahr could only wryly comment, "That son-of-a-bitch could sleep hung up on a meat hook, and I can't sleep at night!"

The Scarecrow, Tin Man, Lion, and Witch weren't even allowed to escape the set at lunchtime. Their makeups were considered potentially off-putting to the appetite of anyone eating in the Metro restaurant. The actors were instead requested to "order in"; the commissary would deliver. Hamilton, unable to eat much of anything for fear of ingesting some of her makeup, brought her lunch from home. She best summed up the problems of stifling makeup and cumbersome wardrobe when she remembered, "We were *always* so uncomfortable *all* the time. You had to watch yourself going up and down the steps and running in and out. It made you so *tired* at night." Hamilton also had to balance her tall witch's hat, manipulate her cloak to avoid tripping on its hem, and try to keep her makeup from staining her costume. The Wicked Witch's laugh was her own invention, but the shrill cackle blew out several sound tubes while she was recording her dialogue. And her false fingernails popped off in a shower of celluloid whenever she grabbed anything too quickly.

The constant script revisions created further headaches. Bolger said later, "Everyone seemed to be doing the writing. Every day, we would receive pages of new dialogue as a result of something the director didn't like . . . We never [knew] whether what we had prepared the night before would actually be shot or whether we would have to redo everything when we got to the studio the next morning." At Fleming's request, Mahin continued to work on the script throughout the shooting, often providing what he referred to as "little tag lines" to put a laugh at the end of a sequence. The writer sometimes consulted Haley for old vaudeville bits to give the Cowardly Lion, although Lahr himself came up with the classic "Unusual weather we're havin', ain't it?" when awakened by a snow shower in the poppy field. The diplomatic Mahin would later be called upon to arbitrate a Langley/Ryerson/Woolf dispute over the *Oz* screenwriting credits; he personally refused any credit at all.

Another problem that plagued the *Oz* actors and staff was the heat from the lights. Meinhardt Raabe remembers a conversation with chief unit electrician A. W. Brown. "He told me that *Oz* used 'the most lights, the most electricity of any picture' that had ever been made. They had two huge energizing generators outside our [sound stage] to provide the extra current. We had more than 150 thirty-six-inch arc lamps hanging from the ceiling to produce 'natural sunlight.'" The Munchkinland set, with its giant artificial flowers and thatched roofs, required "a fireman going around with a meter all day long, checking to see where there were any hot spots . . . He would find [one] and say, 'turn out that light!' to lessen the concentration on a particular spot." The lights also resulted in several cases of "klieg eyes" for members of the *Oz* unit. The swelling and pink inflammation caused by the powerful rays could only be eased by several days of rest.

Wallace Worsley recalls: "Air conditioning was fairly primitive at that time, even though we had the best there was. But [when the lights got too hot], we would stop for two or three hours [and] open all the doors to clear the set of smoke before we made the next take—another reason *Oz* took so long." Bolger's memories were the same, and he elaborated, "When you opened the doors of the enormous stages they had at MGM, it took a long time to close them again and get reorganized for shooting. Everything was time consuming."

"*All* the shots were complicated," remembers Worsley and, as Haley said in a 1939 interview, "We were lucky when we got four setups shot in a day. Normally, that's half a morning's work. It took all afternoon to get the right take on one of Toto's scenes. Time is what ate up all the money . . . Sometimes, we'd all have to sit around for an hour—I'd be reclining on that board—while Judy was studying social science or something like that." Judy Garland, as a minor, was required by law to spend three hours of her eight-hour day with a tutor. Years later, she laughed and said, "I got all mixed up . . . I'd do a scene

A 1939 magazine photo showed a costumed Garland, her stand-in, and their school teacher at lunch in the MGM commissary.

84

(right) Fleming and LeRoy relax on the Oz set with actress Norma Shearer. The latter was made up for her role in the concurrent MGM production Idiot's Delight. *(below) The legendary Louis B. Mayer, head of MGM, beams paternally at two of his most prized personalities. Mickey Rooney was one of the top box-office attractions in the country in 1939. Oz, and the musicals made with Rooney, would soon elevate Judy Garland to the same status.*

and then be rushed off by the schoolteacher to study arithmetic for eight minutes, and then they'd call me back to do another scene. And then back to seventeen minutes of history. I wound up reciting more history in the scenes . . .''

The delays, cast replacements, discarded footage, and parade of directors took its toll on the *Oz* unit. At one point, MGM decided all the effort wasn't worth the results being achieved and decided to close down the production. LeRoy was forced to argue it back from abandonment: "They wanted to stop it—they said 'it's just for kids'—'it's costing too much.'" Arthur Freed purportedly told the executives, "If I had two and a half million dollars, I'd buy this picture from you. It'll be worth more than that someday." MGM

MGM star Wallace Beery and his daughter Carol Ann visit the studio photo gallery where the prop Oz book played an important part in several publicity stills for the picture. Beery himself wanted to play the title role in The Wizard of Oz, *and there reportedly exists a small publicity photo of the actor— distributed as a cigarette pack giveaway/premium circa 1938— that mistakenly lists* Oz *among his credits.*

Andy Hardy mugs with the Scarecrow: Mickey Rooney visited the Oz set during the first days of shooting.

years. Jack Haley characterized the sixteen-year-old as "born to brilliance," and Worsley described her similarly: "She was *naturally* brilliant; in fact, she never had to work hard to do anything. Where other people really had to work at singing or dancing or *any*thing, she picked it up like *that*." Margaret Hamilton thought, "Judy kept us all going. When she came on the set, it was as though the lights got brighter." Garland enjoyed a special friendship with Hamilton during the making of *Oz*. In 1985, Garland's daughter Lorna Luft told an interviewer, "Mama said she had a real hard time pretending to be scared of . . . the Wicked Witch . . . In between takes, Margaret would serve tea to Mama, and they would laugh so hard that Margaret's green makeup would start to run into her cup of tea. Mama said every time she would have to cower at the Witch, all she could think about was this soiled, discolored green crumpet Margaret would give her with all the panache of a great lady—as if she were some kind of Technicolor Queen Victoria."

Thus, *Oz* continued—despite the ominous rumblings from the front office and with laughter and determination in the face of behind-the-scenes strain and on-set difficulties. By the fourth week under Victor Fleming, the cast was playing their scenes in the poppy field. (It had taken twenty men a full week to im-

nervously allowed the picture to continue but lived in fear of any advance adverse publicity. So LeRoy and Freed closed the set to press and visitors; Worsley recalls "there was a cop on the door" through much of the shooting schedule.

What saved the unit was the aforementioned kidding and clowning, coupled with the dedication and enthusiasm of cast and crew. The director was a special catalyst: "Obstacles make for a better picture!" was Fleming's stated motto, and Worsley recalls the difference between Thorpe and Fleming as "like night and day. Fleming was a real interesting character. If he saw a grip doing something wrong, he'd . . . show him how to do it." The assistant also noted that LeRoy "let Fleming do it his own way" and seldom interfered on the set. (As a director himself, LeRoy knew the independent Fleming would hate—and not need—a producer looking over his shoulder.) Meinhardt Raabe remembers Fleming's consideration and how he extended himself even to the Munchkins; the director "got along famously with the little people." And Billie Burke beamed to a 1939 interviewer, "It was fun working on *Oz*. Vic was like a schoolboy, so excited about the film's possibilities."

The unit also enjoyed Judy Garland; there were no signs of the difficulties that would beset her in later

Garland has her makeup freshened between Oz takes on the Tin Woodman set in November 1938. (courtesy Bill Chapman)

In the Emerald City: *(top) Test shots taken in January 1939. The deleted "triumphal return": (middle left) The chorus in the parade. (middle right) The principal cast and honor escort. (bottom left) While extras rest in the background, a test is made* *of the principals. Garland is replaced for the moment by Bobbie Koshay; Lahr's right arm is out of the lion-costume sleeve, and he's holding a cigarette. (bottom right) The quartet is marched to the palace; the scene dissolved here to the throne room.*

(above) The original 1939 Oz campaign book was one of the most painstakingly prepared and lavishly lithographed of its kind. The oversize package was distributed to theater owners for use in publicizing and exploiting the film; it included illustrations of lobby standees, posters, lobby cards, banners, and tie-in products. *(On facing page, top)* The original Oz "24-sheet" was designed for billboard-size spaces. *(bottom)* Lobby cards, usually measuring eleven by fourteen inches, were generally produced in sets of eight: a title card and seven hand-colored stills from the movie. Pictured here is one of the original scene cards used in the initial release of Oz; it offers a moment from the deleted "triumphal return" sequence.

THE TALK OF HOLLYWOOD

In the world's motion picture capital "The Wizard of Oz" is being heralded as Movieland's triumph of 1939. Filmed in Technicolor, set entirely to music and given realism throughout, it faithfully tells the story which has sold nine million copies since it was written by L. Frank Baum in 1900.

(above) MGM prepared a color postcard, "The Talk of Hollywood," to herald the Grauman's Oz premiere in August 1939. (courtesy Michael Patrick Hearn)

(On facing page, top) This splashy flyer was designed to be folded in four and distributed as a theater giveaway in 1939. The exterior included a panel (not shown here) whereon the theater owner could imprint his name and playdates. (left) The interior was solid Oz advertising. (Both sides featured an abundance of gleeful hyperbole.)

Three people of Oz—Jack Haley as the Tin Woodman who wanted a heart, Ray Bolger as the Scarecrow who wanted a brain and Bert Lahr as the Cowardly Lion who wanted courage. All are former Broadway musical comedy stars.

Wearing the magic ruby slippers which she gets when her house falls on a witch in the land of Oz, Dorothy (Judy Garland) meets the Scarecrow.

'The Wizard of Oz' Makes the Movies

THIRTY-NINE years after his original debut, "The Wizard of Oz" is again coming out of Hollywood to amuse and intrigue the world. L. Frank Baum, a newspaper man who lived in Hollywood and in Coronado, California, first created the character and the other people of the fantastic land of Oz in a book, "The Wizard of Oz," written in 1900. It has since sold 9,000,000 copies, and 20 years after Baum's death—at Hollywood in 1919—his Oz books are selling at the rate of 100,000 a year. Now Metro-Goldwyn-Mayer has made it into a super-color production, with a cast including Judy Garland as Dorothy, who is blown to the land of Oz by a Kansas cyclone, Frank Morgan as the Wizard, Ray Bolger, the dancer, as the Scarecrow, Bert Lahr as the Cowardly Lion, Jack Haley as the Tin Woodman, and Billie Burke as the Good Witch.

A new score has been written to supplant that of the stage musical comedy version in which Dave Montgomery and Fred Stone scored a great success in 1904. The picture, which is to be released soon, took a year to make, employed 9200 actors, and had to be cut down from a half million feet of color film. These are the first stills to be released from the production, which was directed by Victor Fleming.

On top of the Tin Woodman's cottage is the Wicked Witch (Margaret Hamilton), who tries to prevent the Tin Woodman, the Scarecrow and Dorothy from getting to the Wizard. Dorothy clutches her dog Toto in fear.

The four adventurers knock at the door of the palace of the Wizard of Oz to ask for aid. Frank Morgan, the Wizard, is the man behind the mustachios.

On facing page: (left) The original 1939 insert poster measured fourteen by thirty-six inches; (top right) the smaller, "midget card" poster for 1939 (courtesy Tod Machin); (bottom right) the cover of the 1939 Exploitation Book, part of the original campaign folder.

(This page) Part of the Oz campaign: this layout appeared in the St. Louis Post-Dispatch picture section of July 16, 1939. Most similar color features included Kodachrome photographs exclusively provided for the use of the specific publication.

(top left) During early promotion for The Wizard of Oz, *Judy Garland appeared on the cover of* Modern Movies *(March 1939) in a dress created for her by the film's costume designer, Gilbert Adrian. (top right) Garland, Lahr, and Haley as depicted by Earl Christy for* Screen Romances *(August 1939). (bottom*

left) Ray Bolger sat for cover art for Minicam *(August 1939). The Kodachrome was taken by MGM's Eric Carpenter, and an accompanying article was written by camera chief John Arnold. (bottom right) Judy Garland as Dorothy made an engaging portrait for* Movie Life *(August 1939).*

The amount of lighting equipment required for Technicolor photography in 1938–39 is everywhere apparent in this production still of the Witch's castle.

plant some forty thousand artificial flowers into the set floor on Stage 29.) In early December, Fleming took the unit back to the Witch's castle where, among other scenes, he reshot the sequences originally done by Richard Thorpe. Margaret Hamilton was there called upon to "torch" Ray Bolger while delivering the line, "How about a little fire, Scarecrow?" Fleming supposedly encouraged her, "Light him as if he were a cigarette." Bolger's suit had been chemically fireproofed, but Hamilton was understandably on edge. The scene took five takes to complete; "Let's try it again," Fleming would call . . . and then add, pointedly: "Miss Hamilton, *please* look as if you *enjoyed* it." According to Hedda Hopper, the Wicked Witch "fainted dead away . . . after she had done her bad deed."

One of the film's most memorable special effects was accomplished on the same set when the Wicked Witch melted away. "It was so doggone simple," according to Buddy Gillespie. "We just had her on a little hydraulic lift [and] dropped her down through the

floor. Her black costume was fastened down to the floor. We had a little dry ice, or liquid smoke, that came out to make it look as though she were melting. And she went down and down and down! Her black hat stayed on the floor, and her costume just spread out and covered up the hole."

It was during these Winkie sequences that one of the Witch's guards inadvertently stepped on Terry/Toto. The dog was, with some effort, temporarily replaced by another terrier. (A second dog was already being used in some instances as Terry's stand-in for rehearsals, and a tiny stuffed animal was supposedly pressed into service for lengthy color and lighting tests.) Terry was a trouper, however, and returned by midmonth for the Munchkinland sequences. Meinhardt Raabe recalls the dog as "so well trained. She performed completely in response to hand signals from her trainer who was out of camera range. [The dog] was attentive to Dorothy all the time, as if she was intimately devoted to her, so . . . it was not obvious she was being directed by anyone."

The melting of the Wicked Witch.

Meanwhile, vocal arranger Ken Darby was preparing for the prerecordings of the "Munchkinland" number:

> Herbert Stothart called me in and said, "We need some Munchkin voices . . . a lot of [the midgets] can't sing very well, and a lot of them are German and can only speak [that] language. And we have to create a sound . . ." So I got my arithmetic going, and I figured it out. Film speed is ninety feet per minute. I got together with [Supervising Sound Recorder] Douglas Shearer; we recorded a metronome click track at the speed Herbert Stothart and I agreed would be the right tempo for the Munchkin sequence, along with a tone on the piano giving the key in which we wanted the music to finally be recorded. The arithmetic went like this: There are twelve halftones in an octave. I divided twelve into ninety feet per minute and got a quotient of seven and a half feet for each semitone. Next, I multiplied this by four, which gave me thirty feet per minute, equal to a major third. Then, subtracting thirty from ninety, we found we needed a machine that would play back our click track and piano key at sixty feet per minute and slow the vocal performance of the singer proportionately. That sounds like a lot of malarkey . . . but that's the way it had to be done."

It was Shearer's responsibility to create the special machinery that would make the recording at the slower pace. Then, according to Darby, "We slowed down 'D-i-n-g d-o-n-g t-h-e w-i-t-c-h i-s d-e-a-d . . . ' I had all these so-called Ken Darby Singers in there, and when we played them back at ninety feet per minute, it was what you hear in the picture. Herb could put his downbeat to it and conduct to the click track we had made originally; it was in the right key, and the orchestra didn't have to change pitch." (Darby also recalls, "[For] the Winkies, we did the reverse, and it gave them a sepulcher kind of a sound.")

Construction on the Munchkin set began the week of December 5. It stood ninety feet high, built to scale (one-quarter normal size) and included dozens of tiny houses and shops, a public square, a bridge over a tiny stream, a fountain, little pathways and streets, and the beginning of the Yellow Brick Road. According to studio publicity, forty painters worked a week in more than sixty colors to give the set the proper and special glow: it was to be the first Technicolor scene *Oz* film audiences would see. Cedric Gibbons told an interviewer, "To fashion a 'Munchkinland' which a little girl from Kansas might have dreamed, we began with a premise that the smallest things she had ever seen were probably ants. And how do ants live? Under grass and tree roots. So, with toadstools and anthills as our architectural pattern, we made proportionately larger grass and flowers, such as hollyhocks twenty feet tall." Meinhardt Raabe remembers the unique situation created by the Munchkin lily pond: "They put a lot of bluing in the water, as if it was reflecting a real sky. Then they had these little white ducklings floating around. But the ducks absorbed the color . . . and turned out to be blue ducks! So the technicians had to drain the pool and paint the bottom blue, so it would have the correct blue cast."

Darby's music rehearsals and prerecordings began December 9 and continued through December 22. There were eight sessions in all, including (at one point or another) Judy Garland, Billie Burke, the King's Men Octet (three of whom were vocal doubles for the Lollipop Guild), the Debutantes (a girls' trio who sang the parts of the Lullaby League), thirteen principal singers, forty-five musicians, and several of the midgets. Lorraine Bridges was later called to redo the singing for Burke's Glinda; among the other principals was Pinto Colveg, who won fame as the voice of Walt Disney's "Goofy."

The days spent on the Munchkin segment brought new problems to the *Oz* unit. As early as December 1, one of the little people had to be dismissed from the picture: Marjorie Raia was "too young for working purposes." Another midget, Elsie Schultz, was injured in a car accident on December 21 and had to quit the film. Choreographer Bobby Connolly came down with influenza in the midst of rehearsals and was away for several days; Albertina Rasch was brought in to continue staging in his absence.

The makeup process for the little people was as difficult as for the principal cast—and the crew had over 120 midgets to prepare each day. Raabe says that, initially,

> Jack Dawn designed each individual makeup. He drew the makeup on a person according to what your part was going to be. Then they took a still

Glinda invites the Munchkins to "come out, come out" and greet Dorothy and Toto at the beginning of their sequence in the film. Metro musical arranger Roger Edens stands just left of center at the base of the photograph; Victor Fleming stands to the left of the camera boom with his hands on his lower back. (December 1938)

Meinhardt Raabe (left) explains that, as Munchkin Coroner, he has "thoroughly examined" the Wicked Witch of the East.

picture and put that into a file so, the next morning when you went to work, one of the assorted makeup men would get your picture out of the file and make you up exactly like Jack Dawn had done. Some [Munchkins] had higher cheekbones, mustaches . . . we all wore a skullcap and whatever hairstyle they wanted [was] put on over the top.

Dawn's assembly-line routine for the midgets involved thirty or more makeup artists; William Tuttle remembers the crew "carrying these trays of supplies along the line. You'd sit in one chair and get a beard on, sit in another chair, get a nose on, another chair, you'd get ears on." Raabe says, "We showed up at six A.M. for makeup, seven—into costumes, eight o'clock—ready for shooting, until six o'clock at night. Then, by the time you went back to the costume department, took off your costume, hung it up, and had the makeup department clean you off, it was eight o'clock before you could eat dinner. It was not an easy job . . . but we enjoyed it."

There *were* happy, memorable aspects to the work for the little people. Hazel Resmondo, having her first show-business experience at age thirty-three, remembers walking out on the set in her costume for the first time: "It was all so beautiful, I started to cry." One of the pleasanter events during the two weeks of actual Munchkin filming was a special open house thrown by the studio. "The major stars at MGM all brought their children in to see our little Munchkin City," relates Raabe. "The children would get our autographs and we, in turn, would get Poppa or Momma's autograph." Among visitors to the Munchkin set (whether on that day or on others) were Joan Crawford's niece, Victor Fleming's eldest daughter and stepdaughter, Wallace Beery and daughter Carol Ann, Myrna Loy, and Norma Shearer. Raabe also remembers seeing Spencer Tracy, Hedy Lamarr, and Mickey Rooney and, in her *Examiner* column on Monday, December 19, Louella Parsons wrote that another special guest had surreptitiously crept into Munchkinland:

Greta Garbo isn't as indifferent to studio gossip as she would have the world believe. For a week, everyone on the lot has been talking about little

Yvonne Moray, the thirty-inch midget on the *Wizard of Oz* set, and saying how much she looks like GG in miniature. Well, Saturday, the door to [the sound stage] opened and who should walk in but Garbo. She stayed just long enough to give the pint-sized Yvonne the once-over and then walked out. Whether she thought Yvonne looked like her or not, she didn't say.

The *Oz* unit remained so busy that only two days, December 25 and 26, were taken off for the Christmas holiday—and December 25 was a Sunday. Just prior to the break, Judy Garland gifted the Munchkins with candy and personally autographed pictures. Many of the little people would remember for years the warmth of the young star. "She was very sociable . . . a nice young girl," says Mary Ellen St. Aubin, whose husband Parnell was a Munchkin soldier. Raabe agrees: "We were accepted as equals by her. She would sit down on the steps on the set with the rest of us and chat every day." Almost fifty years later, the Munchkin Coroner would describe his association with Judy as "the single most exciting thing of my life."

The little people worked hard at adapting to the *Oz*

(above) Myrna Loy meets Munchkin Olga Nardone during a break in Oz filming. The two actresses are positioned over a portion of the Yellow Brick Road. (right) The camera dollies in for a close shot during the "Munchkinland" routine. (December 1938)

Jackie Cooper. All of which Billy thinks is sissy—he knows he's the better man." When Garland recalled the situation in 1967, she didn't name Curtis but remembered telling the gentleman in question she couldn't go out with him because, "'oh, my mother wouldn't like it.' And he said, 'Aw come on . . . bring yer maw, too!'"

Over the years, stories have proliferated about the general after-hours misbehavior of the little people of *Oz*. The legend was perhaps inaugurated by Judy Garland during a 1967 interview with Jack Paar. She jokingly referred to the midgets as "*drunks*! . . . They put them all in one hotel in Culver City, and they got smashed every night. And [MGM would go in and] pick them up in butterfly nets! . . . [and] slam a tulip in their noses!" Such sentiments were later echoed by John Lahr (quoting his father in the biography, *Notes on a Cowardly Lion*) and by Mervyn LeRoy in his autobiography, *Take One*. Wallace Worsley still rolls his eyes and exclaims when reminiscing about the Munchkins. "Oh, Lord! They were a mixed breed! A limousine would drive up—they'd take about twelve or fourteen of them—and the doors would open up, and they'd tumble out in the morning. And some of them were drunk, and some of them hadn't been to sleep all night . . . they'd been carousing around. They

Munchkins Harry and Daisy Doll visit director Jack Conway on the set of Song of the West *in December 1938. In 1930, Conway had directed Doll in MGM's* The Unholy Three.

experience. Their oversize, encompassing costumes and the height of the set floor made it impossible for them to easily maneuver onto or off of the stage platforms. A half-dozen personnel were assigned to lift them into place and to assist them in the bathroom—a frequently embarrassing state of affairs. One midget, who refused assistance and who was, according to Bert Lahr, "never sober," fell into the latrine one afternoon and couldn't get out. Original *Oz* publicity actually capitalized on this story, albeit judiciously phrasing the narrative. Hedda Hopper, however, blithely went ahead and claimed in her column that the incident happened to Billy Curtis, "and Nelson Eddy rushed in and saved him from drowning."

On a couple of occasions, a few children were used to add to the crowds of Munchkins in some of the long shots. Tutors were then required to work with the children, and this led to other problems. According to Hopper, "The minute a scene is finished, [the teachers] grab the kids for their lessons and, nine times out of ten, what they find on their laps is a midget." Another writer continued, "When the midgets rebelled, the teachers became firm. Some of the midgets began speaking shrilly to the women in a foreign tongue. Luckily, none of the women could understand what they said." Hopper also noted that Munchkin Curtis was "trying to date up Judy Garland, but she prefers

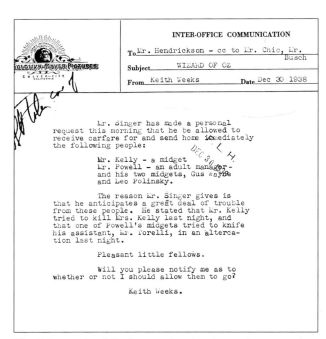

The little people of Oz *have endured an increasing reputation for misbehavior during their after-hours activities in Culver City in 1938. Investigation has shown that it was a rambunctious few who gave a bad name to the whole group, but this memo seems to indicate that at least a few of the Munchkins did have their "temperamental" moments.*

INTER-OFFICE COMMUNICATION

To_ W K CRAIG-cc F L Hendrickson,K Weeks,MLeRoy

Subject_ MARGARET HAMILTON

From_ FRED DATIG   Date__ 1-5-39

         The above suffered first
degree burns on her face and second degree burns
on her hand in a scene which was being photographed
by us for our production WIZARD OF OZ on December
2 8th.

         Mr. Katz has advised that
M iss Hamilton is not to be taken off salary during
the period she is incapacitated.

         It is estimated she will
be able to resume her work in a week or ten days.

A memo discusses Margaret Hamilton's on-set accident during the film made of her departure from Munchkinland. MGM's estimate that she would resume work "in a week or ten days" was decidedly optimistic. Her burns kept Miss Hamilton away until the second week of February.

were pretty hard to keep track of . . . the costumers had an awful time!''

What surfaces through the many anecdotes and memories is a grain of truth. There *were* altercations, episodes of inebriation, and lewd incidents, but only a small proportion of the midgets participated in such events. In truth, the most serious episode in conjunction with Munchkinland didn't directly involve the little people at all.

During an afternoon take of the Wicked Witch's exit from the tiny village, Margaret Hamilton was severely burned when the fire effect surrounding her trapdoor/elevator was set off a couple of seconds too soon. Her hat, broom, and hair caught fire, her face and hand were badly burned. Only fast action by the men working under the set prevented the flames from causing any other damage to the actress. Hamilton's green makeup was toxic, made with copper; the pain caused by the alcohol needed to antiseptically clean her face was something she would remember for the rest of her life. She was driven home with masses of salve covering her burns and wrapped in mummylike facial bandages. Despite urging (if not guilty) calls from the studio, she was unable to return to work until nearly mid-February.

Meanwhile, Munchkinland shooting was completed on December 30. The majority of the little people finished their work on December 28 and were dismissed from the picture; only twenty were required on December 29 and 30 while Fleming filmed the very beginning of the sequence. On dismissal, many of

This unique float, designed by Mrs. David R. Coleman, was the MGM/Culver City entry in the 1939 Tournament of Roses Parade in Pasadena, California. Adhering to the theme "Golden Memories," the Oz float was made of chrysanthemums and multicolor pompons and served to publicize the picture some seven months prior to its premiere. Four of the Munchkins appeared as themselves. Dorothy was played by Judy Garland's stand-in, Bobbie Koshay; the Scarecrow by Bolger's stand-in, Stafford Campbell; the Tin Man by Haley's stand-in Harry Master; and the Lion by Pat Moran.

the Munchkins returned to their homes around the country. (The studio had immediate difficulty with Leo Singer, who protested first that it was unfair to release most of the troupe and hold only twenty. Then he argued that he could not live up to a clearly stated clause in his original agreement that all the little people be kept available in Hollywood for two weeks after the shooting of their sequence for any retakes or additional scenes.)

Some of the Munchkins found further work in California. Jerry Maren, one of the Lollipop Guild, did a short for Metro, *Tiny Troubles.* Billy Curtis and a dozen others played pygmies in *Tarzan Finds a Son,* and several little people, including Munchkin "Mayor" Charley Becker, rode the Culver City/MGM *Oz* float in the Tournament of Roses Parade on January 1. The Singer Midgets stayed in Los Angeles, preparing a promotional vaudeville tour that was to end at the New York World's Fair; there had been some thought of including a *Wizard of Oz* concession at the Queens, New York, extravaganza and reassembling the entire Munchkin village out East. Though the idea was heavily publicized, it was quickly abandoned.

Meanwhile, preparations had continued on the scenes that would follow Munchkinland. Because he was not needed for any work with the midgets, Bert Lahr spent a week vacationing in Palm Springs and returned to Hollywood in mid-December. He immediately joined the other three principals in rehearsals for "The Jitterbug," which would shoot early in January. On December 22, Lahr, Garland, and Bolger rerecorded the opening portion of that number, with Jack Haley chanting the rhythmic dialogue originally done by Buddy Ebsen in October. Prerecordings were made for the Emerald City music the following week; the routines would be filmed in mid-January, and several different vocal arrangements were prepared for Frank Morgan and the chorus for "The Merry Old Land of Oz" and its special material "Renovation Sequence."

The *Oz* actors began the New Year back on Stage 26, now the Haunted Forest. When a cold kept Judy Garland at home for several days, Fleming shot scenes involving her three companions, Toto, and the Winged Monkeys. Tests had been done in October and December of the Monkeys' approach, landing, and departure; these sequences were finally taken over five days between January 5 and 19.

There were around a dozen costumed actors who played the Winged Monkeys, although careful film editing made it appear that there might actually be the thirty-six claimed by studio publicity. Whatever their number, the Monkeys "struck" the picture for several hours one morning when informed they were being paid by the day for their work and not by each actual stunt "take" of their flying and landing. Jack Haley remembered that an emergency call went out to the Screen Actors Guild for a representative to rush to the set and straighten out the situation. (At one point, a couple of Monkey actors had to be hospitalized when their support wires snapped and they crashed to the set floor.)

The remainder of the Monkey troupe was done in miniature. Meinhardt Raabe visited the Haunted Forest set before he left Hollywood and says, "The whole ceiling of the building was hung with little monkey puppets. You could see the wires leading out to pulleys on the side so they [could be] manipulated by peo-

The principal cast and (beyond the perimeters of the photograph) three hundred Emerald City extras prepare to say good-bye to the Wizard. (Starlet Lois January appeared as the woman whose cat was chased by Toto— thus preventing Dorothy from a balloon "return to the land of E Pluribus Unum.")

Wardrobe women hung up and filed away Emerald City costumes at the conclusion of shooting.

been completed earlier that week for the trick Horse-of-a-Different-Color: one white, one yellow, one purple, and one red animal. The Society for the Prevention of Cruelty to Animals forbade the actual dying of the horses, so the art department tinted them by using lemon, grape, and cherry gelatin powder. (The horses then had to be kept from licking the powder off themselves and from rearing at the sight of their oddly colored compatriots. But the basic effect succeeded admirably.)

Oz publicity labeled Emerald City "the largest interior set" of the picture. It covered twenty-eight hundred square feet, and its primary appointments were made of glass. Wallace Worsley remembers it as "a beautiful set . . . just incredible." During the third week of January, Frank Morgan drove the horse cab through the Emerald City marketplace, and the set was next used for the principals and ensemble to react to the Wicked Witch skywriting overhead. (The special-effects footage of her actual message would not be completed until May.) Between 300 and 350 extras participated in these production sequences; during the fourth week of January, they were also present

ple on the side of the set to simulate all these flying little monkeys." Raabe also recalls seeing a double for Judy Garland in a flying harness, preparing to be carried into the air by two of the "live" Monkey actors.

The rest of the first two weeks of January was used for dress rehearsals and filming of the elaborate "Jitterbug" song and dance. According to publicity, a marksman spent three hours shooting a .22 caliber bullet at the blade of an ax. The whine of the bullet as it glanced off the blade was recorded, a number of these recordings edited together and amplified, and the resultant sound furnished the buzz of the jitterbug. A group of trees similar to those in the earlier orchard sequence also figured in the staging for the routine. Bobby Connolly directed the choreography of the trees by using "two long sticks to tap the time on the controls by which the technicians operated the trees. They were enclosed in a housing through which they could not hear the music and made the trees dance by signal, much as an aviator 'flies blind' with his radio."

By Saturday, January 14, the principals had reached the Emerald City and worked for the first time with Frank Morgan as the Gatekeeper ("Who rang that bell?!"); Bobby Connolly simultaneously rehearsed the ensemble in the processional portions of "The Merry Old Land of Oz" and triumphal reprise of "Ding! Dong! The Witch Is Dead." Tests had also

Character actress Sarah Padden appeared in several MGM films in 1938–39. This is a shot of her test for the role of Aunt Em; according to an interoffice memo, Clara Blandick was assigned the part the next day. Padden's first name is misspelled on the test board.

for the Wizard's balloon ascension. Billie Burke appeared at the conclusion of the scene and told a 1939 interviewer about Fleming's directions for her entrance. "I come down one flight of stairs and go up another. Vic came up to me. 'Billie,' he'd say, 'I want you just to float.' Float! I felt really apologetic that I must touch earth at all."

Behind the scenes, LeRoy and Freed were finally casting the roles of Aunt Em and Uncle Henry; the *Oz* unit expected to shoot the Kansas sequences by late February. Character actor Harlan Briggs was announced as Uncle Henry on February 1, but eight days later word came that Charley Grapewin (Freed's original choice) had "postponed his retirement" to play the part. Meanwhile, May Robson supposedly refused the role of Aunt Em as brief and undemanding, so tests were done of MGM character contract player Sarah Padden on January 31. The next day, however, the role went to Clara Blandick.

Oz was, as of February 1, officially in its fifth month of production. MGM's consternation had continued to mount over the time and expense involved, and confused statements hit the press throughout January as to the expected completion date of the project. Metro first announced a March release. A few days later, they noted that the film would be before the cameras until late March. Finally, on January 23, the trades mentioned in passing that Victor Fleming would be tied up with *Oz* "until late spring."

On the set, Fleming continued to film the Emerald City sequences. Between late January and mid-February, the cast progressed through scenes in the Palace hallway, throne room, and foyer (the latter for "If I Were King of the Forest"). Noel Langley remembered how firm the director was in his control of certain aspects of the performances, specifically with Frank Morgan. "He made Morgan cut down on the burlesque, play it straight . . . and it made the man furious. Every time Fleming would shout, 'Is everyone ready?' for a scene, everyone would shout, 'Yes' except for Morgan who, under any circumstances, would shout 'No!' He protested on every scene." Bert Lahr, too, recalled how Fleming would "cut out bits of comedy that were funny, but too much burlesque for fantasy. He wanted to keep a certain mood."

Both Judy Garland and Ray Bolger were ill and off the picture for several days during the second week of February, but there were other Hollywood events that would have more far-reaching effects on the *Oz* set. On February 13, David O. Selznick and George Cukor made a joint announcement that the latter would relinquish his post as director of *Gone With the Wind*;

the search for a replacement was to begin at once. Cukor had been shooting the picture for about three weeks and had expressed dissatisfaction with the script he'd been forced to use. Clark Gable, playing Rhett Butler, had in turn expressed dissatisfaction with Cukor. Selznick first approached King Vidor for the job; when he demurred (feeling, as well, that "the script needed so much work"), Selznick turned instead to Gable's good friend, Victor Fleming.

The exhausted Fleming, having worked three and a half months to achieve the improbable in *The Wizard of Oz*, initially wanted nothing to do with *Gone With the Wind*. He finally accepted the assignment out of loyalty to Gable and, on February 15, the trades announced that he would take over the picture. They also noted that *Oz* would be completed by King Vidor who, as he told film historian Clive Denton in 1973, "was glad to do *Oz* rather than *Gone With the Wind*."

Fleming wanted to finish as many of the *Oz* Technicolor scenes as possible before departing for Selznick International. At an office conference on February 16, he refused to begin *Wind* as requested on February 20 and demanded suitable lead time to get acquainted with the material. He also insisted on the use of John Lee Mahin as script adjunct; Fleming, too, found the *Wind* script unacceptable.* The director ultimately waited until March 1 to begin shooting the picture and worked steadily until April 26, when he collapsed. (Sam Wood guided *Wind* for two weeks until Fleming's return.) The pressure on Fleming to salvage *Gone With the Wind* after performing the same function on *Wizard of Oz* was overwhelming; as early as mid-January, an (unconfirmed) comment in Louella Parsons's column indicated that the director was ill and off *Oz* for several days. Jack Conway and W. S. Van Dyke supposedly filled in for him.

Fleming's final days on *Oz* involved the Wizard's presentation scenes in the Emerald City throne room. The script included one of Langley's most pointed and dry jokes. When the Scarecrow was given his diploma, he joyously proclaimed, "The sum of the square roots of any two sides of an isosceles triangle is equal to the square root of the remaining side!" Langley's "proof" that the Scarecrow had a brain sounded like a learned statement but was, in fact, inaccurate. (The Pythagorean theorum offers that the square of the length of the hypotenuse—or longest side—of a right triangle is equal to the sum of the squares of the lengths of the other two sides.)

---

*Mahin had been working since January 10 on a Hedy Lamarr vehicle, *Lady of the Tropics*, but his *Oz* script revisions would be filmed into March.

DATE Jan 26- Feb 10

PRODUCTION 1060

SET 71

STAGE 14

PICTURE Wizard Of Oz

TITLE OF MINIATURE Ext. Kansas Farm ----Miniature

Details of Min.Set Area

Scale

Backing White Proj. Sky

REMARKS   Shots of Kansas Farm from various angles showing tornado approaching and engulfing house.

Estimated Construction & Special Effect.
Preparation   7600
Spcl. Camera Mounts   5000. *
Operation   5500
Elect.Operation   3600
Add & Changes   *
Total Approp. 21700.
Final Cost 27089.83

No.of Bldgs.or Units
Day Nite Dawn Sunset

Dressing & Min.Props --Kansas Farm built two times. Change in design. Overhead Gantry crane to carry tornado tubes. Two tornado tubes. White backing. Moving cloud frames. Moving foreground glasses for clouds. Rigging for dust.

CONSTRUCTION   10492.87
Total Construction Cost XXXXXXXX Total Spcl.Effects

OPERATION   Construction Dept.Daily Cost

Average Crew		Foreman	Mechanics	Helpers	Labourers
	Morning		10	1 ptr.	1 grip
	Afternoon	1	18		4 grips
	Nite				

Total Operation Cost 12423.84

ELECTRICAL   Average Load
Wind Machines & Fans 2 wind machines - 6 fans
Average Daily Crew A.M. -10- P.M. 14
Total Operating Cost 4173.11

CAMERA DEPT.
Cameraman Fabian
Extra Cameras
Lens 35--40-- 50mm.
Speed 48
Approx.No.of Feet of Film Printed

1060-71
Wizard of OZ
Ext. Kansas Farm Min.

Aug.20 -Test water vortex
Nov.5 -Test cloth tube.
Jan. 26-Test of Set. Small tube.
" 27-Take long shot background
" 30-Correction in sky and dust.
" 28-Retake correction in clouds
Feb.2 -Cut 2
Feb.3 -Correction in dust control
Feb.4 -Correction in dust and length of travel
" 6 -Cut 3 BG. for front porch
" 7 -Test of long shot-cut.
" 8 -Change in set.
" 9 -Correction using small tube
"10 -Test using large tube rotating
"11 -Correction foreground clouds
"13 -Correction dust and clouds

For the Tornado used in Kansas Farm sequence a Gantry Crane travelling the length of Stage # 14 was hung from the bottom of roof trusses.The Gantry car supported a canvas cone in the shape of a Tornado which was rotated by a D.C. motor on a speed control. The motor assembly was arranged to tip sideways and was controlled from the car together with its cross travel. The approach was controlled by a motor winch on the stage floor. The base of the tornado cone was fastened to a car travelling on a predetermined track and containing arrangement for dust. This car was moved by operators below set. Set was built on platform and was 3/4 scale. Sky was projected moving clouds on white backing. This was augmented by cotton clouds on moving foreground glasses. Air was piped around set for wind effects. Wind machines were also used.

*** NOTE: SPECIAL CAMERA MOUNT ON GANTRY CRANE ($5000.00) NOT
          INCLUDED IN ESTIMATE. RE-DESIGN OF SET AND REBUILDING
          NOT INCLUDED.

(top) A frame blowup: the tornado makes its initial sweep across the Kansas landscape. (above) The special-effects cost-breakdown sheets, filled in by Buddy Gillespie and his staff, describe the procedure used to achieve the shot.

Before leaving the *Oz* unit, Fleming also oversaw some of the special-effects footage of the approaching tornado for the Kansas sequence. Tests had been done in August, November, and January before Buddy Gillespie and his crew were able to create a realistic funnel cloud; the final result—equivalent to a thirty-five-foot-long muslin stocking—was photographed over ten days in February. (The footage proved so striking that MGM used different takes of the *Oz* tornado for the climactic scenes of *Cabin in the Sky* in 1943 and in *High Barbaree* in 1947.)

The director also spent a day with King Vidor, who remembered, "Victor was a good friend, and he took me around to look at all the sets that had been built and hadn't [yet] been used." According to Vidor, Fleming left *Oz* that night to prepare *Gone With the Wind*; the *Oz* unit gave him an on-set farewell party on February 17.

With Vidor at the helm, the third week of February was devoted to some of the black-and-white scenes on the Kansas farm. The cast was augmented for several days by twelve hogs, a cow, four horses, a mule, twenty chickens, three ducks, and thirty pigeons for barnyard episodes before and during the tornado. The first time Judy Garland walked the pigpen fence and (as scripted) fell in, she landed among the baby pigs and was immediately charged by their mother. Assistant director Al Shenberg rescued her, but Judy and Toto had become so close that the dog also jumped into the fray to defend the young actress. Shenberg was forced back into the pigpen to save Toto from the much larger swine.

Vidor must have finished all the farmhand footage during the week of February 19, as a memo in the MGM files states that Jack Haley's last day on *Oz* was Sunday, February 25. Supposedly only Kansas scenes

(above) February 1939: "Zeke," "Hickory Twicker," and "Hunk Andrews"—the three Kansas farmhands—stand outside the MGM sound stage in more comfortable garb than they had worn for the preceding three months as citizens of Oz. (right) One of the scenes directed by King Vidor: (from left) Clara Blandick, Judy Garland, Terry, Margaret Hamilton, and Charley Grapewin in the Kansas farmhouse parlor.

remained to be shot after that, but Vidor remembered in 1973 that he directed color footage for *Oz* as well; it's possible this included miscellaneous "pick-up" shots and takes or retakes of "If I Only Had a Brain" and its surrounding dialogue (originally filmed by Fleming the preceding November). Studio records show that Ray Bolger rerecorded the song on February 28, and script notations indicate that several portions of the scene were rewritten around the same time. (Bolger's extended eccentric dance routine was staged by Busby Berkeley who—except for one picture in 1931—didn't work at MGM until December 1938. That places his arrival at the studio a month *after* the Bolger/Garland scenes were taken by Fleming. *Oz* choreographer Bobby Connolly had left Metro for a Mexico vacation on February 10; Berkeley, who'd had Connolly as a protégé at Warner Bros., was a logical choice to do or redo the Bolger dance in late February/early March 1939.) In 1985, Bolger remembered at least one aspect of the filming: "They put me on a wire so I'd look like I had shot up in the air. They got me up about a hundred feet—and then someone yelled 'Lunch! One hour break!' and they all walked out."*

Among Vidor's final scenes were those with Miss Gulch, Dorothy, Toto, and Professor Marvel. Frank Morgan's costume in those segments provided a genuine "believe it or not" anecdote and an almost ghostly benediction for the *Oz* unit. Marvel's shabby, Prince Albert–style coat had been selected from a rack of old clothing purchased by MGM. When Morgan idly turned out the pocket one day, he found the name L. Frank Baum sewn into the lining, and both Baum's widow and the Chicago tailor who made the jacket later verified that it had belonged to the author of *The Wizard of Oz* many years before. LeRoy presented the coat to Mrs. Baum when filming was completed.

Vidor's special joy in *Oz* came when he shot the "Over the Rainbow" sequence. He later enthused,

> I get a tremendous kick out of knowing I directed that scene. Whenever I hear the record played, I remember that I was in on the beginning. I had very much the feeling of adapting the movement of silent films to the staging of a musical number. Previously in most sound musicals, someone stood up in front of the camera and sang directly to [it]. In directing "Over the Rainbow" I was

*Whatever the circumstances behind the number and scene, it is apparent in the finished film that the whole segment was pieced together from shots taken at various times. The length of Judy Garland's braids changes from long to short to long in the dialogue before the song; they're then short for "If I Only Had a Brain" and long once again for the wrap-up chorus of "We're Off to See the Wizard."

Three days after the *Oz* premiere, Mervyn LeRoy "officially" expressed his gratitude to King Vidor for his uncredited direction of some of the picture.

able to keep the movement of Judy Garland flowing freely very much in the style of a silent scene.

With much of the cast already dispersed, the final days of *Oz* filming were quiet ones. Principal photography was virtually complete by the second week of March; the trades noted on March 6 that Judy Garland had gifted photographer Hal Rosson with a "new plug-less radio" in appreciation of his work. Suddenly, if peacefully, five months of trauma and trial were over. But it would be several more months before the cast, crew, media, and public would know what had been wrought.

The Victor Fleming Scrapbook

For many years, Victor Fleming's secretary also served her employer as an informal archivist, compiling for each of his films a scrapbook of stills, production pictures, clippings, and memorabilia. Some of the photographs she scalloped for his Oz collection are reproduced on the next four pages through the generosity and courtesy of Fleming's youngest daughter, Sarah, and the cooperation of William Tompkin.

(below left) Billie Burke meets Norma Shearer in Munchkinland in December 1938. Judy Garland is dimly visible in the distant center background. (below right) Choreographer Bobby Connolly and Ray Bolger flank Jack Haley, the latter minus the top half of his Tin Man costume and funnel hat. Haley wards off chills with towel and robe; his shiny makeup, polished legs, and the background setting indicate that this picture was taken during his first three days in Oz in November 1938. (bottom)

Garland's apparent veneration for Victor Fleming was quite genuine. Here, she and the director pose with journalist Adela Rogers St. Johns, one of Garland's great admirers. More than thirty years later, she would describe the star as "our one great genius" and write a glowing (if biographically inaccurate) portrait of her talents and appeal in Some Are Born Great (1974).

(above) Candid clowning with two old vaudevillians. (above right) "Well, Scarecrow, what would you like for Halloween?" Bolger cowers on the lap of Margaret Hamilton in a moment of mock consternation. (right) Dorothy and the Scarecrow get musically acquainted on the Yellow Brick Road. (November 1938)

(left) Whether ad libbing jokes or just giving the Lahr inflection to his musical couplet in "The Merry Old Land of Oz," the Cowardly Lion delights his coworkers. This is the "Renovation Sequence" of the film, wherein the quartet is (respectively) restuffed, polished, and coiffed for their audience with the Wizard; "I got a permanent just for the occasion" is the Lion's later comment.

(right) Warner LeRoy, son of the Oz producer, is awed by the Munchkin village and representatives of their army. Dorothy Gale looks on. (December 1938)

(left) The Munchkins— half in and half out of makeup and costumes—enjoy their catered luncheon. MGM provided their noon meal on a soundstage adjacent to the Oz unit. (December 1938) *(right) Director Fleming inspects the Haunted Forest in January 1939. The ultimately deleted "Jitterbug" number has just given way to the approach of the Winged Monkeys, suspended midflight at center and top left of the scene. (below) 'Twas the week before Christmas: Judy Garland reads the December 26, 1938, issue of Life while relaxing outside an Oz soundstage. She is ogled in turn by three of her coworkers.*

CHAPTER 7

Post-Production and Previews

Even with the completion of principal photography, *The Wizard of Oz* was far from finished. It took nearly four months to edit, complete the special-effects scenes, compose, orchestrate, and record the musical score, and prepare *Oz* to be previewed and (eventually) premiered. For several weeks, Victor Fleming did double duty, directing *Gone With the Wind* at Selznick International by day and working on *Oz* at MGM with editor Blanche Sewell by night. They assembled a two-hour, rough-cut print by March 15; to this, Buddy Gillespie and his crew added the final moments of special-effects footage during April. During the same period, some of the live action footage was finally melded with the matte paintings done by Warren Newcombe and his staff. Wallace Worsley remembers Newcombe's team as the "best in the business" at creating such art and, in the case of *Oz*,

they provided many of the most striking scenic vistas in the finished picture.

Herbert Stothart, George Stoll, and their coworkers were meanwhile involved in four weeks of arranging both the background score and the accompaniments for songs that had been filmed to only piano and voice tracks. By April 11, they were ready to begin recording, and their ten sessions during the next three months utilized anywhere from thirty to fifty-three musicians and as many as forty vocalists. (The St. Joseph's Choir, directed by Roger Wagner, did the final voice tracks for the Munchkins on April 12 and 13.) The arrangers peppered the score with interpolated musical jokes and appropriate underscoring. Schumann's "Happy Farmer" was used in the Kansas sequences; the Mendelssohn "Scherzo in E Minor" accompanied Toto's escape from the Witch's castle.

This billboard was posted outside MGM in late February 1939 to alert passersby to the forthcoming film.

ATE   Jan. 23-May 1

RODUCTION   1060

3T   87

AGE   14

ICTURE   Wizard of OZ

ITLE OF MINIATURE Ext. Witch Skywriting

etails of Min.Set Area

3cale

acking   Glass tank

3MARKS

Shots of witch writing "Surrender Dorothy or Die-WWW"
in sky with smoke from broom. Shot as matte to be printed into
Technicolor sky.

ressing & Min.Props

6'x6' glass tank and rigging
witch in various angles

3TRUCTION

Total Construction Cost 738.66   Total Spcl.Effects

PERATION   Construction Dept.Daily Cost

Average Crew		Foreman	Mechanics	Helpers	Labourers
	Morning	1	3		1 grip
	Afternoon	1	3		
	Nite				

Total Operation Cost 3999.55 (Includes fullsize process)

LECTRICAL   Average Load

Wind Machines & Fans

Average Daily Crew A.M.-4 P.M.-3-

Total Operating Cost 1797.35   (Includes full-size process)

MERA DEPT.

Cameraman   Fabian

Extra Cameras

Lens   25--40---2"

Speed   24

Approx.No.of Feet of Film Printed

Preparation

Spcl.Camera Mounts   400.

Operation   800.

Elect.Operation 300.

Add & Changes

Total Approp. 1500.

Final Cost   *** 6535.56
(see attached)

1060-87
Wizard of OZ
Ext. Witch Skywriting

Jan. 23 -Tests
" 31 -""
Feb.1   -Shots-drift corrected
"   2 -Correction for better letters
Mar.25 -Retakes new layouts
" 27 -Retake on R
" 28 -Corrections SUR
" 29 -Take of SUR
" 30 -Surrender Dorothy or die WWW
" 31 -Retake
Apr. 1 -DOROT toHY
APr.10 -1¼" scale witch on Tower track.
" 12 -Retakes --entire layouts for white matte
" 13 - Retakes
" 14 - " "
" 15 - " "
" 28 -Retakes using first layout
" 29 -Continuation
May 1 -Test using foreground glass

For Witch Skywriting a 6'x6' x4" tank with glass bottom
was framed 12' above the stage floor with camera shooting up
and thru glass into 2" of white translucent water. The smoke which
formed the letters was a black liquid released under slight
pressure thru a stylus made with a hypodermic needle upon which
a small black profile of witch was fastened. This was moved by operators from above forming the letters required. Wind drift was
made by causing slight drift of water across tank. Black and white
shots wer printed into color sky.

*NOTE: Original estimate did not include number of separate cuts
as added by director. Originallly planned as single cut.

ATE March 23

RODUCTION   1060

3T   60

TAGE   14

ICTURE   WIZARD OF OZ

ITLE OF MINIATURE Title Insert

etails of Min.Set Area

cale

acking   #5 grey

EMARKS

Insert of title on glass ball as it falls away from camera
and bursts on floor. To be used reversed.

ressing & Min.Props

Ball and rigging
Camera set-up

ONSTRUCTION

Total Construction Cost 227.30   Total Spcl.Effects

PERATION   Construction Dept.Daily Cost

Average Crew		Foreman	Mechanics	Helpers	Labourers
	Morning	1	4		1 grip
	Afternoon	1	4		1 grip
	Nite				

Total Operation Cost 159.66

LECTRICAL   Average Load

Wind Machines & Fans

Average Daily Crew A.M. -10-

Total Operating Cost 239.37

MERA DEPT.

Cameraman   Fabian

Extra Cameras

Lens   50 mm.

Speed   64

Approx.No.of Feet of Film Printed

Estimated Construction & Effect.

Preparation

Spcl.Camera Mounts

Operation

Elect.Operation

Add & Changes

Total Approp.

Final Cost   636.23

*Buddy Gillespie was required to fill out cost- and time-
breakdown forms for each of the special effects he and his
department created for* The Wizard of Oz. *(top) One of the
more spectacular segments of the film was the Wicked Witch's
skywriting episode as she flew over Emerald City. (at left and
above) Another effects sheet and a frame blowup from the
actual test footage give an example of one of the many attempts
to achieve an unusual opening title for* The Wizard of Oz.
*Gillespie's description of the filming explained, "A large glass
ball filled with white liquid with title painted on top surface was
dropped from the runway of Stage 14 to the floor covered with
black cloth. Camera rigged to shoot at speed. Shot printed
reverse. Ball formed from splash and travelled toward camera
coming to stop with title before lens."*

played backward to achieve the range of weird noises heard in the Haunted Forest.

In a 1939 feature on "the wizards of *The Wizard*," the *Christian Science Monitor* compared the number of soundtracks for an ordinary picture (three: dialogue, music, and incidental sounds) with the *Oz* average of twelve tracks for each ten-minute (or so) reel of film. The *Monitor* further broke down its description by listing the sounds needed in *Oz* Reel 5 (the apple orchard/the discovery of the Tin Woodman/the Wicked Witch on the cottage roof). These included:

a) Dialogue
b) Supplementary dialogue especially recorded, including the voice of an apple tree
c) Track including sounds of tree picking its own apples and movements and footsteps of Tin Man.
d) Tree slapping Judy Garland's hand, tree snapping its fingers, apples hitting the ground, sounds of Tin Man, and whistle sounds.
e) Sounds of Judy's footsteps.
f) Straw Man's movements.
g) Sounds of an oil can being squirted.
h) Sounds of Judy picking apples. Movements of the tree.
i) Bird sounds.
j) Dog sounds, yips, growls, barks, whines.
k) Witch sounds—very weird.
l) Musical background score.
m) Records of two songs.

(top) Herbert Stothart was credited with "musical adaptation" of The Wizard of Oz. *In this case, it meant that he assisted in the composition of the underscoring, oversaw the arranging and orchestration, and co-conducted (with George Stoll) the orchestra. (above) Film Editor Blanche Sewell worked side by side with Victor Fleming to assemble the various "rough cut," "sneak preview," and final release versions of* Oz.

Moussorgsky's "Night on Bald Mountain" was played during Dorothy's rescue, and "In the Shade of the Old Apple Tree" and "Reuben and Rachel" were heard, respectively, during the apple orchard and cyclone scenes.

In addition to the music, there were hundreds of other elements to be added to the film soundtrack. Douglas Shearer and the sound department spent weeks collecting, coordinating, and compiling the required components. The engineers even traveled to Catalina Island to record thousands of feet of bird calls. These were then combined, rerecorded, and

Shearer eventually had five shifts working to complete the various soundtracks, and *Daily Variety* called it the "biggest [job] of its kind since dawn of the talkies."

Through all this, the *Oz* stars were involved elsewhere. Frank Morgan began filming *Balalaika* and, on March 9, simultaneously celebrated his twenty-fifth wedding anniversary and twenty-fifth anniversary as a performer. He was quoted in the press, "To fool both your wife and the public for 25 years is quite an accomplishment, if I do say so!" Jack Haley returned to Twentieth Century-Fox and his regular radio duties. Bert Lahr, without a studio contract, considered a Broadway show. On April 3, the trades reported that Metro "had allowed Ray Bolger's contract to expire." Although it was rumored that Bolger would sign with another studio, the end of the month found him discussing a Broadway return as well. Judy Garland went on to another brief personal-appearance tour that was ultimately extended to five weeks due to public re-

Frank Morgan's twenty-fifth anniversary in show business is celebrated by singer Gertrude Niesen (one of the actor's radio cohorts on the "Good News" program that season), actress Rita Johnson (with whom Morgan appeared in the 1939 film Broadway Serenade)*, and MGM star Lionel Barrymore.*

sponse. Business everywhere was, according to the *Hollywood Reporter,* " 'above' sensational." Police were required to control the crowds when Garland played Loew's State in New York, and in Cleveland she broke the theater attendance record. By the end of April, she was back at MGM rehearsing for *Babes in Arms,* in which she would once again work with Margaret Hamilton. The latter had just completed a role in Warner Bros.' *Battle at City Hall.*

But by early May Garland and Billie Burke were—if only briefly—called back to *Oz* for a few pick-up shots. (These had been delayed because Burke had suffered a compound fracture in her foot while filming *Bridal Suite* in early March.) The MGM files note that other *Oz* retakes were done as late as June 30; it must have seemed at times as if the picture would never be completed. There were even problems in trying to determine an appropriate format for the *Oz* opening credits: *Daily Variety* wrote on April 22 that thirty-two different lettering and color-scheme designs had been broached. For a while, LeRoy considered starting the film in black and white (for the studio name and Leo the Lion), switching to color (for the title), and dropping back to monochrome (for the individual credits). He felt that running the entire opening in color would "stand out inharmoniously" against the "Kansas gray" of the first part of the film. After at least three other ideas for the credits were fully developed, it was finally decided to use the black-and-white background panorama of clouds seen in the finished film. (LeRoy had already been through the headaches of the black-and-white-to-color change in the body of the film itself. The moment of transition between Kansas

and Oz involved a delicate and painstaking method whereby the footage was stencil-printed frame-by-frame in order to effect a seamless switch. Only the Land of Oz outside the farmhouse door appeared in color; the interior and Judy Garland remained in sepia-tone.*)

By mid-June, *Oz* was ready for its previews. These test screenings were "sneaked," unannounced, into a regular theater program somewhere outside greater Los Angeles, and audience reaction helped determine what further polishing and editing were required. LeRoy and Fleming knew that at least a quarter-hour of *Oz* needed to be deleted to get the film down to a manageable running time. The average picture ran a little over ninety minutes in 1939; *Oz* was, even after three months of post-production work, still close to the two-hour mark.

There are apparently no existing records that list all the dates and towns used for the *Oz* previews. It is fairly certain that the film was first seen in either Santa Barbara or San Bernadino, and that it was after this showing that "The Jitterbug" production number was cut from the picture. Theories abound as to the reasons; one (inaccurate) claim against the routine was that it provided too strong a showcase for Bert Lahr and interfered with the concept of *Oz* as a stellar vehicle for Judy Garland. Another unconfirmed report states that enthusiastic patrons bounced out of their seats and danced along with the song in the theater aisles! As Margaret Hamilton remembered it, "An executive told me, 'We're [cutting] it, because we don't want [the picture] dated.' I looked at the man and I said, 'How long do you expect this thing to go on?' And he said, 'Oh, about ten years.' And I said, 'You're out of your mind!' " The "Jitterbug" footage has not been seen since 1939 but, from surviving home movies taken by Harold Arlen during a portion of dress rehearsal, it seems *most* likely that the upbeat, off-hand, jubilant song was scrapped simply because it was highly inappropriate at that moment of dramatic tension in the film. The staging spotlights Bert Lahr no more than Garland, Bolger, or Haley, and the number is not so much dated as inessential.

Supposedly cut at the same time was Ray Bolger's extended solo dance during "If I Only Had a Brain." The entertainer commented in 1985, "My wife and I were so disappointed [but] the executives thought it was too much fantasy . . . [with] the idea of the wind scooping [the Scarecrow] right up in the air."

An *Oz* sneak preview was definitely held at the Pomona Fox Theater on June 16, for the picture was

*The stencil-printing process and sepia-tone were only utilized in the original release prints of *The Wizard of Oz.*

115

Witch (cont'd)
Take your army to the Haunted Forest, and bring
me that girl and her dog! Do as you like with
the others, but I want her alive and unharmed!
They'll give you no trouble, I promise you that.
I've sent a little insect on ahead to take the
fight out of them. Take care of those ruby
slippers. I want those most of all. Now, fly!
Fly! Bring me that girl and her slippers! Fly!
Fly! Fly!
                              LAP DISSOLVE TO:

LS - Dorothy - Scarecrow - Tin Man and Lion
walking forward thru Haunted Forest - Lion yells -

MCU - Lion growling - Jitterbug on his nose - he
looks down at it - speaks - CAMERA TRUCKS back -
Tin Man slaps the bug away -
                    Lion
What's that? What's that? Take it away - take it
away - Take it away!   (cries)
                    Tin Man
Hold still - hold still -

MLS - Scarecrow - Dorothy - Tin Man and Lion -
Dorothy jumps as Jitterbug bites her leg - Tin Man
speaks - all start forward - Tin Man yells - Dorothy
takes bug off his neck - Bug bites Scarecrow - he
jumps in the air - falls to ground - jumps up again -
CAMERA PANS the Four to right - the reset to quivering
trees and noise - CAMERA TRUCKS back - Dorothy and
others tremble and move about as they sing -
                    Dorothy
Oh! Something bit me, too!
                    Tin Man
Now come on - you're acting silly -- (yells)
                    Scarecrow
Oh, come on now - everybody -- (yells)
                    Dorothy sings
Did you just hear what I just heard?
                    Lion sings
That noise don't come from no ordinary bird.
                    Dorothy
It may be just a cricket
Or a critter in the trees.
                    Tin Man
It's giving me the jitters
In the joints around my knees.

CS - Scarecrow and Tin Man - CAMERA PANS to right to
Lion and Dorothy - each sing -
                    Scarecrow
Oh, I think I see a jijik
And he's fuzzy and he's furry
I haven't got a brain
But I think I ought to worry!   CONTINUED

                    Tin Man
I haven't got a heart
But I got a palpitation.
                    Lion
As Monarch of the Forest
I don't like the situation.
                    Dorothy
Are you gonna stand around
And let 'em fill us full of horror?
                    Lion
I'd like to roar 'em down --
But I think I lost my nerve.

LS - Dorothy - Lion - Scarecrow and Tin Man
running around in - the tree quivering -

MS - Scarecrow - Tin Man - Lion and Dorothy
huddled together - looking o.s. -
                    Tin Man
It's a whozis.
                    Scarecrow
It's a whozis?
                    Lion
It's a whatzis.
                    Tin Man
It's a whatzis?
                    Lion
Whozat?
                    Tin Man
Whozat?
                    Scarecrow
Whozat?

MCS - Scarecrow - Tin Man - Lion and Dorothy -
Dorothy steps forward - sings - CAMERA PANS right
as she dances back near Lion -
                    Dorothy
Whozat?
Who's that hiding
In the treep top?
It's that rascal
The Jitter Bug.
Should you catch him
Buzzin' round you
Keep away from
The Jitter Bug!
Oh, the bats.....

MS - Scarecrow - Tin Man - Lion and Dorothy -
Dorothy singing - CAMERA PANS - TRUCKS back as
all dance -
                    Dorothy
....and the bees
And the breeze in the trees
Have a terrible, horrible buzz
But the bats and the bees   CONTINUED

                    Dorothy
And the breeze in the trees
Couldn't do what the Jitter Bug does
So be careful
Of that rascal
Keep away from --
                    Scarecrow - Tin Man and Lion
-- The Jitter Bug!
Oh, The Jitter -
Oh, the Bug
Oh, the Jitter -
                    All
Bug-bug-a-bug-bug-bug-bug-bug-a-boo!

MS - Lion runs over by tree - tree catches hold
of Lion's tail - Scarecrow runs in - releases
lion - tree grabs Scarecrow - he finally gets
free - CAMERA PANS left as Scarecrow runs over
to Dorothy held by another tree - Tin Man starts
to chop at tree - Limb of tree hits him over the
head - Tin Man staggers - throws ax o.s. - Lion
enters - CAMERA TRUCKS as the four dance -
                    All
In a twitter
In a throw
                    Scarecrow
All the critters just began
To nod about and pose
                    Tin Man
Thar she blows!

LS - Dorothy - Tin Man - Scarecrow and Lion
dancing -

KLS - Dorothy and Group dancing - Trees of the
forest moving in rhythm -

MS - Lion and Tin Man dancing -.

CS - Lion and Tin Man dancing -

LS - Tin Man - Lion - Dorothy and Scarecrow dancing -

KLS - The Four dancing -

ELS - The army of Winged Monkeys flying over
haunted Forest -

MLS - Dorothy and Group dancing - look up o.s. -
react -

ELS - The army of Winged Monkeys flying over
Haunted Forest -

(top) The travelers meet the human Jitter Trees of the Haunted Forest in a five-minute song and dance, "The Jitterbug." The slit in the back of the tree at the right gave its operator the ability to easily slip in and out of the trunk casing; it was his job to move the branches of the tree as if they were arms.

(above) Excerpts from the rough-cut script detail "The Jitterbug" as it was sung and filmed; the Wicked Witch's speech to the Winged Monkeys at the top of the first page actually remains in the finished film, although no explanation is ever given for the nonappearance of the "little insect."

Ray Bolger's extended solo dance to "If I Only Had a Brain" was cut from Oz before its premiere and "lost" until discovered in the MGM vaults by Bud Friedgen and Michael Sheridan. Jack Haley, Jr., later incorporated it in its entirety in That's Dancing! (1985).

reviewed the following day in the Pomona *Progress* under the headline, "Child's Book Is Made Into Adult's Film." The critic was enthusiastic about *Oz*, his sole reservation being "the movie is not for children, at least in the form previewed here last night to a near-capacity audience . . . Children are subjected to a strain far beyond any they might get by reading words on a printed page . . . even the Kansas twister is too realistic." But he called the production "spectacular . . . in the most gorgeous colors imaginable [and with] the best cast fact or fancy could provide." The reporter noted in a side comment that "Judy Garland was among others in the studio party last night, and the little songstress obligingly autographed everything handed her as she made her way from the theater. In the picture, she was little Dorothy, and she was all little Dorothy could ever hope to be."

Garland later remembered that it was in Pomona that "Over the Rainbow" was cut from *Wizard of Oz.* Arthur Freed confirmed such a probability in 1972 when he told his biographer, Hugh Fordin, that the song was taken out "after the second preview . . . [MGM studio manager] Eddie Mannix said it slowed down the picture." LeRoy recalled in 1973 that "six MGM executives" wanted to cut the song; "they asked why we had to have Judy sing in the farmyard." Both LeRoy and Freed took credit for arguing "Rain-

bow" back into the film. Freed even gave Louis B. Mayer an ultimatum: "The song stays or I go." Through their combined efforts, "Over the Rainbow" was reinstated.

According to a studio memo, *Oz* was previewed again on June 27, and in his 1973 interview LeRoy mentions a "sneak" in San Luis Obispo where "the audience sat in silence for almost a minute at the end of the screening . . . Then they broke into cheers."

By July 5, with at least three previews for guidance, the editing work was done. George Stoll telegraphed Herbert Stothart (on vacation in Wisconsin) that *Oz* was "definitely cut" and that final scoring needed to be wrapped up by July 7. (The musical track was actually completed on Sunday, July 9.) Not at all coincidentally, Victor Fleming had finished at Selznick on July 1 and officially reported back to Metro on July 5. The next day, *The Wizard of Oz* was turned over for negative cutting.

The film then ran 101 minutes, and several scenes had been excised to achieve that length. (In Pomona, three weeks earlier, the picture had lasted 112 minutes.) Gone by July 6 were: the sequence in which the Wicked Witch turned the Tin Man into a human beehive; the Emerald City production number/reprise of "Ding! Dong! The Witch Is Dead"; a long montage of scenes as Dorothy returned to Kansas from Oz; and

(facing page, below) In the rough cut of The Wizard of Oz, *the Wicked Witch made good on her threat to turn the Tin Woodman into a beehive, and Dorothy, Toto, and the Scarecrow had to take cover. (right) The rough cut script gives the beehive sequence as it was filmed and first edited together. (A notation is made that the trick shot of animated bees had not been provided for editor Blanche Sewell; it's possible that the whole concept was abandoned before this could be executed.) (below) The Scarecrow looks on as Dorothy consoles the Tin Woodman who has inadvertently killed a bee.*

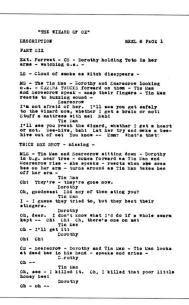

Dorothy's brief reprise of "Over the Rainbow" in the Witch's castle.* Fleming also did considerable tightening within the footage that remained. Eliminated was a brief exchange between Dorothy and Professor Marvel referring to the "poppies on the wallpaper" of her Kansas bedroom. The Wicked Witch's skywriting message was trimmed from "Surrender Dorothy or die WWW" to just the first two of those words. Also removed were several of Bert Lahr's comic bits; a couple of lines from the fighting apple trees; a portion of the chase in the Witch's castle; a brief middle stanza of "If I Were King of the Forest"; and a couple of extra repeats of the chanted "Lions and tigers and bears, oh my!" by Dorothy, the Scarecrow, and Tin Man.

Some of the editing resulted in inconsistencies in the finished picture. When the "human beehive" segment was taken out, Fleming found it necessary to "flop" the scene that immediately preceded it so that Garland, Bolger, and Haley would maintain continuity with their positions in the subsequent scene. The moments shown in mirror image were slightly fuzzy on screen (because the film negative had to be duped and then reprinted on its opposite side), but the deleted portion was at least adequately bridged. In another instance, Frank Morgan had been given a bit of business as the Soldier guarding the Wizard's Palace: he suddenly excused himself from a conversation with Dorothy and her friends to go and "change the guard"—and then adjourned to a tiny, revolving sentry house. While inside, he simply turned his fake mustache upside down and quickly returned to the conversation. The entire bit was cut out but, in the release print, Morgan was initially seen with his mustache pointed up and then—after a cutaway shot to the other characters and with no explanation—with his mustache pointed down. Finally, Fleming also took out two brief scenes of Jack Haley's Hickory, at work on a wind machine to ward off cyclones. The unseen invention was still discussed in the picture, however: Aunt Em berated the farmhand for "tinkering with that contraption," while Hickory vowed that "Someday they're going to erect a statue to me in this town!"

*The reprise featured a portion of the original bridge to the song: "Someday I'll wake and rub my eyes/And in that land beyond the skies/You'll find me./I'll be a laughin' daffodil/And leave the silly cares that fill/My mind behind me." (Before the Kansas scenes were shot, Harburg had replaced that lyric with "Someday I'll wish upon a star . . . " etc.)

(above and on the following two pages) Four publicity stills detail the progression of the "triumphal return" sequence, even though the number was cut from the release print. Note the broomstick of the Wicked Witch, proudly brandished by the Scarecrow. (For several Technicolor views of the triumphal return, see page 87).
(right) Script pages from the rough cut edit of Oz describe the number as it was originally shot and assembled.

```
                              Leader
              Hail to Dorothy!  The Wicked Witch is dead!
                              Winkies
              Hail!  Hail to Dorothy - The Wicked Witch is dead!
      26      CS - Dorothy, with Tin Man, Lion and Scarecrow in
              back of her - she speaks -
                              Dorothy
              You mean, you're...you're all happy about it?
      27      CS - The Leaders raises up his head - speaks to
              Dorothy o.s. int.f.g. - other Winkies in back of him -
                              Leader
              Very happy - now she won't be able to hit us with a
              broom...
      28      CS - Dorothy, with Lion, Tin Man and Scarecrow in back
              of her - Dorothy turns to the Tin Man -
                              Leader o.s.
              ....anymore!
                              Dorothy!
              The broom!
      29      MLS - The Leaders gives the broom to Dorothy as the
              Scarecrow, Lion and Tin Man react with joy -
              CAMERA TRUCKS forward as Dorothy speaks to them -
              the Winkies speaks -  CAMERA PULLS back as they form
              an arch with their spooks - they sing - Dorothy and
              her friends dance beneath, then exit out to b.g. -
                              Dorothy
              May we have it?
                              Leader
              Please!  And take it with you!
                              Dorothy
              Oh -- thank you very much!  Now we can go back to
              the Wizard and tell him the Wicked Witch is dead!
                              Leader
              The Wicked Witch is dead!
                              All
              The Wicked Witch is dead!  The Wicked Witch is dead!
              Hail - Hail - the Witch is dead
              Witch oh Witch - the Wicked Witch
              Hail - Hail - the Wicked Witch is dead
              Hail - Hail - the Witch is dead
              Witch oh Witch - the Wicked Witch....
                                        LAP DISSOLVE TO:
      30      ELS - In Emerald City - Streets are thronged with
              people - the procession enters from b.g., led by
              a band -
                              All sing
              Hail - hail - the Wicked Witch is dead!
      31      ELS - The Band marching along the crowded streets -
              they turn, exit out to left f.g. -
                              All sing
              Ding Dong!  The Witch is dead.
              Which old Witch?
              The Wicked Witch!
              Ding Dong!  The Wicked Witch is dead!
      32      ELS - The Procession comes forward through the
              crowded streets - surrounded by flower girls are
              Dorothy, the Tin Man, Lion and Scarecrow - the
              Scarecrow is carrying the Witch's broomstick -
                              All sing
              Wake up, you sleep head
              Rub your eyes
              Get out of bed
              Wake up, the Wicked Witch is dead!
```

```
      33      MLS - CAMERA TRUCKS back with the Tin Man, Lion,
              Dorothy and the Scarecrow as they come forward through
              the singing crowds - they wave, smile, etc -
                              All sing
              She's gone where the Goblins go
              Below -- below -- below!
              Yo ho, let's open...
      34      LS - The Procession passes girls lined up in front of
              the palace - the four pass along in front of them
              at left - all wave greetings -
                              All sing
              ...up and sing
              And ring the bells out
              Sing it high
              Sing it,...
      35      ELS - Full shot of the area in front of Palace - the
              Procession files around in it to the right -
                              All sing
              ...low
              Let them know
              The Wicked Witch is dead!
              Which old,...
      36      ELS - CAMERA BOOMS back to left with the Procession
              as it comes forward -
                              All sing
              ...Witch?
              The Wicked Witch
              Ding Dong!  The Wicked Witch is dead!

      NO      DESCRIPTION

      37      MLS - CAMERA PANS right with the Procession as it
              marches toward the palace - CAMERA BOOMS around to
              one of the huge crystals as the Tin Man, Dorothy,
              Scarecrow and Lion enter through the palace gates -
                              All sing
              Wake up, you sleepy head
              Rub your eyes
              Get out of bed
              Wake up, the Wicked Witch is dead.
              She's gone where the Goblins go
              Below - below - below.
              Yo ho, let's open up and sing
              And rings the bells out
              Ding Dong!  The merry-oh
              Sing it high --
                                        LAP DISSOLVE TO:
      38      INT. THRONE ROOM - LS - Throne - Oz's voice booms
              out as the CAMERA PULLS back to reveal the Scarecrow,
              Dorothy, Lion and Tin Man standing in front of it -
                              Oz's Voice
              Can I believe my eyes?  Why...
      39      MLS - The Four trembling with fear - CAMERA PULLS
              back as Dorothy comes forward with the broomstick
              and places on the steps on to throne - she speaks -
                              Oz's Voice
              ...have you come back?
```

In addition to trimming the picture for reasons of length, Fleming realized—from the Pomona review and the reaction of all the preview audiences—that he needed to tone down some of the more overtly threatening aspects of Margaret Hamilton's expert characterization. (L. Frank Baum's granddaughter Florence wrote Oz author Ruth Plumly Thompson on July 16 that "we saw the sneak preview about three weeks ago . . . It was very good, although the Witch was so terrifying that some small children had to be taken out. However, that is being remedied.") Fleming cut at least a dozen of Hamilton's lines from various scenes in the picture, including such harrowing declamations to Dorothy and Company as "I'm here for vengeance," "Can you *imagine* what I'm going to do to you?," "I'm going to start in on you *right here* . . . one after the other," and (after Dorothy fell asleep in the poppy field and her friends tried to rouse her) "Call away! Call away! She won't hear *any* of you again! And there's *nothing* you can do about it, either!"

By the end of July, MGM was again scheduling extra work shifts, this time at the studio laboratories: over five hundred prints of *Oz* were needed to accommodate the film's opening dates in August. Metro officially copyrighted the picture on August 7; it was almost ten months to the day since the first cameras had turned under Richard Thorpe. *The Wizard of Oz* had cost MGM—at that point—nearly three million dollars.

(on facing page) Publicity photos for Oz *were taken over luncheon with Maud Gage Baum and Judy Garland in Spring 1939.*

PART TWO

The Oz Diary Continued: Promotion and Reception

CHAPTER 8

The Oz Campaign

It isn't surprising that MGM fired some of its biggest promotional salvos in heralding *The Wizard of Oz.* With the set closed to the working press throughout much of the shooting schedule, only brief items about the film had appeared in the trades and columns; there were no interviews, photographs, or features released during the actual production. The studio publicity department decided instead to create one enormous burst of press just prior to the release of the picture.

The rationale behind their approach was first publicly explained in a *Daily Variety* notice on May 8: "Conclusion was reached [that] a wrong impression of [*Oz*] as a child's fantasy might be reached by a part of the public if they saw indiscriminate art on it." In early April, MGM held major discussions on the *Oz* press campaign. It was decided that the New York office would plant all national and fan-magazine art, covers, and special layouts; the West Coast would dispatch all rotogravure and newspaper material. The *Variety* report explained, "Effort is [thus] being made to have a release and art in hands of editors . . . in every part of the globe where the company releases on July 1st . . . first time in recent years Metro is releasing all . . . publicity on a picture . . . on a given date . . . Feature of the campaign will be exceptional amount of color art as well as double the normal number of stills used on a feature picture."

MGM spent several months as well discussing the best way to showcase *The Wizard.* After missing the originally planned opening at Christmas 1938, the studio set its sights on a preview near Easter 1939. In late February, they considered booking *Oz* in its initial engagements as a "road show"—two screenings daily, with reserved seats, advance-purchase tickets, and higher prices. Their hope was that this would impress upon the public the importance of the film and help recoup some of its overwhelming cost. When editing and scoring took four months, the plans for Easter were dropped, but as late as May 28 the idea of the road-show format was still alive. It was abandoned

Judy Garland did a series of publicity poses while wearing contemporary-teenager outfits created for her by Oz *designer Adrian in 1938. The photographs were utilized in conjunction with* Oz *publicity. (courtesy Bill Chapman)*

shortly thereafter in favor of a different marketing approach that would cash in on the mass publicity campaign: a "saturation booking," with the film opening simultaneously in hundreds of theaters over a period of just a few weeks. Release date was set for August.

In early May, the studio issued one of its first *Oz* promotions by providing a series of free postcards (and free mailing) to any and all visitors on the MGM lot. According to *Daily Variety* (May 12): "Postcards bear many different shots from the picture, and any number can be mailed by the lot oglers. More than 300 went out the first day with studio fondly hoping that 200,000 will carry a personal message plugging the picture all over the world by the time it is released."

The "ban" on preliminary release of *Oz* press ma-

Metro-Goldwyn-Mayer has produced more than seven hundred feature films.

★ ★ ★ ★

Many of us will never forget such exciting screen panoramas unfolded after the titles: "The Big Parade", "Ben-Hur", "Mutiny on The Bounty", "The Good Earth", "The Great Ziegfeld", "Grand Hotel", "David Copperfield", "The Citadel", "Goodbye Mr. Chips"... to mention but a few.

★ ★ ★ ★

And many of us will agree that "The Wizard of Oz" tops them all.

The magic tale spun by L. Frank Baum, read the world over by millions, will soon delight the eyes and warm the hearts of all who go to the movies. For they'll all go.

★ ★ ★ ★

Here is a most resourceful shadow-show, combining every cleverness that has been discovered by the craft, with all the art of perfect casting, dialogue and song.

Follow the yellow brick road to Oz along with Dorothy. Meet the Scarecrow, the Tin Woodman, the Cowardly Lion on the way. Defy the Wicked Old Witch, weather the cyclone and the mystic wood; revel in the Land of the Little People, and see the dazzling Emerald City.

★ ★ ★

And as you go, sing "If I Only Had a Brain", "Over The Rainbow", "The Merry Old Land of Oz", and all the other graceful, pleasant ditties that echo through the scenes.

★ ★ ★ ★

"The Wizard of Oz" is a World's Fair in itself. A World's Fair in Technicolor.

★ ★ ★ ★

Decorate with laurel—the director, Victor Fleming; the producer, Mervyn LeRoy; the screen playwrights, Noel Langley, Florence Ryerson and Edgar Allan Woolf.

★ ★ ★ ★

And the music-makers, E. Y. Harburg and Harold Arlen.

And toss a garland to Garland, our own Judy, and hail the mummery and minstrelsy of Frank Morgan, Ray Bolger, Bert Lahr, Jack Haley, Billie Burke, Margaret Hamilton, Charley Grapewin and the Munchkins of Munchkinland.

★ ★ ★ ★

How you'll laugh at the Cowardly Lion.

★ ★ ★ ★

And you'll know that the producer of such a fine, brave, different work is also a lion.

★ ★ ★ ★

But not cowardly.

—_Leo_

Judy Garland tells Frank Morgan (THE WIZARD)

DOROTHY OF METRO-GOLDWYN-MAYER'S "THE WIZARD OF OZ"

ANYBODY CAN BE A WIZARD AT JELLY-MAKING!

"ALL YOU HAVE TO DO IS STICK TO _CERTO!_"

Judy Garland and Frank Morgan appearing in M-G-M's new technicolor production "The Wizard of Oz"

❶ WATCH CLOSELY, MR. MORGAN—AND YOU'LL SEE SOME _REAL_ MAGIC! THIS _CERTO_ IS NOW GOING TO TRANSFORM FRUIT JUICE INTO JELLY—_PERFECT_ JELLY!

SA-AY! WHAT _IS_ THIS _CERTO?_

❷ _CERTO'S_ WHAT MAKES JELLIES JELL AND JAMS JAM, MR. MORGAN, AND IT _ALWAYS_ WORKS— EVEN WITH HARD-TO-JELL FRUITS LIKE STRAWBERRIES AND PINEAPPLE!

SOUNDS LIKE POWERFUL MAGIC, ALL RIGHT! BUT LISTEN, JUDY—HOW LONG'S THIS GOING TO TAKE?

❸ JUST 15 MINUTES! SEE? I BOILED THE JELLY _ONLY ½ MINUTE!_ AND I NOW POUR 11 GLASSES FROM ONLY 4 CUPS OF JUICE—_HALF AGAIN MORE_ BECAUSE NO JUICE BOILED AWAY!

SMART GOING, JUDY— VERY SMART INDEED!

❹ AND WAIT TILL YOU _TASTE_ THIS JELLY! THAT SHORT BOIL SAVES FLAVOR, TOO—MAKES JAMS AND JELLIES TASTE LIKE THE RIPE, FRESH FRUIT!

NO WONDER YOU JELLY WIZARDS STICK TO _CERTO_, JUDY! AND YOU WERE RIGHT ABOUT THE TIME, TOO! YOU FINISHED THE JOB IN 15 MINUTES FLAT!

WHY 3 OUT OF 4 JELLY CHAMPIONS USE CERTO:

1. Certo is the "tried and true" pectin that takes the guesswork out of jelly-making!
2. Certo alone gives you 79 recipes—a separate _tested_ recipe for every fruit!
3. Certo reduces boiling time to ½ minute for jellies—only a minute or so for jams!
4. Certo jellies retain fresh fruit flavor—no "boiled-down" taste!
5. Certo gives you _half again_ more glasses —makes _all_ fruits jell _perfectly!_

MRS. C. ARLT of St. Paul, Minnesota, whose jams and jellies won 8 prizes at last year's Minnesota State Fair. Like 3 out of 4 Jelly Champions, Mrs. Arlt always uses Certo!

Look for the tested recipes under the label of every bottle of Certo —a product of General Foods.

Insist on CERTO THE "TRIED AND TRUE" PECTIN THAT TAKES THE GUESSWORK OUT OF JELLY-MAKING!

Greatest best-seller of modern fiction (9,000,000 copies). L. Frank Baum's "The Wizard of Oz" long remained untouched by Hollywood producers.

★ ★ ★ ★

Magnificent courage was required—and well-nigh unlimited facilities—to translate the mystic Land of Oz into vivid screen entertainment for the young-in-heart of _all_ ages.

A cast of 9200 is headed by the brightest stars of stage and screen—Judy Garland, Frank Morgan, Ray Bolger, Bert Lahr, Jack Haley, Billie Burke, Margaret Hamilton, Charley Grapewin and Toto, the dog for whom the entire country was searched and who plays one of the most important roles in the film.

★ ★ ★ ★

Only M-G-M had the resources to attempt the tremendous Technicolor production that this masterpiece demanded. Two years of production work that required nearly every one of M-G-M's thirty sound stages...necessitated sixty-five gigantic sets...6275 technicians representing 165 arts and crafts — glass-blowers, color-mixers, cellophane experts, flower-makers, powder and fire handlers, water-tinters, beard-dyers, wig-makers, animal trainers, strange noise developers, and others too numerous to mention.

★ ★ ★ ★

Trees had to dance. Monkeys had to fly. A tornado had to sweep through the heavens and bear a real Dorothy away to a land of her imagining that was as excitingly real as life itself—yet utterly unlike anything ever seen on earth!

★ ★ ★ ★

Munchkinland alone took months to build...with its 92 tiny houses, flowers as big as palm trees, fountains, river and market place. The hundreds of midgets who play the Munchkins were gathered from 42 cities in 29 states.

★ ★ ★ ★

Emerald City, populated by tiny folk resembling china dolls, costumed in every shade of green, required four tremendous sets, 4260 people, 50 expert glass-makers, and over 22,000 separate glass objects, some as large as a living room.

★ ★ ★ ★

The Haunted Forest has trees which move their limbs and encircle you as you pass and pluck their own fruit. Thousands of birds make weird sounds you have never heard before.

★ ★ ★ ★

Over 2000 water-color sketches were required for cast make-ups. The musical score demanded a symphony orchestra of 120 pieces, and a chorus of over 300 voices. 212,180 separate sound effects were used. 3210 different costumes were created—and M-G-M's tremendous wardrobe department toiled for six months to turn them out.

★ ★ ★ ★

The result—nearly 100 miles of actual film footage...a quarter of a million feet of sound track...over a half-million feet of Technicolor film to give you 100 minutes of unparalleled entertainment: THE WIZARD OF OZ—filmed as L. Frank Baum himself would have wished it.

—_Leo_

(left and right) "The Lion's Roar" was a syndicated ad column appearing in many magazines from the 1930s to the 1950s; it frequently ran as a sidebar to the table-of-contents listing. There were two different Oz columns in the monthly series. (center)

The Certo ad shows the extremes to which Oz tie-in publicity was carried. It ran in magazines and newspapers between July and October 1939.

This postcard was sent out by MGM in response to fan mail received for Judy Garland in 1939. In addition to promoting The Wizard of Oz, its reverse side also instructed Garland partisans as to the procedure for acquiring her photograph.

terial extended to its musical score as well. Harry Link was the West Coast representative for Leo Feist music publishers and, while working to promote the film songs, he was also required to keep the material under wraps until the studio wanted it to be heard. Orchestras, vocalists, and record companies were prohibited from utilizing any of the numbers and, when bandleader Larry Clinton managed to record a 78 rpm single of "Over the Rainbow" and "The Jitterbug" for Brunswick in April, MGM requested the disc be withdrawn; Clinton had, intentionally or not, jumped the release date for the music. An early deal whereby RCA Victor would record all the *Oz* songs for an album fell through around the same time when the company simply got tired of waiting for Metro to give a go-ahead on the project. Recordings of the *Oz* score were eventually produced and released in the autumn by Decca (who had Judy Garland under contract).

There was a reason for MGM's musical procrastination: they wanted to debut the tunes on their own "Good News" radio program, a weekly hour of song and comedy sponsored by Maxwell House Coffee and heard Thursday evenings over NBC. The *Hollywood Reporter* broke the news on June 20 that "Good News" for June 29 would "sound a booming exploitation note for the studio's long awaited—and so very

expensive—*Wizard of Oz.*"

Garland, Bolger, Lahr, Arlen, and Harburg were assembled for the special broadcast; Mervyn LeRoy was scheduled to appear in a couple of "scenes" but bowed out at the last minute, and his lines were taken by a professional actor. "Good News" emcee Robert Young filled in for Jack Haley and sang a half chorus of "If I Only Had a Heart"; Garland sang "Rainbow," and Bolger and Lahr did portions of their songs. The latter also got to reprise the full "If I Were King of the Forest" routine, including a musical tag unused in the finished picture. The rest of the program featured a re-creation of part of the "Munchkinland" routine; a number of sketches fictionalizing events attendant to the creation of the movie; conductor Meredith Willson, his orchestra and chorus in an *Oz* medley; and "Good News" regulars Frank Morgan and Fanny Brice. The former did a monologue and chorus of "The Merry Old Land of Oz"; Miss Brice was featured in her revered "Baby Snooks" character as her "Daddy" Hanley Stafford explained the *Oz* story to her. "Good News" even honored Fred Stone for his participation in the original stage musical.

The program won enthusiastic response. *Variety* termed it "a hardy plug" and commended the "catchy musical numbers" and "slick job" done by the radio writers: "For once, the broadcast may have left radio listeners with an urge to see the screen vehicle." The critic particularly liked Lahr's "King of the Forest," "We're Off to See the Wizard" ("looms as picture's march hit"), and "Rainbow." The *Hollywood Reporter* concurred that "Rainbow," "warbled so terrifically

Rehearsal for the "Good News" radio program, June 29, 1939. Among the participants (standing, left to right): Bert Lahr, Ray Bolger, MGM executive L.K. Sidney, Oz lyricist E.Y. "Yip" Harburg, composer/conductor Meredith Willson, music publisher Harry Link, and, seated at the piano, Judy Garland and Oz composer Harold Arlen. Neither Sidney nor Link was heard during the actual broadcast. (courtesy Edward Jablonski)

Ray Bolger and Judy Garland appeared in a quieter moment with one of the fighting apple trees in this exclusive Kodachrome. *It was used as the cover of the* New York Sunday Mirror *magazine section, August 20, 1939.*

MOVIES

DAZZLING BRILLIANCE MARKS M-G-M'S COLOR VERSION OF

The Wizard of Oz

To amuse his neighbors' children, a Chicago journalist named L. Frank Baum made a habit, in the late 1890's, of telling them fairy tales of his own invention. Baum's friends persuaded him to write his stories down. In 1900, Bobbs-Merrill published his book, *The Wizard of Oz*. Since then, *The Wizard of Oz* has become a children's classic. Fred Stone and David C. Montgomery became famous stars in the operetta version of *The Wizard of Oz* in which they played as Scarecrow and Tin Woodman for 506 performances in 1903-04. Frank Baum wrote 13 more books dealing with the Land of Oz before his death in 1919. Thereafter the series was carried on by Ruth Plumly Thompson, who still gets out an Oz book every year. About a million copies of the original *Wizard of Oz* were sold. Sales for the entire series total a little over 5,000,000.

What distinguishes Baum's stories from most such fables are 1) a modern U. S. heroine and 2) absence of any really horrifying ogres, monstrosities or bewitchments. Heroine of *The Wizard of Oz* is a friendly Kansas girl named Dorothy who finds herself in Oz when she gets blown off her uncle's farm by a cyclone. There she encounters a cowardly lion, a tin woodman and a perambulating scarecrow.

Although *The Wizard of Oz* was not meant to terrify children, it terrified Hollywood by unique production problems. The picture cost $3,000,000. Shooting lasted from September 1938 until last May. Now completed, *The Wizard of Oz* will not be ready for general release until this fall.

Characteristic of innumerable dilemmas was that posed by flying monkeys. M-G-M borrowed wings of giant condors from museums, attached them to midgets dressed in monkey suits, who were hung on wires and manipulated from an elaborate control board. As the Cowardly Lion, Bert Lahr wore an 83-lb. costume. When Judy Garland (Dorothy) got a cold, the five-day delay in shooting cost M-G-M $150,000. Other members of a notable cast are Jack Haley as Tin Woodman, Ray Bolger as Scarecrow.

WHEN DOROTHY AND SCARECROW MEET TIN WOODMAN, HE IS SOMEWHAT RUSTY, SHE SYMPATHETICALLY OILS HIM UP

Arriving in Land of Oz, Dorothy is ecstatically greeted by Munchkins. This is because her house, blown away by cyclone, has fallen on witch-queen to whom they objected.

Good Witch Glinda (Billie Burke) explains to Dorothy that the only way she can get back to Kansas is to visit the Wizard of Oz and persuade him to make the proper arrangements.

The two-page full-color spread in Life *(July 17, 1939) was one of the first pieces of* Oz *prerelease publicity published in a national magazine.*

On way to Emerald City where Wizard lives. Dorothy meets up with Scarecrow, Tin Woodman and ferocious-looking Lion who turns out to be pitifully timid. They proceed together.

In poppy field near Emerald City, quartet is doped by bad witch, who later uses flying monkeys. She dislikes Wizard intensely, is a bad influence on the countryside generally.

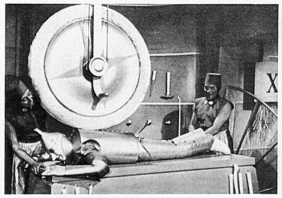

Woodman gets polished before going in to see Wizard. He means to ask for a heart which he lacks. Scarecrow wants brains to replace straw. Cowardly Lion feels the need of courage.

In presence of Wizard (Frank Morgan), Lion, Woodman, Dorothy and Scarecrow are taken aback to hear that, before requests are granted they must bring him bad witch's broom.

EMERALD CITY GIVES QUARTET FINE SEND-OFF BEFORE THEY START JOURNEY TO BAD WITCH'S COUNTRY. THIS SEQUENCE ALONE COST M-G-M $100,000

*Included (bottom Kodachrome above) was a miscaptioned but beautiful panoramic view
of the deleted "triumphal return" sequence.*

This specialized Oz advertising filled a full page of many Sunday comic sections in a number of major newspapers in August 1939. (MGM publicists estimated that nearly fourteen million readers would see such a prominent display.)

(left) This exclusive ad and layout was prepared by MGM for McCalls (September 1939) and incorporated two exclusive Kodachromes. (right) A somewhat different promotional concept was designed for The Saturday Evening Post (August 26, 1939) and featured its own exclusive Kodachrome.

(left) Another MGM variation of the Oz ad was created for Life (August 28, 1939), again with a unique color photograph. (right) The cover of the souvenir program for the Oz premiere at Grauman's Chinese Theatre, August 15, 1939. (courtesy Dick Martin)

The front page of the Chicago Sunday Herald *and* Examiner Screen & Drama *section for July 16, 1939, was reserved for this film publicity. The illustration at top was an exclusive* Kodachrome; the remaining photos were standard stills, hand-colored specifically for this feature.

Is It a Scarecrow? No — It's Ray Bolger Dancing in "The Wizard of Oz"

Mat 872 5-60

An excerpt from the 1939 campaign book: (left) Ray Bolger publicity photos were made available in newspaper matte format for easy reproduction by local publications.

by Judy Garland . . . is a cinch for the hit class." (Its estimation was correct; soon after the song's debut on "Good News" and general availability to other radio programs, it began to appear on the Hit Parade, where it endured for several months. "Rainbow" spent seven weeks at number one—the most frequently played and heard song in the nation.)

After the success of "Good News," Harry Link traveled to major cities to plug the songs with different bands and singers. Lyricist Harburg did the same thing

Photoplay Studies was a periodical distributed to students enrolled in film-appreciation courses. The September 1939 issue was devoted to Oz and included articles supposedly written by LeRoy and Fleming, a summary of the movie plot, and varied questions designed to motivate film analysis.

This cartoon was designed to compete with the more famous "Ripley's Believe It or Not!" features.

A memorable fantasy of childhood, *The Wizard of Oz*, which Montgomery & Stone made into a musical extravaganza many years ago, is now a Technicolor picture. Among odd characters met by heroine Dorothy (Judy Garland) in her fantastic trip to the Land of Oz are *The Scarecrow* (Ray Bolger) who wants a brain, *The Wizard* himself (Frank Morgan), *The Cowardly Lion* (Bert Lahr) who seeks courage, *The Tin Woodman* (Jack Haley)

(above) This two-page promotional feature appeared in Motion Picture *for August 1939. Nearly all the fan magazines carried some form of Oz publicity, ranging from photo stories to lengthy articles about the production process. In all cases, at least one or two of the stills provided by MGM were exclusive to each magazine.*

Music to make you sing . . . laughter to make you happier than you have been in years . . . the story beloved by the young-in-heart of all ages now comes to the screens of the world, peopled with the brightest stars of stage and screen.

It's Metro-Goldwyn-Mayer's most magnificent achievement, requiring 9200 actors, every one of the 30 giant sound stages on the studio lot, 65 tremendous sets and the brain and brawn of 165 separate arts and crafts . . . to bring you one hundred minutes of scintillating entertainment.

It's All A Dream!

—an enchanting nightmare . . . a jolly tale
of fun and fantasy. They've called it—

THE WIZARD OF OZ

You remember the fascinating fairy tale, the story of
Dorothy (Judy Garland) who fell asleep with her little
dog Toto and awakened in a strange and wonderful
land . . . how she decided to go to the great Wizard
(Frank Morgan) and ask him to send her back to
Kansas . . . the odd friends who joined her: the Scarecrow (Ray Bolger), the Tin Woodman (Jack Haley),
the Cowardly Lion (Bert Lahr). You remember, too,
the Good Witch of the North (Billie Burke) and the
wicked, Wicked Witch (Margaret Hamilton). Here
they all are—brought gaily to life by M-G-M

(above) "It's All a Dream" was the title of the sepia-tone spread in Movie Mirror *for August 1939.* (left) An elaborately designed Oz *magazine advertisement was prepared for the bottom halves of two facing pages.*

**METRO-GOLDWYN-MAYER'S GLORIOUS
TECHNICOLOR PRODUCTION WITH**
JUDY GARLAND (as Dorothy), FRANK MORGAN
(as the Wizard), RAY BOLGER (as the Scarecrow),
BERT LAHR (as the Cowardly Lion), JACK HALEY
(as the Tin Woodman), BILLIE BURKE (as the Good
Witch), MARGARET HAMILTON (as the Bad
Witch), CHARLEY GRAPEWIN (as Uncle Henry),
and the Munchkins. Screenplay by Noel Langley,
Florence Ryerson and Edgar Allan Woolf. Music
and Lyrics by Harold Arlen and E. Y. Harburg.
A VICTOR FLEMING Production. Produced by
MERVYN LE ROY. Directed by VICTOR FLEMING.

both in New York and in London; the film was scheduled to open abroad late in the year. In August, several orchestra leaders devoted portions of their regular radio programs to *Oz* segments, and MGM also prepared a full *Oz* radio show on transcription disc as part of their "Leo Is On the Air" series. The thirteen-minute promotion included songs and excerpted dialogue from the film soundtrack.

The studio didn't overlook a single opportunity to promote *The Wizard of Oz*; they even considered (but rejected) the idea of sending Bert Lahr to the International Lion's Club convention in Pittsburgh in July. By August, Metro had distributed unusually lavish campaign and exploitation books to theater owners across the country who would be playing *Oz*. The books offered examples of poster art, promotional ideas and gimmicks, and news of commercial tie-ins. *Film Daily* raved about the scope of the first book: "Here is one of the most comprehensive exhibitor aids ever issued on a production . . . an encyclopedia of contests, ballyhoos, stunts and displays available for showmen . . . to assure highly effective promotion . . . this volume will be followed soon by a merchandising exploitation supplement . . . a massive two-color section containing an imposing list of national manufacturers who are tied in on the production."

A few days earlier, on August 2, MGM's full-page *Variety* ad named nearly a hundred cities and theaters where *Oz* was set to open—"the greatest list of simultaneous bookings ever made on any film." Spurred by the success of the *Oz* sneak previews, the studio labeled the film "one of the greatest pictures of all time, perhaps the greatest picture ever made." On August 11, MGM announced the results of their "$250,000 Campaign" in a two-page spread in *Film Daily.* The copy included the pronouncement: "The industry is talking about nothing else but the greatness of . . . *Oz.* The preview confirmed advance reports it is

The August 27, 1939, issue of the Baltimore Sun Times *included one of the many black-and-white newspaper spreads that drew public attention to the screen version of* Oz.

one of the biggest box-office sensations of all time. 400 happy theaters are about to play it . . . " The spread went on to list thirty national, juvenile, and fan magazines that would carry *Oz* ads, many in full- or two-color; nearly as many newspapers that would run full-page, full-color comic-section ads; and ninety-nine newspapers already running "teaser" ads on the forthcoming film. More than thirty different magazine and newspaper features were also scheduled to appear during the late summer or early fall ("never such a barrage of pre-release publicity").

Variety summed up the extent of the nationwide *Oz* publicity in a brief feature on August 16 and noted that, when all the different film ad outlets were totaled, the circulation figure reached almost ninety-two million. A humorous note was struck in the midst of the promotional brouhaha when a *Hollywood Report-*

These unusual black-and-white portraits accompanied a brief review of Oz *in* Screen Guide *for September 1939.*

The Family Circle *was among the first magazines to recognize the appeal of (and interest in) the MGM picture, as evidenced by these two "cover story" issues: July 21 and September 15, 1939.*

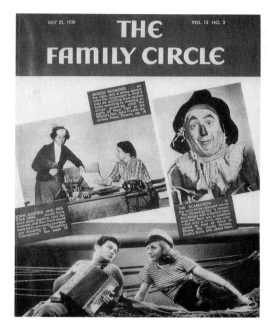

er columnist on August 4 wryly quoted a Metro press agent as having dreamed "the ultimate in press agent dreams . . . he passed a huge newsstand with thousands of mags and papers, and every one of them front-covered *The Wizard of Oz*." More than two months later, the same column pointed out that *Oz* screen-writer "Florence Ryerson . . . subscribed to a clipping service (at three cents a clip) to get the 25 or 30 [*Oz*] notices she expected but to date over 6,000 clips have

poured in, and she is still trying to find a way to stop the service!"

Press hyperbole or not, such an item is indication of the breadth and success achieved by the *Oz* campaign, brilliantly overseen by Howard Strickling, Howard Dietz, and their associates. The concentrated and virtually unprecedented press onslaught had the desired effect; to paraphrase Metro's own statement in the *Film Daily* ad, the public *was* waiting.

Five Oz *advertising buttons were shown in the 1939 campaign book.*

CHAPTER 9

Hollywood Party

Heralded by full-page trade paper ads and large displays in the Los Angeles daily press, *The Wizard of Oz* received its gala Hollywood send-off on Tuesday evening, August 15, at Grauman's Chinese Theatre. The elaborate care taken in the making of the picture extended to the premiere as well. It was one of the grandest celebrations of its kind (or, per *Daily Variety,* "another well-planned and well-directed entertainment"). Public interest was heightened by both the publicity campaign and (especially) the extraordinary critical praise won by the film after its press preview earlier in the month (see Chapter 12: The Reviews).

MGM received ticket requests days in advance and, by August 14, the *Hollywood Reporter* offered that the evening would "chalk up at least one mark—the largest number of reservations from players and their children to ever attend a pic debut. And that's one phase of the film folks' lives that usually is not exposed to the papers." When listing in advance the possible premiere celebrities, the press made much of the expected participation of the "original" Scarecrow, Fred Stone; the niece of his late partner, David C. Montgomery; the Royal Historian's granddaughter, Ozma Baum; and Maud Gage Baum herself. Metro also noted a request it had from one of the midgets who played in the film: he and his girlfriend wanted to attend the *Oz* opening but, between them, they needed only one seat at the theater.

Mervyn LeRoy was on site at Grauman's at dawn on August 15, overseeing the setup of the premiere much as he had the film itself. When a worker asked why, LeRoy quipped, "Where's the fun in a circus if you don't see 'em unload the animals?" At one o'clock that afternoon, fans were already arriving to claim seats in the ten-tiered banks of bleachers put up on either side of Hollywood Boulevard. The stands cost two hundred dollars to erect and stretched from Orchard Avenue to Orange Grove Drive; all five thousand available spaces were filled long before the scheduled 8:30 P.M. showtime. The overflow—three thousand more zealots—spilled out onto adjoining

The official studio invitation to the Grauman's premiere.

sidewalks, and Grauman's itself expected an additional two thousand patrons, ticket-holders who had paid $2.20 per reserved seat.

In addition, every window in the Hollywood Roosevelt Hotel across from the forecourt was jammed with gaping admirers, as were the roofs of the neighboring buildings. More than a hundred policemen were required to handle the traffic and throngs on the street, while klieg lights played patterns in the sky.

MGM had assigned Elmer Sheeley of the studio art department to create special premiere decorations outside the theater, and he converted the Grauman's forecourt into a Kansas cornfield, complete with cello-

The August 15 premiere was attended by a host of stars and many of those who had been involved with the film. (right) Director Victor Fleming and his wife Lu (right) celebrated with playwright Robert E. Sherwood and his wife Madeline. (below right) "Lollipop" kid Jerry Maren played the Munchkin Mayor at Grauman's and extended a welcome to Chico Marx. (Behind them, from left, are Bert Lahr, MGM actress Ann Rutherford, and Mrs. L. Frank Baum.)

phane cornstalks and a stuffed Scarecrow. A Yellow Brick Road extended through the set piece to the theater entrance, and a group of midgets was recruited to once again dress as Munchkins and greet arriving members of the audience in the courtyard.*

When Ella Wickersham reported on the evening two days later in the *Los Angeles Examiner,* she could only acknowledge, "It was bound to happen. For with each succeeding film premiere outdoing the last one in brilliance, it became inevitable that one would eventually out-Grauman Grauman, out-Hollywood Hollywood and, so far as the comfort of the 10,000 fans was concerned, out-bleacher all previous premiere bleachers. Such was the distinction of the premiere for MGM's *The Wizard of Oz.*"

She was far from alone in her estimation. Even the local parking-lot attendants called it the biggest opening in five years, and all the Los Angeles press offered elated accounts of the festivities.

The loudest audience responses outside the theater were won by Wallace Beery, Fred Stone, and Hedy Lamarr; the arrival of the latter caused the only moment of really uncontrollable crowd reaction all evening. The *Hollywood Reporter* complimented, "the

*For the next few days, MGM continued to make up and costume the little people and send them over to Grauman's to meet patrons during the film's engagement at the theater.

celebs gave beautiful cooperation . . . only blight on the proceedings was the directorial manner assumed by Orson Welles as he instructed still men how to make their shots." Other stars in attendance included Edgar Bergen, Harold Lloyd, Eleanor Powell, Virginia Bruce, Ann Rutherford, Allan Jones, May Robson, Bonita Granville, Buddy Pepper, Douglas Fairbanks, Jr., Virginia Weidler, and Eddie Cantor. MGM was represented for the occasion by Ida Koverman, executive secretary to Louis B. Mayer, along with Eddie Mannix, Hunt Stromberg, Joseph Schenck, Howard Strickling, and Ben Thau.

Most important was the presence of those who had

actually been involved in the film. The *Oz* alumni on hand included Ray Bolger, Bert Lahr, Billie Burke, Charley Grapewin, Mervyn LeRoy, Victor Fleming, Arthur Freed, Herbert Stothart, and Edgar Allan Woolf.

Frank Whitbeck was master of ceremonies for MGM, and he paraded the stars, film moguls, and industry craftsmen onto a dais and past a KMTR radio microphone for quick greetings and comments. A fourteen-piece orchestra provided *Oz* songs as background accompaniment from beneath an emerald-green canopy, and Fred Stone told listeners how he'd named one of his daughters Dorothy after the heroine of *The Wizard of Oz.*

Ella Wickersham also noted the presence of famed theater critic Ashton Stevens, who had reviewed the original stage *Wizard* on its 1902 opening night in Chicago. "It was positively heart-warming to hear the trio [of Stevens, Stone, and Maud Baum] discussing those exciting days."

Mrs. L. Frank Baum was much feted at Grauman's that evening, and both MGM and the media enjoyed the fact that the house she and Baum had shared in Hollywood was only blocks from the theater (at 1749 N. Cherokee Avenue).* Emcee Whitbeck saved one

*"Ozcot," as it had been called, was built in 1910, and the author's later books (including eight of the Oz series), were written there. A 1939 press release noted that the "site was selected because the Baums wanted to live in a sleepy little country village near a big city. At the time, famous Hollywood Blvd. was a row of homes, and the only place to 'eat out' was the Hollywood Hotel. Movie companies made scenes of the streets and timidly asked permission to use the Baum back porch for a shot."

(above) Wallace Beery escorted his daughter Carol Ann. (right) Though he received no screen credit for The Wizard of Oz, associate producer Arthur Freed had plenty to smile about. His first film as a full-fledged producer, Babes in Arms, had been triumphantly previewed a week earlier. (It would mark the beginning of his career as head of MGM's "Freed Unit," producing—as stated in an end credit for That's Entertainment [1974]— "the most outstanding series of musicals in motion picture history." Thirteen of his subsequent forty-four films would star Judy Garland.) Freed attended the Oz premiere with his wife Renee and daughter Barbara.

(above) Mr. and Mrs. Mervyn LeRoy (center) arrived with Mrs. Darryl Zanuck and director Ernst Lubitsch.

Bert Lahr and fiancée Mildred Schroeder had great cause to celebrate. His work as the Cowardly Lion was already being singled out in preview reviews as the highlight of the picture.

Eddie Cantor and daughter Janet were surrounded by Ozians when they arrived. Cantor was one of the early Oz boosters. After a private screening of a portion of the picture in February, Cantor was "still raving" several days later, according to the Hollywood Reporter. "Eddie says it is the greatest entertainment he has ever seen and rates the Harburg/Arlen score as the most outstanding contribution to original screen music in years!" ("Rambling Reporter" column, February 24, 1939)

of his greatest salvos of the premiere for Mrs. Baum's introduction to the radio audience:

> Tonight—with all the brilliance, the fanfare, the music and excitement—must be the realization of a beautiful dream for one woman . . . the companion, the inspiration, the wife of the man who created the now-famous character of the Wizard of Oz and all the lovable characters of Munchkinland. Through her life, Mrs. Baum has had reason to be proud of the honors that were bestowed upon her husband. Upon his death, the pain and loneliness of his passing were made easier in the knowledge that she had shared the life of a man whom his legion of friends called "one of nature's gentlemen." Tonight, Mrs. Baum, we of Metro-Goldwyn-Mayer are proud to have you here . . . to dedicate this premiere to your husband and to the books he wrote—and to the happiness he brought to millions of children. Ladies and gentlemen, we are honored in presenting to you—Mrs. L. Frank Baum.

Reading from a tiny card on which she'd prepared a statement, Maud Baum responded, "One of the greatest thrills of my life will be to see the Land of Oz, with all its queer people that Mr. Baum created, come to life under the magic of Metro-Goldwyn-Mayer in their marvelous production of *The Wizard of Oz*." She was

genuinely excited and moved by the evening and would, for years, preserve much of the memorabilia from the *Oz* premiere in an oversize scrapbook.*

Inside Grauman's, the picture was given a rousing reception and, at its conclusion, mounted policemen were—for the first time at a Hollywood premiere—called out to control the crowds still waiting outside behind the chain-iron valances. Final stragglers didn't depart until midnight. Meanwhile, the stars, celebrities, and press adjourned to the Trocadero nightclub for a post-premiere party, and Hedda Hopper observed that, when Bert Lahr made his entrance, Mervyn LeRoy jubilantly kissed him on both cheeks (as had Frank Morgan in the film).

The Wizard of Oz was the talk of the town as a motion picture, but for days afterward much intraindustry press praise was extended to the premiere itself. The *Hollywood Reporter* editorialized on August 29:

---

*Included in her souvenirs were two other mementos that harked back to life with her husband. One was a telegram sent the day of the opening by her son, Harry Neal Baum, in which he wrote, "With you, am thinking of Dad tonight at his latest success." The other was a congratulatory message from Frank O'Donnell, president of Reilly & Lee, the Oz book publishers: "Last night's premiere must have been one of the biggest thrills of your life." On the strength of her participation in the premiere and the success of the film, Mrs. Baum traveled to New York in September 1939 to discuss her husband and the original Oz book on the "Ripley's Believe It or Not!" CBS radio program.

WEDNESDAY, AUGUST 16, 1939 ★★★ NO. 123

HOLLYWOOD SEES 'WIZARD OF OZ'

Celebrities are shown attending the gala premiere of "The Wizard of Oz," M-G-M fantasy which opened amid lights and fanfare last night at Grauman's Chinese Theater. Left to right, Paula Stone,

Mrs. Frank L. Baum, widow of the story's author; Ray Bolger, who portrays the role of the scarecrow in the film, and Fred Stone, who appeared as the wizard in the 1902 stage production.

Billie Burke, widow of the late Florenz Ziegfeld, and Dalies Frantz, concert pianist, are shown stopping to talk

with midgets who performed as Munchkins in the movie. The little people were on hand to lend color to the premiere.

Talking with the costumed Munchkins from the Land of Oz, some of the screen's younger players are shown above. They

are Bonita Granville, in center; Terry Kilburn, Leni Lynn and Buddy Pepper, standing. Ten thousand fans attended.

. . . Time was when crowds that packed the sidelines [at a film opening] were looked upon as yokels, were herded in and shoved about and given very rude treatment. Today, however, it is realized that these people—most of them from out-of-town—are finally rated as important ambassadors of good will . . .

At the *Wizard of Oz* premiere, MGM cashed in on this potential good will mine, not only with the introduction of grandstand bleacher seats for the fans, but were also successful in arousing a laggard civic pride, resulting in Police Chief Hohmann assigning a mounted police squad for the occasion, thereby cutting red tape and departmental restrictions so that every cooperation was extended in intelligent and sympathetic handling of that opening-night crowd.

The awnings over the Chinese walkway had been removed so that stars could be seen from every vantage point. Lights were turned on when the show was out so that late-comers might still look at the stars.

The amount of good will that accrues from this new type of Hollywood showmanship cannot be estimated . . .

In addition to the general raves for *The Wizard* and its send-off, there was also media vindication for Mervyn LeRoy. He had been the victim of a lot of industry backbiting and envy over his position and unprecedented six-thousand-dollar weekly salary at MGM, and there was much negative gossip about both his abilities as a producer and the likelihood of a successful screen adaptation of *The Wizard of Oz*. By mid-August, however, with reaction to the film's preview all over town and plans for the gala premiere continuing apace, the motion-picture colony had adjusted its opinions. No one pointed this out any more proudly than *Hollywood Reporter* editor W. R. (Billy) Wilkerson in his front-page "Tradeviews" column on August 16:

Several weeks ago it was a flop. Today it's being rated as one of the greatest of hits.

That's Hollywood.

The anvil swingers and the rumor boys have been working on *Wizard of Oz* for many

(left) The Los Angeles Herald-Express *for August 16, 1939, devoted several columns to photographs of the Grauman's festivities (even though their first caption inaccurately states that Fred Stone played the Wizard, not the Scarecrow, in the* Oz *stage musical). (courtesy Allen Lawson)*

It is not very often that the people who help make great pictures get great credit, so here goes, and thanks to all the Wizards who made "The Wizard of Oz" possible.

Thank you,

VICTOR FLEMING

AND

ADRIAN	FRANCES EDWARDS	RAY O'BRIEN
ARTHUR APELL	HARRY EDWARDS	SHEILA O'BRIEN
HAROLD ARLEN	NAT FINSTON	WEBB OVERLANDER
POP ARNOLD	ARTHUR FREED	W. E. POHL
JOHN ARNOLD	CHIPS GAITHER	BARRON POLAN
GEORGE BASSMAN	CEDRIC GIBBONS	ROY RAYMSEY
CHRIS BERGSWICH	BUDDY GILLISPIE	GERALD F. ROCKET
MARGARET BOOTH	ERNIE GROONEY	JACK ROHAN
MALCOLM BROWN	YIP HARBURG	HAL ROSSON
A. W. BROWN	TOM HELD	FLORENCE RYERSON
GAVIN BURNS	JANE HARRISON	CHARLES SCHRAM
ULRICH BUSCH	BILL HORNING	BLANCHE SEWELL
WILLIAM CANNON	HENRI JAFFA	DOUGLAS SHEARER
GEORGE CAVE	SAM KRESS	AL SHENBERG
CHARLES CHIC	NOEL LANGLEY	LEE STANFIELD
SAMMY COHEN	BETH LANGSTON	GEORGIE STOLL
BOBBY CONNOLLY	JOHN LEE MAHIN	HERBERT STOTHART
JOE COOK	DONNA MASON	KEITH WEEKS
KEN DARBY	BETTY MASURE	EDWIN B. WILLIS
ALAN DAVEY	NORBERT MILES	EDGAR ALLAN WOOLF
JACK DAWN	WARREN NEWCOMBE	WALLACE WORSLEY

P.S. And thanks to the never tiring exploitation heads:

HOWARD STRICKLING   HOWARD DIETZ   FRANK WHITBECK

SI SEADLER   ANDY HERVEY

and to you

ARTHUR FREED

you know how thankful I am.

"THE WIZARD OF OZ"

A METRO-GOLDWYN-MAYER PRODUCTION

Both the Hollywood Reporter *and* Daily Variety *ran eight pages of self-promotional Oz ads subsequent to the West Coast premiere. (It was—and remains—standard practice for producing studios or some of those involved in a film to so tout their activities to the rest of the picture community.) This is Mervyn LeRoy's opening "thank you" page from the Oz layout.*

Among the Oz trade paper ads was this one for Margaret Hamilton. Many film critics commented on her terrorific performance and its effect on young audiences.

MARGARET HAMILTON

as

THE WITCH

"Miss Hamilton's grotesque witch is neatly drawn to gain dramatic effect."
—HOLLYWOOD REPORTER

"Margaret Hamilton does a really amazing job both as Miss Gultch and the Wicked Witch of the West."
—L. A. EXAMINER

"Margaret Hamilton triumphs as the Bad Witch."
—L. A. TIMES

"Margaret Hamilton is magnificently evil as the dreadful witch."
—VARIETY

Management
AD SCHULBERG - SAM JAFFE, Inc.

months. The word was around very early in its production that "Louie" Mayer and "Nick" Schenck were at odds because of its production, that because of it the production was stopped; that not until Arthur Loew came out here and did a rave on the idea for his foreign market was the trick started again.

Later, the boys started to work on Mervyn LeRoy. Why was he taking so long? Why was he spending so much money? Why hadn't someone seen some of the picture? "The thing must be a bust," claimed an anvil-wielder, "if it was good, it would not be kept under cover for so long." The fact was that sound was easily 40 percent of Mervyn's job, and its perfection was quite a task, even after the actual photographing was finished.

But the rumor army and the anvil brigade have now seen it, and even those boys are more than "charitable" with their appraisal. They actually believe it will take in a lot of money.

The *Wizard* was a great gamble. No company but Metro would have taken it. No company other than Metro could afford to have taken it. It's just those gambles that, many times, give the picture business its much needed boost. This picture will do a lot for Metro, for Paramount, Warners, 20th, and every other company be-cause it will bring people out to see it who will enjoy it; it will get people talking about pictures, people who have been too quiet on the subject for a long time; it will put a good clean taste in the mouth of every ticket buyer and send the industry's worst critics to the box office.

There are enough credits in the picture for everyone who had anything to do with it to feast on, but the big chunk must justly go to pint-sized Mervyn LeRoy, who engineered a whale of a job in maneuvering all forces to such a happy conclusion.

LeRoy himself reveled in the response to *Oz*, and he specifically acknowledged the praise of one film fan on August 24 when he wrote Maud Baum:

Words fail me to tell you how happy your wonderful letter made me feel. Really, from the bottom of my heart, the picture's success is complete knowing that you loved it as I do, and that you especially liked Judy and the Tin Man and the Lion and Scarecrow as well.

But, most of all, as you stated it, we were able to retain Mr. Baum's "kindly philosophy" . . . and we, in turn, are grateful for Mr. Baum's wonderful and remarkable imagination which made the picture possible . . .

CHAPTER 10

"Capitol" Times in Manhattan

Judy Garland didn't attend the Grauman's celebration. She wasn't even in California. But her *Oz* premiere would be an even bigger event, thanks to her own growing stardom, the public anticipation for the film, the MGM promotional forces, and, especially, the companionship of Mickey Rooney. On Sunday, August 6, she, Rooney, Roger Edens, and Metro publicity aide Les Peterson left Los Angeles and trained East for a series of four one-day theater appearances in East Coast cities. These shakedown dates were planned as a warmup for the *Oz*/Garland/Rooney Broadway debut at Loew's Capitol Theatre.

The idea of the double act had come about late in July. MGM was determined to launch *Oz* with all the power they possessed and figured no one was better than Rooney to spearhead a New York City campaign for the picture. He was, at that time, the box-office sensation of the nation. Garland, of course, had already proven her appeal and affinity for live performance for MGM on a couple of earlier tours, and the pairing of the two would serve as a "live" preview of the just-completed *Babes in Arms* (which Metro would open cross-country in the fall).

The act debuted at the Capitol Theatre in Washington, D.C., on Wednesday, August 9. The duo took the stage at 2 P.M. for their first show; the planned twelve-minute routine stretched to forty, thanks to the response from a capacity crowd. The theater manager finally had to plead with the audience to leave as an additional six thousand patrons were waiting outside to get in for the second performance.

The clamor continued all day, and fifteen thousand admissions were ultimately tallied, with thousands more turned away. "The kids" did their fourth and final show midevening and, as a result, Loew's and the theater manager were taken to juvenile court the following week. The theater had violated the local child labor law that forbade girls under eighteen years of age

from appearing on stage after 7 P.M. (Settlement came quickly when Loew's eastern division manager paid a twenty-five-dollar fine.)

For the next three days, Garland and Rooney performed on the Connecticut Poli Theater circuit: August 10 in Bridgeport, August 11 in New Haven, and August 12 in Hartford. Everywhere they went, response was as it had been in Washington.

Meanwhile, preshow publicity in New York was mounting. In addition to the expected *Oz* press pieces (both photographically and in interviews with LeRoy,

Judy Garland and Mickey Rooney signed autographs for Los Angeles fans as they prepared to leave for the East Coast Oz *premiere. (On facing page) This ad in* The New Yorker *(August 19, 1939) called attention to the New York premiere and the "live" stage show with Garland and Rooney.*

149

On the first stop of their pre-Broadway tour, the show teens were greeted by fans and band in Washington, D.C.

Lahr, and Haley), much anticipatory excitement was created by the idea of a live stage show at the Capitol—the first there in several years—and the plans to fete Rooney and Garland. More than seventy metropolitan New York, Westchester, and New Jersey Loew's theaters participated in a quickly arranged contest to select 150 teenagers as the "official Garland/Rooney welcoming committee." The seventy-five girls and seventy-five boys—a couple chosen at each theater—would greet the stars upon their arrival at Grand Central Station and attend a special luncheon with them at the Waldorf Astoria Hotel. The idea created much furor, and the ballot boxes in the respective theater lobbies were immediately crammed with applications.

Not every teenager was keen on the contest. The *New York Times* took delight in reporting an exchange at a Loew's theater in Brooklyn when an unctuous master-of-ceremonies discussed the chance to meet Mickey Rooney with "a moppy-haired, low-heeled young female of jitterbug demeanor." She scowled, "Naw, I go out with a fellow, and he's a lot cuter than that little squirt." Undaunted, the relentless emcee offered the chance to meet Garland to "a young man of the same species." He replied, "Na-a-a; I'd radder see de Dodgers."

Such opinions were distinctly in the minority, however. Loew's gleefully announced that around two hundred fifty thousand ballots had been received by

Friday, August 11. On that evening, the names of a boy and girl were drawn at each theater, and the weekend was spent in alerting the winners as to the activities planned for the following Monday morning.

August 14 dawned hot and humid but, with band playing and signs aloft, the 150 teens marched down Broadway and turned east on 42nd Street to Grand Central Station. All had been asked to dress up for the occasion, and the girls also sported Mickey Rooney buttons and ribbons; the boys had similar Judy Garland decorations and high paper hats. The waiting room at Grand Central was draped with bright, blue-satin banners, the newsreel and newspaper photographers were out in force, and the Loew's/MGM press corps directed the media traffic.

But what astounded everyone—greeters, drumbeaters, and innocent commuters—was the additional turnout of fans: a "screaming, delirious, perspiring, roped-off mob . . . , bigger," according to the *New York Daily Mirror,* "than the mob that met Mae West two years ago or the hooligan crowd that gathered last winter to tear the sarong off Miss Dorothy Lamour." There was a crowd of several thousand on hand an hour before the train from Bridgeport was due. By the time it arrived at 12:10 P.M. (forty minutes late), the number of waiting enthusiasts totaled ten thousand. Twenty-five detectives and 250 patrolmen were quickly summoned to the scene.

The majority of the crowd was held back in the

(left) "Seein' Stars" was a regular feature in many Sunday newspaper comic sections. On August 13, 1939, it paid homage to the forthcoming Wizard of Oz. (courtesy Rob Roy MacVeigh) (below left) A hand-tinted portrait of Dorothy in the Toronto Star Weekly, September 30, 1939. Though this appeared more than three months after Garland's seventeenth birthday, the accompanying caption gave her age as fifteen. More accurately, it also celebrated the diminutive entertainer as "one of the brightest singing stars in the film firmament of Hollywood." (below) The popularity of the Harburg/Arlen Oz score led to this illustrated folio in early 1940. Marketed through Leo Feist Inc., the booklet included sheet music and lyrics to the principal film songs. (The fifty-cent cover price is here covered by a music store ink stamp.)

(On facing page) "Wizard of Oz Par-T-Masks" were manufactured by the Einson-Freeman Company and distributed by W. L. Stensgaard & Associates. The Oz collection was accompanied by a handout flyer, "8 Ways to Have Fun at a Hallowe'en Party with Wizard of Oz Masks." There were possibly masks as well of Glinda, the Wicked Witch, and Nikko, although these were likely used primarily for display or promotion. (This page, right) "Judy Garland as Dorothy in The Wizard of Oz" was an all-wood composition doll manufactured in three sizes (thirteen inches, fifteen-and-one-half inches, and eighteen inches) by the Ideal Novelty & Toy Company in 1939. The doll was sculpted by Bernard Lipfert and featured large brown "sleep eyes," a human-hair wig (mohair in the case of the smallest version), and a rayon-and-organdy dress adapted by Mary Bauer from Adrian's design. (Some Dorothy dolls wore a red-and-white or green-and-white checked dress or a red dress with a white apron.) (courtesy Woolsey Ackerman)

(above) Ideal also issued "The Strawman by Ray Bolger of The Wizard of Oz" rag doll in 1939. (courtesy Mildred Martin) (left) This thirteen-inch figurine has a carved wax head, cloth dress, and crepe-paper-over-wire-armature body. It was sold in the 1980s as "possibly" a display item from the 1940 Academy Awards ceremony but has also been seen in a Christmas 1939 photograph taken in Judy Garland's home.

OIL *say* OIL
be your
Valentine

COME WITH ME
AND BE MY
VALENTINE

I MAY BE
A " SCARECROW "
BUT I'LL FIGHT
TO KEEP YOUR HEART

MY VALENTINE

I'M NOT
LION
WHEN
I SAY—

IF I HAD
COURAGE
I WOULD ASK YOU TO

BE MINE

These bright and colorful Valentines were issued for use in February 1940 and 1941 by the American Colortype Company. Each has at least one fold-back tab, enabling it to stand on its own, and is identified on the reverse as licensed by Loew's, Inc. "From the Motion Picture—Wizard of Oz."

Oh, what delights await you! MUSIC AND DRAMA AND LAUGHTER.

The Greatest Magic Film Ever to be Made.

THE WIZARD OF OZ

A Metro-Goldwyn-Mayer Picture from the famous story by L. FRANK BAUM

Songs by E.Y. Harburg & Harold Arlen

Directed by VICTOR FLEMING

Produced by MERVYN LeROY

Screen Play and Adaptation by Noel Langley, Florence Ryerson and Edgar Allan Woolf

ONE YEAR in the making!

FOLLOW THE YELLOW BRICK ROAD THAT LEADS TO THE WIZARD OF OZ

FRANK MORGAN as The Wizard

BERT LAHR as The Cowardly Lion

JACK HALEY as The Tin Woodman

JUDY GARLAND as Dorothy

RAY BOLGER as The Scarecrow

MAUD G. BAUM

1749 N. CHEROKEE STREET   HOLLYWOOD

This colorful stationery was designed for use by Loew's and MGM officials and Maud Gage Baum in 1939. (courtesy Michael Patrick Hearn) (inset at right) "The Wizard of Oz Children's Writing Paper" was a boxed set of widely-ruled stationery. Each sheet featured, in color, an Al Hirschfeld Oz caricature. (Hirschfeld drew advertising art for a number of MGM films in the 1930s and 1940s.)

THE WIZARD OF OZ

COPYRIGHT 1939 BY LOEW'S, INC. PRINTED IN U.S.A.

Children's Writing Paper 10 sheets 10 envelopes

WHITMAN PUBLISHING CO. RACINE, WIS.

BILLIE BURKE as Glinda

MARGARET HAMILTON as The Wicked Witch

(above) Bobbs Merrill had published The Wizard of Oz since 1903, and they were quick to issue a special "movie edition" of the book in 1939. The endpapers contained film scenes and publicity stills. (middle far left) The illustrations by Leason for The Wizard of Oz Picture Book are indicative of the approach Walt Disney might have taken had he obtained screen rights to the story. (Racine: Whitman Publishing Co., 1939) (middle left) Another Oz abridgement, published by Grosset & Dunlap in 1939, was illustrated with sketchy, childlike drawings by Oskar Lebeck. (bottom) The Wizard of Oz Paint Book and The Story of The Wizard of Oz (Whitman, 1939) were illustrated by Henry E. Vallely. The storybook was later reissued in a smaller format as a Cocomalt premium.

STORIES OF THE LAND OF OZ 10¢ each

Here are nine books about the strange and marvelous Land of Oz and its fascinating people . . . the Scarecrow, Cowardly Lion, Tin Woodman, lovely Princess Ozma, the Wizard, Tik-Tok, The Gnome King, and many others . . . as well as Dorothy and her dog Toto.

Six of the books are abridged versions of the large Oz books; three are complete as L. Frank Baum wrote them. All are generously illustrated in color by John R. Neill. For sale at most bookstores, department stores, and 5-and-10-cent stores everywhere at only 10c each.

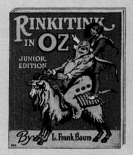

If your neighborhood bookstore, department store, or 5-and-10-cent store cannot supply these books, send $1 to Rand McNally & Company, 536 S. Clark St., Chicago, and we will send you all nine of them postpaid.

RAND McNALLY & COMPANY • Publishers

| New York | Washington | CHICAGO | Los Angeles | San Francisco |

The back cover of Child Life *for September 1939 showed all nine of the little Oz books issued by Rand McNally to take advantage of an Oz-conscious nation. The books—six adaptations of full-length Baum Oz novels and six complete Baum Oz short stories (two-to-a-volume)—were also available in a boxed set: The Wonderful Land of Oz Library.*

The "Official Reception Committee" for Garland and Rooney at Grand Central was headed by six specially selected New York-area teenagers. (below) Jack Haley served as emcee for the special Oz luncheon and radio broadcast at the Waldorf-Astoria.

terminal waiting room by the police lines. The reception committee was organized in an honor guard of two lines, just past the station gates on the platform leading to the train ramps. More police, the press, and six specially recognized committee members were allowed on the platform of the Garland/Rooney train itself. Finally, when all the other passengers had detrained, the stars appeared, stunned by the heat, the myriad press, and the anticipatory bedlam inside the station itself. They went through the lines of reception committee, and order was maintained until the duo passed under the portal into the terminal itself. The band struck up again, klieg lights were turned on, flashbulbs exploded, and confetti swirled down around them. The noise—in applause, cheers, and whistles—was happily riotous. (When a reporter managed to yell in Rooney's ear, "How do you like it?" the teen grinned and shouted back, "*Swell!*")

He and Garland paused briefly to pose for cameramen—who later described her as a "red headed looker"—and were then hurried through the station as smoothly as possible. Rooney gave out with Andy Hardy's well-known love-cry, "Woooooo-*woo!*" when tumbling into a waiting cab, and the kids, their mothers, Roger Edens, and entourage taxied to their Manhattan headquarters at the Waldorf for further interviews.

The press was suitably wowed by the crowd, its response, and the genuine quality of warmth evidenced by Garland and Rooney. The story of their arrival was front-paged in the New York papers and among the next day's headlines was a happy, perspective-seeking

No, It Wasn't Julius Caesar

―――――

Nor Was It One-Way Corrigan,
Nor Napoleon, Nor Lindbergh.

On Wednesday, Garland and Rooney were once again joined by the 150 teenagers for the Waldorf luncheon. The event was orchestrated by Howard Dietz, who dubbed it "the first cocktail-less cocktail party for movie stars." He organized the reception committee members in an upstairs room at the hotel to rehearse the songs from *Oz* so they could serenade the stars, and he invited Jack Haley over to emcee the party.

August 17 was opening day at the Capitol. This photograph looks northwest across Broadway, with the corner of 50th Street in the left foreground. (51st Street cuts in just to the right of the Capitol marquee.) People lined up five abreast from the theater box office under the marquee, north to the corner of ·51st and Broadway, west down 51st Street to Eighth Avenue, south on Eighth Avenue to 50th Street, east on 50th back to Broadway, and around the corner in front of Howard's Clothes.

(Haley had spent the preceding week promoting *Oz* between his own stage shows at Loew's State.) Guy Lombardo, His Royal Canadians, and Louis Prima were on hand to provide live music and, as soon as they struck up, a couple of the teens started dancing. Not to be outdone, Rooney grabbed Garland and they took to the floor, too; they were fast surrounded by a jitterbugging throng. The young stars danced with their guests as well, and the teens kept them at it for thirty minutes while the lamb-chop-and-milk lunch went untouched.

Publicity flourished . . . and *Oz* had yet to open. The Waldorf was daily besieged by fans. The press noted that Loew's exploitation executive Oscar A. Doob had taken to signing his first name "Ozcar." Garland and Rooney were announced as the only two people "empowered to issue and legalize membership" in the Merry Munchkins of Oz. "To be a Munchkin," explained a press release, "you greet people by putting your thumbs in your ears and wiggling your fingers and exclaiming, 'Oz about it, pal?!'" With all of the hype, there was some danger that the picture and stars wouldn't be able to live up to the expectation that was being generated.

On Thursday, August 17, the lines began forming outside the Capitol at 5:30 A.M. and, by the time tickets went on sale at eight o'clock, the waiting crowd was estimated at fifteen thousand. The theater doors were opened at eight forty-five; by nine ten, all five thousand seats were filled, and there were still between ten thousand and twenty thousand people on line, five and six deep, around the entire city block.

Herndon Davis's excellent portrait of Bert Lahr appeared in the New York Herald Tribune *on Sunday, August 13, 1939.*

Captain Joseph Fristensy of the West 47th Street Station had originally ordered forty policemen to the Capitol. He quickly called for twenty more to control potential line crashers and deal with the mob. Ushers were called from inside the Capitol to help the police, and a couple of ticket sellers were sent walking along the line to dispense admissions for the next show in order to prevent a riot at the box office.

There were no incidents, however. About 60 percent of the waiting fans were under eighteen, but the line included equally enthusiastic adults, happy to stand for the chance to get into a subsequent performance. Many brought lunches; some of the older ladies stood and knitted.

When Garland and Rooney arrived at the theater midmorning, they were awed by the moat of fans surrounding the block. According to newsmen, the actor took one look and gulped, "Gee, what goes on?" Garland responded, a trifle proudly, "*We* go on!" "What a mob," Rooney continued. "They told me it would be big, but I never expected anything like this," enthused the girl, and Rooney riposted, "You've got to expect practically anything in the Land of Oz."

Inside the Capitol, the first house "wept, howled with glee, and trembled with fear" during *Oz*, according to the *New York World Telegram.* The crowd then "tramped and catcalled impatiently through a couple of shorts." The *Journal American* continued,

> the youthful customers out front applauded the trailers and shorts as though the noise would hurry these films through and were finally rewarded when the Glamour Boy of Young America—Master Rooney—bounced exuberantly out of the wings with young Miss Garland . . . The personal appearance of the youngsters at the first performance was nothing short of terrific . . . Judy sings a couple of songs with both vigor and enthusiasm . . . The jitterbug audience went even more hysterical when [Mickey] joined Georgie Stoll's band and gave out with the drums. [Stoll was imported from Culver City to conduct for the show.]

The *World Telegram* added that Garland and Rooney "were given a reception which was as spontaneous as it was loud and which certainly indicated how the public felt about the two kids," while the New York *Mirror* opined, "Were there one child in greater New York who wasn't either in the Capitol or trying to get in, that youngster must have been quarantined with the measles. . . . A juvenile tempest raged on Broadway." The *Daily News* raved, "They sang and danced with all the verve and rhythmic bounce of youth," and the *Post* stated, "Yesterday, the Capitol celebrated its departure from peace, dignity, and plenty of seats. To put it mildly, it was terrific. . . . The 15 or 20 thousand fans weren't wrong. Judy and Mickey put on a bang-up show."

The occasionally caustic columnist Damon Runyon devoted an entire column to his experiences at the Capitol; he had to fight through the crowds to get into the theater and then stood near the stage for the live portion of the program. "It has been our experience that these personal appearances of movie celebrities are generally most inadequate to say the least, but we wound up enjoying [Garland and Rooney]. Judy is a plumpish little girl with a great set of pipes, and Mickey is all rhythm."

The happy madness impressed not only the notoriously hard-boiled journalists but, as noted in the *World Telegram,* "Broadway showmen who happened by stared in amazement." The *New York Herald Tribune* delivered the quietest appraisal but seemed to sum up general media opinion when it concluded, "If Hollywood must come 'in person', this is the way it should do it."

While the press was filing its opening-day stories, the hordes of people continued to get on line at the Capitol. The theater manager finally announced that Judy and Mickey would do an extra show that evening, and the final tally for August 17 was seven performances to thirty-seven thousand customers. The Hollywood *Reporter* added, "So many people were turned away that the overflow filled almost all the other Broadway houses, jammed the restaurants, soft drink parlors, and candy stores."

That night and the next day, Manhattan newspapers splashed the events at the Capitol all over their front pages. To compound the excitement, the breaking notices for *The Wizard of Oz* were again jubilant and largely raves, considered worthy of column after column of review space. Louis B. Mayer had come to New York to cast a cool corporate eye at the kickoff and was overwhelmed by the response. He, Nicholas Schenck, and their associate J. Robert Rubin dined at Lindy's on August 17 and telegraphed Mervyn LeRoy in Hollywood, "We had the best lunch ever. Had the crowds for dessert."

The week continued as it began. Garland and Rooney maintained a weekday schedule of five shows a day (coupled with seven screenings of *Oz*); on weekends, they did seven shows a day (coupled with nine screenings of *Oz*). Between performances, the duo seldom left the theater after their late morning arrival. Meals were brought in from the Waldorf, al-

CAPITOL, N. Y.

Judy Garland, Mickey Rooney, The Martins (8), George Stoll orch (23); 'Wizard of Oz' (M-G), reviewed in VARIETY *Aug. 16.*

Four years have elapsed since the Capitol on Broadway dropped stage shows with a loud thud. Now it steps back into the picture, even if only temporarily, with the attention-getting combination of Judy Garland and Mickey Rooney behind the foots and 'The Wizard of Oz,' featuring the femme juve. on the screen. It's colossal b.o., attested to by the record-breaking attendance opening day (Thursday), and an excellent entertainment buy for old and young alike.

The Garland-Rooney personal is serving a three-fold purpose for Loew's and Metro. First, it's giving 'Oz' a rousing b.o. sendoff in the metropolis; (2) it's serving as a swell trailer for the forthcoming 'Babes in Arms' (M-G), which co-stars the kids, and (3) it indicates the b.o. potentialities of occasionally showcasing Metro players on the Capitol's stage.

There's a vast difference between the current biz at the Capitol with that of its last stage show. Latter held Lou Holtz, Belle Baker, Block and Sully, Moore and Revel, and Tip, Tap and Toe, but the public was apathetic. It was stronger on paper than is the current layout, but the names of Rooney and Garland are evidently magic, plus the benefits accruing from the dandy exploitation campaign on 'Oz.'

A crowd of around 10,000 waited in line for the Capitol's doors to open Thursday (17) morning. This was before the appearance of reviews on the film, so it was either the lure of Garland-Rooney or another instance of the public 'smelling' a good film, or both. In any event, once inside, they're getting their money's worth from both stage and screen.

This is not merely a personal of two film players, but a solid act running nearly 26 minutes. It's grade-A showmanship by both kids. They sing, dance and Rooney drums. They're young, fresh and on the upbeat in the public's affection and imagination—a tousle-haired imp and a cute, clean-cut girl with a smash singing voice and style.

Miss Garland has had quite a bit of stage experience and her stage presence is to be expected, but Rooney surprises with his easy manner in front of a live audience. He sticks to his puckish character and only once does he come close to having his smart-aleckness rebound against him. This is in his clinch duet with Garland on 'Oceans Apart,' introed as Rooney's own composition and coming as their finale. It appears as though he would become too rough, but he manages to stay just within bounds.

She carries the brunt of the vocals, socking out 'The Lamp Is Low' and then 'Comes Love,' from 'Yokel Boy,' at the outset. She leads into Rooney's impersonation of a scene between Clark Gable and Lionel Barrymore in 'Test Pilot,' with Rooney then slipping behind the drums for a jam session. He's far from being a topflight skin-beater, but it's swell novelty coming from him and aimed at the jive hounds. Considering his mixed sartorial get-up opening night, Rooney might also have soloed 'Sam, You Made de Pents Too Long.'

They insert a major plug for 'Babes in Arms' via two songs from that film, 'Good Morning' and 'God's Country.' Latter is a slap at the dictatorships, naming Stalin, Franco, Il Duce and Der Fuehrer, and indicates controversy if the picture is released with that song intact.

Rooney clowns his singing, but indicates some vocal ability. He also shows promise as a hoofer in a shag routine with Garland. In 'Country' he works in a comic impersonation of F.D.R., without, however, mentioning names, and then both lead neatly into the 'Oceans' encore. The audience appreciation is loud and long throughout.

Loew's smartly brought personable George Stoll, Metro musical director, on from the Coast to direct the pickup stage orch. Latter holds 21 musicians, plus a pianist for a singing octet, and though rehearsed for only three days is tiptop. First five minutes of the 31-minute stage show is taken up by the orchestra. The Martins (8) and their smooth orch-vocal blend on 'We're Off to See the Wizard,' from 'Oz.' The mixed octet, named after its pianist, Hugh Martin, has practically nothing to do after the opening, the stage then being taken over and held thereafter by the two film juves.

Band is spotted on the stage in a very smart setting, spread out to seem even larger than it is, and reminiscent of the Capitol's once large symph. Musicians are tuxed, but Stoll sticks to an ice-cream suit. It's a touch of Hollywood nonchalance. *Scho.*

Variety (August 23, 1939) gleefully reviewed the Capitol stage show.

though more publicity was generated when it was reported that the kids sometimes preferred the five-cent hamburgers from a stand near the Capitol stage door—a dozen a day for the boy, nine for the girl. (Loew's reassuringly announced that the hamburgers—as an occasional dietary deviation—had been pronounced nutritionally adequate by the theater house physician and the mothers of the two stars.) The Capitol management also set up a sunbath solarium and roof playground/garden as a retreat from stage and dressing rooms. It was usually midnight when the entertainers were done for the day and, even then, protective detectives and uniformed police were needed to get them through the vigilant crowds.

Sometimes they would be escorted out between shows for further promotional gigs. On August 19, Rooney hosted a supper party on the Waldorf Starlight Roof for socialite Brenda Frazier. On August 23, Garland joined him in a photo session for a *Daily News* color magazine cover. On August 27, there was a fast trek to the World's Fair, where they appeared for newsreel and experimental television cameras with

Mayor Fiorello LaGuardia. It took twenty policemen to clear a path through the fans, and a crowd of five thousand gathered to watch the duo film a promotional short to extol the availability of clean and inexpensive housing for tourists coming to New York.

Understandably, the pace affected all the principals at one juncture or another. At a matinee on August 24, conductor Georgie Stoll was felled by illness just as he was about to enter the orchestra pit. When Rooney ran on and saw that Stoll was missing, he moved upstage to the band and conducted the musicians himself—and continued to move between the band and fore-stage for the remainder of the performance. Garland collapsed midshow in the wings on another occasion, momentarily giving way to the strain. Rooney ad-libbed a couple of comedy routines and, within a few minutes, a revived costar caught his eye from backstage and then strode out to continue the show. (Rooney later wrote, "If I hadn't mentioned her collapse, no one in the audience would have known. That's the sort of trouper Judy was.") Rooney himself was accused by some of the press of unwinding in a

Garland and Rooney clown backstage at the Capitol with visitor Artie Shaw. The bandleader was one of the great passions of Garland's teen years.

variety of Manhattan nightspots after his final evening performances (which MGM quickly denied). There was also trouble on one occasion, apart from the stars, when persistent autograph seekers scuffled at the hotel with Waldorf staff.

But mostly it was all delight, and the press continued its laudatory statements about *Oz* in arts editorials and columns. The *Post,* observing the universal glee of audiences leaving the theater, printed the lyrics to "We're Off to See the Wizard—à la Delancey Street" as they'd heard it sung by some of the patrons in a heavy New York accent. Another columnist reported the reaction of a four-year-old girl who, seeing her first combination film-and-stage show, thought that *Oz* and its cast were "tops [but] I liked those round actors much better than the flat ones."

Rooney and Garland loved the excitement they were creating, and Mervyn LeRoy frequently called them backstage from Los Angeles to share the exultation. Fred Waring had Garland on his radio program as a special guest, dedicating the broadcast to her and playing the *Oz* score. The hold-over success of the film in New York meant the duo had to cancel appearances in Philadelphia, and there were even rumors

that their Broadway triumph had garnered them an invitation to appear in England before the King and Queen.

Garland's one disappointment was that the performance schedule kept both her and her costar from really seeing the World's Fair. She recalled in 1960, "Then Mickey in some way arranged to have the fair officials delay the closing time one night. They kept the whole fair open for us for two hours. We raced from one exhibit to the next. We saw everything. We rode on everything. I still remember it as the most wonderful night of my life."

The Capitol hit an all-time attendance high for the first week of *Oz,* although (as would be the case everywhere), the box-office gross wasn't always of record-breaking caliber due to the fact that youngsters always paid lower admission prices than adults. Still, at a time when twenty-two thousand dollars per week was considered average for the Capitol, *Oz* did sixty-eight thousand its first week and better than fifty thousand its second. *Women's Wear Daily* offered some investigative journalism as encouragement to those who despaired of the day-long lines at the theater. They found it usually took around thirty-one minutes to travel around the block from the end of the line on Broadway and 50th Street to the box office on Broadway and 51st. According to the report, the teenage throngs created the greatest jam-ups from morning until midafternoon, and adults began to dominate the crowds after three o'clock. There was seldom a wait to get into the evening performances.

After two weeks at the Capitol, Rooney was called back to Hollywood to begin work on the eighth Andy Hardy feature, *Judge Hardy and Son.* But *Oz* was a sensation, and the crowds were still strong at the Capitol, so MGM arranged to have Ray Bolger and Bert Lahr join Garland on stage for another week. Rooney's last performances were Wednesday, August 30 and, between the evening shows, he and Garland were escorted a block west to Madison Square Garden to appear as a special attraction at the Harvest Moon Ball. Columnist Ed Sullivan wrote that the teens were at first stupefied by the engulfing, welcoming ovation from the audience of twenty thousand but quickly settled in to a top-form performance. Also on the bill were Jack Haley, Bolger, and Lahr (who had arrived in town on August 28 for Capitol rehearsals), Alice Faye, Tony Martin, Sonja Henie, Adolphe Menjou, John Garfield, Anna Neagle, Irene Castle, George Raft, and the Jimmy Dorsey band. But the Capitol team was reported as the unquestioned highlight.

The next morning at the first show, Rooney strode down the aisle of the Capitol to present Garland with a

Bolger, Garland, and Lahr were reunited for closing week at the Capitol.

bouquet of roses. The gesture backfired when the audience spotted him and stampeded; the show was held up and the actor made a fast retreat. But the remainder of the week went smoothly, and the new Garland/Bolger/Lahr triumverate gave the girl an opportunity to switch her material. Although retaining "Comes Love," she also added Roger Edens's arrangements of "F. D. R. Jones" and "Blue Evening." Lahr did his renowned Arlen/Harburg "Song of the Woodman" from *The Show Is On* (1937), and Bolger followed with an eccentric dance, a comedy routine, and a pantomimed/choreographic version of a recent prizefight in which he played both boxers and the referee. For a finale, the trio sang "The Jitterbug," explaining its deletion from *Oz* due to the length of the film. (When reviewing the new bill at the Capitol, *Variety* observed, "It appears there may have been other reasons. [The number's] good but not up to the other portions of the film.")

General response to the revised show was glowing, and the Capitol box office continued to flourish. The gross for the week was forty thousand dollars; Bolger and Lahr each made three thousand five hundred for the engagement. (Rooney had received five thousand dollars per week for his stint, and Garland got the same weekly salary as her *Oz* costars. Ironically, her cumulative salary for the three weeks she spent at the Capitol came to more than she was paid for the entire five months she worked on *Oz!**)

*Garland's salary for *Oz* totaled $9,649.98 (five hundred dollars per week for nineteen weeks and two days). Bolger made seventy-two thousand dollars for twenty weeks' work; Billie Burke received $6,333.32 for her six weeks and two days. Frank Morgan and Bert Lahr received twenty-five hundred dollars per week, Jack Haley twenty-two hundred and fifty dollars per week, Margaret Hamilton, one thousand dollars per week.

Garland, Lahr, and Bolger continued at the Capitol through September 6, at which time *The Wizard of Oz* concluded its New York debut. The picture moved into local second-run engagements later in the month; Garland and Bolger returned to Los Angeles, and Lahr prepared to rehearse for Cole Porter's new show *DuBarry Was a Lady,* in which the comic would share top billing with Ethel Merman.

New York City went on into an autumn that had already seen the beginnings of World War II. But *The Wizard of Oz* and its attendant hoopla had helped to—if only momentarily—ease the situation. A wire service report at the end of August endeavored to explain the crowds and their reaction:

> . . . nothing like [it] has happened in New York since *Snow White and the Seven Dwarfs*—and beyond that, the memory of man runneth not to the contrary. In the face of such public response, critical praise is beggared. All that local scribes can do is try to analyze reasons behind the popularity of what is already a historic box-office phenomenon.

The journalist went on to speculate that a lot of business was accounted for by the fame of the book, the publicity campaign, and the presence of Rooney and Garland. But he continued:

> These factors . . . have little to do with the satisfaction felt by patrons who enter the theater expecting a lot for their money. Actually, *The Wizard* is considered by seasoned observers as a triumph of showmanship. All the technical resources of the movie medium are put at the service of fantasy here and are used with marvelous skill.
>
> More than skill, though, is the delight in tricky make-believe which is the spirit behind the film. That spirit communicates itself fully to spectators until it's all a funfest with the audience "joining in" as it seldom does . . .
>
> . . . there is wholly the quality of magic in the triumph of this picture, which succeeds where so many film fantasies have heavily failed. It is as much an individual achievement as its literary original.

CHAPTER 11

From Coast to Coast

Special "premieres" of *The Wizard of Oz* were held in at least two other theaters in August 1939, and the first of these actually preceded both the Los Angeles and New York openings. The film began a five-day engagement at the Strand in Oconomowoc, Wisconsin, on August 12 and was even advertised locally as celebrating its "World Premier Showing." Though no reason for the "honor" was given, the Milwaukee film distributor advised theater owners Harley and Ruth Huebner that they were indeed the first to exhibit the picture.

The rationale behind the Oconomowoc booking was probably the same as that attendant to the early *Oz* debut in Spirit Lake, Iowa, where the film opened on August 17. According to *Variety*, the resort town was selected in anticipation that the "Spirit Lake reaction . . . will serve as a key to *Oz*'s possibilities in the entire middle west . . . Newspapermen, critics and editors have been invited to the opening . . . and H. W. Lambert of the Metro exploitation department is in the Iowa burg working on the *Oz* engagement."

By the third week in August, *Oz* had begun to "break" in major cities all over the country, and *Variety* pulled out its powerhouse adjectives to report the grosses. *Oz* was "big" in Baltimore, "great" in Denver, "terrific" in Indianapolis, "outstanding" in Kansas City, and "swell" in Providence. It "led the way" in Philadelphia and was acclaimed the "Wizard of Hub" in Boston. "Spurred by critical raves" and promotion, *Oz* "smashed all opening day records for years" in San Francisco, and the situation as described in Louisville summed up other overall reaction: "*Wizard of Oz* is the big topic along the main stem this week and is causing plenty of oral comment . . . Film patrons . . . are passing the word along in great fashion that at last here is a pic production that rings the bell on all points. It's getting a big play from youngsters and oldsters . . . making biz mighty sweet." *Film Daily* estimated that business for *Oz* was above normal box office by 85 percent in Los Angeles, 88 percent in Indianapolis, 82 percent in Denver, 73 percent in Nor-

folk, 70 percent in Louisville, 60 percent in Akron, 57 percent in Toledo and Reading, 56 percent in Rochester and Kansas City, 55 percent in Dayton, and 167 percent in New York.

Extensive local promotion was a keen support in such success. Syracuse publicity made much of the fact that L. Frank Baum and film composer Harold Arlen were both "local boys," and an Oz costume party was organized via the city's park system. A similar event drew hundreds of contestants in New Orleans, and the press and local film groups were invited to a special preview of the picture; further cooperation came from book and department stores in their extensive Oz book displays and advertisements. In St. Louis, a kiddie coloring contest was established at forty city playgrounds, and a "wizard"/fortuneteller appeared daily in the lobby of the Loew's theater for a week prior to the *Oz* opening. He offered all patrons a free

An ad for the "World Premier" of Oz in Oconomowoc, Wisconsin.

tween Oscar Mayer and Balaban and Katz: I followed the picture through their theater chain. They would have [a poster] in the lobby or billing on the marquee—'In Person Today! One of the Munchkins from *The Wizard of Oz*!' I would get up on the stage in my Oscar Mayer chef's uniform and give a little bit of an introduction . . . what was interesting, what the audience should watch for. And when the people left the theater, we'd present them with samples of Oscar Mayer wieners."

Perhaps the most offbeat *Oz* association came on August 20 when Aimee Semple McPherson and staff staged their version of the film for four thousand worshipers at her Los Angeles temple. The evangelist told the *Oz* story while members of the congregation enacted the principal roles.

In its second week of national release, *Oz* was "mighty" (Chicago), "a big $ maker" (Portland), "a smash" (Omaha), "very nifty" (Los Angeles), and "hefty" (Seattle). "It's *Wizard of Oz* by three lengths" in Lincoln, Nebraska, continued *Variety* and then noted the film topped most of the other movie business in nearly every city it played. As the "current big box office noise" in Minneapolis, the clamor for *Oz* forced the local theater to open its doors two hours earlier than usual. The third and fourth weeks of the picture racked up similar results: amidst other superlatives, *Oz* was "chipper," "socko," "terrific," with "steady profits," and "a heavy winner . . . going great guns" in (respectively) Philadelphia, Cincinnati, Chicago, and Portland.

MGM and Loew's were jubilant and took full-page ads in the trades to underscore the success. One noted the extended playing time *Oz* was enjoying in nine California cities, reprinted a clipping about the New

demonstration of mind reading and concluded each "seance" with the prediction, "It will be your good fortune to see a good motion picture in this theater next week. It's *The Wizard of Oz*." A Seattle department store held an Oz style show and coloring contest, devoting several display windows to Oz-related advertising. In most local competitions, the prizes were tickets to see the film, and all the events—especially the costume parades—drew much newspaper space and free publicity.

A unique promotion for *Oz* involved Munchkin Coroner Meinhardt Raabe, who had returned to work for the Oscar Mayer Company after completing his part in the picture. When the film was ready to open in the Midwest, Raabe recalls, "a deal was made be-

For four weeks prior to the Philadelphia Oz *debut, the Boyd Theatre displayed this exhibit, conceived by theater manager Maurice K. Gable. (Four of the Munchkins, fully costumed by MGM, toured the entire city and garnered additional publicity.) (above left)* Oz *teaser ads.*

The Music Box theater owner mistakenly directed his local newspaper typesetter to costar comic Ted Healy instead of Jack Haley for this engagement of Oz.

York premiere, and featured a caricatured Leo the Lion, swinging on a giant OZ. Another paraphrased the general theater abbreviation for Standing Room Only: instead of S.R.O., the lingo was adjusted to "S.R.Oz." The third included a sketch of a "human" box-office window, reeling and drunk with money. It was accompanied by the simple legend, "Ozified."

The film moved on to smaller locales with similar promotional ballyhoo and results. From mid-September until early October, an MGM publicity caravan for *Oz* canvassed seventeen smaller towns in the Indianapolis and Chicago exchange territories, literally parading down main streets and winning much front-page newspaper space. In several Indiana locations, schools were closed for the day so that students could enjoy the festivities. The Metro caravan then went on to work the hamlets serviced by St. Louis, Minneapolis, Omaha, Kansas City, Long Island, and New Jersey.

Business for *The Wizard of Oz* was superlative from the onset and, by the end of 1939, it ranked as one of the top money-making motion pictures of the year. In its first release, the film returned $3,017,000 to MGM, and the figure would have been higher but for an odd combination of uncontrollable factors. As noted earlier, the film broke attendance records in many areas, but the accompanying box-office figures—while excellent—were not of the same record-breaking caliber. At least one-third of the *Oz* audience

*Front page flash from N.Y.
World-Telegram (typical
of news coverage) as New
York went wild!*

10,000 Wait in Line To See Wizard of Oz

Fans Circle Block Standing Four Abreast

Thousands of women and children, with a few men sprinkled among them today surrounded the block in which the Capitol Theater is located, waiting in line to see the Wizard of Oz on its opening day.

The line began to form before 8 A. M. and when 6,000 marched into the theater, when the doors opened at 8:45, there still remained a line in which there were 4,000 movie fans, police estimated, and 20,000 by the estimate of the theater's press agent.

The line, which 100 police controlled, began at the box office; extended north to 51st St., east to Eighh Ave., south to 50th St. and west to Broadway.

For most of its length people were standing four abreast. Broadway showmen who happened by stared in amazement. They commented that the Wizard was the biggest hit since Snow White and might turn out to be even a greater draw.

OH BOY!

AND NOT ONLY NEW YORK..BUT THE WHOLE COUNTRY AND IN LOS ANGELES..NOW IN ITS 40TH DAY OF PLAYING TIME..15 DAYS IN SAN DIEGO..DOUBLE TIME (7 DAYS) IN WHITTIER.. 14 DAYS IN LONG BEACH AND GLENDALE..7 DAYS IN INGLEWOOD, HUNTINGTON PARK, SANTA MONICA AND OCEAN PARK..IT'S THE SAME STORY EVERYWHERE..! "THE WIZARD"— A WIZ FOR DOUBLE BUSINESS, DOUBLE PROFITS!

A full-page trade-paper ad called attention to the initial box-office success of The Wizard of Oz. *A caricature of MGM's trademark, Leo the Lion, is swinging on the Oz.*

In the Not-So-Merry Old Land of Oz

This editorial cartoon was probably the first to use the public awareness of MGM's Oz characters in a comment on a national or world situation. The Wicked Witch is Hitler, the Winged Monkey is Mussolini, and Dorothy and her companions represent European Civilization, Poland, Britain, and France. (Utica Observer-Dispatch, *August 31, 1939*)

Loew's Weekly *was a four-page give-away flyer provided to New York theater patrons; the September 21, 1939, cover announced the general exhibition of* Oz.

was comprised of children, who paid less in admission prices than adult patrons. And, while business was always strong enough to warrant extended engagements for the film, the picture was not "held over" in some cases because, as *Variety* put it, there was "too much biz backed up." Nineteen thirty-nine was a bumper year for motion pictures, and the glut of incoming films required exhibition space. Finally, much of the potential foreign market for the film was cut off by the beginning of World War II in September 1939.

When the roughly one-million-dollar cost of film prints, distribution, and advertising was added to the final *Oz* production tally of $2,777,000, the box office receipts of $3,017,000 were not enough to put

the picture in the black. *The Wizard of Oz* probably lost around seven hundred fifty thousand dollars on its initial release.

But in spite of the financial loss *The Wizard of Oz* was considered a triumph for MGM. Studio workers at the time suggested the film was intended as Metro's annual "prestige picture," a summation of creative effort designed not as much for ensured monetary success as for popular and critical acclaim. *Oz* more than achieved that goal and, if the film remained "good" for the ten years of subsequent use the studio purportedly expected to get out of it, there would be more money to be made in the future—virtually all of it clear profit.

(on facing page) Judy Garland and Mickey Rooney at the Academy Awards banquet, February 29, 1940.

PART THREE

Raves and Accolades

CHAPTER 12

The Reviews

The *Wizard of Oz* was first seen by the professional film critics—at least those working out of the Los Angeles area—in a special screening arranged by MGM on August 9. (A New York press preview was held the same day.) According to the *Hollywood Reporter*, the guest list included "75 correspondents representing 40 foreign countries . . . their reviews, written in 25 different languages, will reach an estimated audience of 100,000,000 readers."

The general response from the commentators was more joyous than perhaps even the studio dreamed possible. The next day, James Francis Crow commented in the *Hollywood Citizen-News*. "It isn't very often that the Hollywood preview critics admit their enthusiasms among themselves. It was different when *The Wizard of Oz* was shown to the press . . . The reviewers expressed their opinions to one another freely, and the opinions all amounted to the same thing: *The Wizard of Oz* is a great motion picture. It is not only a magnificent, history-making technical achievement: it is a warmly human, deeply emotional photoplay, too; and when the lights went up after the projection-room showing, many of the critics still had the tears in their eyes. They had been crying with the young star, Judy Garland, at her farewell to the people of the wonderful land of Oz." In detailing the technical switch from black-and-white to Technicolor, Crow opined, "It was just here that the history-making character of [the] film struck this reviewer most forcibly. For surely her first sight of the Land of Oz could have been no more wonderful to Dorothy than the sight of this photoplay itself would have been to the eyes of the film fans of 20 years ago . . . An inexhaustibly entertaining and great motion picture."

Happily underscoring the general reaction, Howard Strickling telegraphed Howard Dietz on August 10: "Press preview *Wizard of Oz* sensational . . . reviews this morning absolutely raves [. . .] will wire complete excerpts later today." A full page of glowing extracts was quickly assembled for the August 14 issue of the *MGM Studio News,* an exhibitor's promotional brochure published by Loew's on a weekly basis. Summing up the first wave of written reaction, the *Hollywood Reporter* noted on August 12, "There is more guessing on the probable gross of *Oz* than of any other picture that has come out of this business in its entire history. The guesses run from ordinary hit business to ticket sales topping even *Snow White*. But one thing all the critics . . . agree on, it will play to a mob of customers and will be the talk of the universe."

A plethora of raves also followed the official Los Angeles premiere at Grauman's, and several local writers took the chance (as was then the custom) to expand on their initial printed comments. Further reaction to the film—both in New York a few days later and then across the country—was much the same.

Though the great majority of critical response ranged from positive to rapturous, there was some dissension. A few major magazine critics disliked the musical-comedy approach to the story and panned what they felt were excesses in performance, treatment, or production. After Aljean Harmetz pointedly quoted from these mixed and negative reviews in *The Making of The Wizard of Oz* in 1977, the scope and impact of those comments swelled to the extent that a myth quickly grew about the mostly resistive press reception originally given the picture. Even the surviving stars came to believe it and were quoted about their memories of the "terrible" 1939 reviews.

But any dour critical observation was much in the minority. Film trade papers and the popular press in major cities especially recommended *The Wizard of Oz*, even when they had minor qualms about some aspects of its handling. *Variety* was particularly declarative in its statement, "There's an audience for *Oz* wherever there's a projection machine and a screen."

On September 11, 1939, the *Hollywood Reporter* announced the winners of its monthly "preview poll" of Los Angeles-area critics. *Oz* won five first-place citations: Best Picture, Best Actor (Bert Lahr), Best Cinematography, Best Musical Score, and Best Original Song ("Over the Rainbow"). In second-place commendations, Victor Fleming was cited as Best Director, and Langley, Ryerson, and Woolf were honored for Best Screenplay; even "We're Off to See the Wizard" came in at third place in the Best Song category. Five days later, the drama editors of the various newspapers in the Scripps-Howard chain also voted *Oz* best picture of the month for August 1939.

And—finally—when *Film Daily* conducted its annual poll of more than 450 American motion-picture critics at the end of the year, *The Wizard of Oz* was named one of the ten best films of 1939.

Here is an excerpted sampling of some of the original reviews of *The Wizard of Oz*. The names of the critics and dates of publication are given where known.

———

After the first press previews in Los Angeles and New York on August 9:

Los Angeles Times (Edwin Schallert, August 10): "Fantasy is at last brought to the screen in full-fledged form, and a victory...is achieved in *Oz* which may well be described as epochal. Here finally is [a fantasy] replete with both imagination and entertainment. It will in the future be regarded as one of the truly important contributions to the motion picture. MGM has gone further than mere effects, remarkable as these are in the Kansas cyclone, and shown that truly radiant, one might say poetic, even, atmosphere may be conjured in settings, ensemble and the management of the realistic human beings of the cinema. Billie Burke might have stepped out of Baum's literary make-believe. She appears almost like a being eternally young. That was indeed skillful casting. The most enormous success of all in the picture is Lahr—an extraordinary impersonation, full of humor of a great pensive robustness. Judy Garland is pert, persuasive and amazingly sympathetic. She even will cull some tears in her later scenes. Morgan is splendid, too, while Hamilton triumphs as the Bad Witch. This picture will spell enchantment for children. It will also have the virtue of taking grownups to Never-Never Land. Its possibilities for world-wide success are enormous. *Oz* is worthy of road-show exploitation and redounds to the credit of LeRoy, Fleming, and everybody."

The *Hollywood Reporter* (August 10): "*Oz* will, beyond question, be accorded recognition as a milestone in motion picture history. It scintillates with artistry, yet it possesses such an abundance of qualities which predict broad audience success that there can be no question of its being headed for spectacular playing time and grosses. The picture will undoubtedly reflect great credit on the industry at large. It is...brilliantly inventive, arrestingly beautiful and dramatically compelling to the eye, the ear, and the emotions. LeRoy has captured a spirit of earthy drama of a strong moral flavor and combined this with out-right fantasy and striking effect. The production is remarkable in every department...which further clinches the picture's claims to highly significant achievement. Judy Garland gives [Dorothy] lyric charm and a wholly competent performance dramatically [which] will undoubtedly advance her career vitally. Lahr's performance is scintillatingly outstanding...Haley's is likewise richly drawn...Numerous scenes will remain long in the audience memory—of whatever age—to mark *Wizard* as memorable."

Daily Variety (August 10): "An amazing achievement in entertainment as well as technical wizardry is this elaborate, magnificent, and thoroughly beguiling screen treatment...Occasionally a film rates the designation 'great,' and this is such an occasion. The picture should pay handsomely on its heavy investment and may very well prove to be one of Metro's all-time top money offerings. The fine pictorial version is first of all a distinguished credit...to LeRoy for the painstaking, imaginative, and showmanly task of organizing the mass of material, the many creative and technical factors which required unusual coordination for success...[Fleming's] direction truly is a grand feat...The performances are superb...Screenplay is a masterpiece of fantasy, cleverly contrived to bring out in rich fullness every entertainment element, dramatic and pictorial...the musical program is exceptionally fine..."

The Film Daily (August 10): "Handsomely mounted fairy story should click solidly at the box office. Leo the Lion is privileged to herald this one with his deepest roar—the one that comes from way down—for seldom if indeed ever has the screen been so successful in its approach to fantasy and extravaganza through the medium of flesh-and-blood...a corking achievement all the way through. It spells surcease from cares, tribulations, and taxes..."

Los Angeles Examiner (Louella O. Parsons, August 10): " [*Oz*] has been done on a magnificent scale with settings that are breathtaking in a production that has few equals in the annals of...motion picture business. LeRoy can easily put this down as his ultimate achievement. Victor Fleming must have loved the Oz stories to give the movie such creative and appreciative direction. Langley, Ryerson, and Woolf have shown great imagination and do a skillful job. The little Garland girl is very good. Lahr has never been funnier. Hamilton does a really amazing job [and] Burke looks like a twenty-year-old...she is a delight to the eye. There are so many lovely touches that linger in our memory after leaving the theater. The music is no small part of the success...The children will eat it up, and it should be revived every year for the benefit of the rising generations."

Los Angeles Herald-Express (Harrison Carroll, August 10): "An amazing adventure in the world of fairy tales...the highest compliment that you can pay is that the film compares favorably to Disney's *Snow White*. The real triumph of the picture is the fantastic land of Oz. The eye is assailed with surprises, each more beautiful or more impressive in its camera magic than the last. The photography is gorgeous, the art direction superb, and the special effects are a source of constant wonder. If there is any jarring note, it is in the early reels where there is a tendency to go musical comedy...the story thereafter becomes straightforward and is vastly more interesting...None will deny that *Oz* is one of the greatest novelties ever offered on the screen."

Motion Picture Daily (Alfred Finestone, August 10): "*Oz* is of the essence of screen entertainment that lives for a long time. It probably will prove to be a popular revival at appropriate seasons. It has been given lavish treatment and impeccable direction...a box-office attraction of major importance. Weakness is apparent in the whimsy itself. Dating from the year 1900, it may or may not appeal to sophisticated adults in the year 1939. Valiant attempts have been made to inject a modern note and, while in itself it clicks tremendously, in the surroundings it appears quite out of place. [But] it's the drollery and spectacle that count...Lahr turns in the No. 1 performance. The makeup job calls for a special award."

Los Angeles Times (Hedda Hopper, August 15): "Well, *Oz* has done it. Made human beings as interesting as Disney's cartoons. It lifts you right out of a drab, work-a-day world and makes you long for your lost childhood. To me, the one who stole the show was Lahr...he's finally come into his own. The music throughout surpasses anything sound has done up to date. *Oz* is truly a great picture."

Hollywood Citizen-News (Philip K. Scheuer, August 15): "No one was more surprised than Hollywood—collective, Hydra-headed Hollywood—when 'LeRoy's Folly' turned out to be fantasy of the year. I can think of no other film with human actors with which to compare the 'reality' of its make-believe. Fairbanks' *Thief of Bagdad,* Fritz Lang's *Siegfried,* the one or two Oz works of the past...were fascinating in their time. Yet today they would not hold a candle to the thing of wondrous beauty, hearty whimsy, and combined sight-sound magic wrought by this 1939 wizard."

Paul Harrison, NEA syndicated columnist: "An exciting flesh and blood fantasy...[*Oz*] will probably play for the next five years."

Movie Digest (August 16): "Dust off the adjectives and prepare for extended runs...all concerned in the production spent lavishly of their imagination and skill. Direction, scripting, musical ingredients, playing, are on a scale of the highest. Add those elements and then multiply for the Technicolor job—so entrancing and engrossing as to make it tough on the next black-and-white picture you view after *Oz.* All this is so memorable because of the simple fact that LeRoy, Fleming, and their aides captured the 'spirit' of the Baum fairy tale classic. Except for a few jarring notes in Lahr's dialogue, a viewing of the picture means being transported to a land of dreams...The picture marks a great break in the screen career of Garland. Technicolor and Judy mate perfectly, and the youngster's real talent takes sympathetically to the role...The pivot of the action is a trouper-studded cast...none overshadowing the other, and all contributing to the general atmosphere of an adventure into the nowhere...Stothart's score is a gem, musical numbers by Arlen and Harburg sparkle...Skillful Bobby Connolly handled the dance numbers on the same clear-cut, while highly imaginative, plane that distinguishes the entire production."

Variety ("Flin," August 16): "*Oz* is likely to perform some record-breaking feats of box office magic. Favorable word-of-mouth on the unique and highly entertaining features of the film should spread rapidly. It's a pushover for the children and family biz. Nothing comparable has come out of Hollywood in the past few years...Some of the scenic passages are so beautiful in design and composition as to stir audiences by their sheer unfoldment. At popular prices, [*Oz*] is a bargain package for eye and ear..."

Picture Reports (August 16): "Surpassing all previous screen extravaganzas in the mammoth scope of its production, *Oz* commands superlatives from critics and public alike. It is truly a magnificent spectacle, a towering achievement in the technical magic of motion pictures. Yet whatever the sum total of its accomplishments, the most significant is the fact that it opens new vistas of pure fantasy to the screen...Every person who had a hand in the making of *Oz* had something up both sleeves. The picture will still be playing to delight a coming generation. About the only criticism is that valuable time is wasted in getting Dorothy off to Oz. Quite unnecessary is the establishment of the farmhands in Kansas as the prototypes of the Scarecrow, Tin Woodman, and Lion. It is footage that could be eliminated in favor of more gorgeous bits of business of the ilk of the Horse-of-a-Different-Col-

or...The music is really delightful. Too much credit cannot be given to Victor Fleming. He brooks no apologies in presenting a fable and keeps events steadily marching forward without pause. The costuming by Adrian is especially fine and those character makeups created by Jack Dawn are alone worth the price of admission. Garland deserves stardom for her performance. She is everything admirers of the character could want her to be, and her role is unusually long and exacting. Bolger, Lahr, and Haley are perfection itself...LeRoy has indeed given *Oz* a magical production. Its universal success will be his praise."

After the Grauman's premiere in Los Angeles on August 15:

Hollywood Citizen-News (Carl Combs, August 16): "Preview critics last week exhausted their unusually large supply of laudatory adjectives in describing the enchantments of *Oz.* Premiere critics today are left with little else to do but echo their praises. [*Oz*] is a milestone in the progress of the entertainment industry. It is like looking through a magic telescope at the illustrations in your favorite Oz book...a super-fantasy, the likes of which Hollywood has never seen. Amazingly enough, all this breathtaking adornment not once eclipses the delightful presence of the carefully chosen players. Judy Garland, rosy-cheeked, starry-eyed, and more alluring than a glamour girl, [has] an almost continuous two-hour job of exploring the wonders of Oz...Lahr's 'King of the Forest' assumes proportions of an aria from *Aida...Oz* is a triumph."

Los Angeles Times (Edwin Schallert, August 16): "A new experience and a new thrill dawned last night. The viewing of this picture with movietown first-nighters does naught but intensify admiration and enthusiasm for its attractions. *Oz* is living up fully and more than fully to the expectations of those who appraised it scarcely a week ago at preview. The film is one of those marvels of moviedom which come all too seldom—a pioneering step and an artistic realization at once. Those who remember the older golden days of Hollywood with their courage and experimentation will be heartened anew and will, perhaps, even hope that *Oz* will put an end to the deadly dull routine of formulae...The story 'carries on' as an exciting adventure...joyous, inspired make-believe. And the audience undoubtedly actually 'rooted' for Dorothy and her companions, for applause punctuated the way." (Four days later, Schallert editorialized on the potential receipts of *Oz:* "Estimates are that [it] will gross at least five million dollars in the international market. It may not quite equal *Snow White* because of altered world conditions and the magic of Disney's name in foreign countries. But this Baum fantasy, as brought to the screen, will be the closest rival of that big money-making cartoon feature. Like that picture, it is also being hailed as a movie milestone—something new, daring, and genuinely path-breaking in the cinema.")

Los Angeles Herald-Express (Harrison Carroll, August 16): "Hollywood conquered another frontier last night when MGM's *Oz* scored a lustrous triumph in the almost unexplored world of fantasy. [The sets and effects] offer something unique in the history of the screen. An acceptable musical touch is the welcome of the Munchkins...in the manner of Gilbert and Sullivan. Three midgets who receive no program credit offer a scene-stealing bit in this sequence...*Oz* is just as much a screen classic as was *Snow White.* You can see it again and again and never tire of its marvels."

1939 products: *(top left)* Whitman's "Game of The Wizard of Oz" *(courtesy Fred M. Meyer); (top right)* The Hollywood Jewelry Company produced an Oz charm bracelet as well as costume jewelry like this Tin Man pin; *(middle left)* "Soapy Characters from the Land of Oz" *(courtesy Rob Roy MacVeigh;* the Kerk Guild also marketed a separate Dorothy soap figure); *(above)* Barney Stempler & Sons created wooden children's coat hangers that pictured (at least) Dorothy, Toto, Nikko, and the Good Witch; *(left)* The Newark Mask Company issued three pressed-gauze or linen masks *(courtesy Rob Roy MacVeigh).*

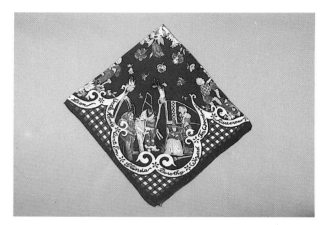

(top left) Illustrations of movie scenes were used for The Wizard of Oz *scarf* (Brian Fabrics, 1939). The scarf was also printed and marketed in a different color scheme. (top right and above) Corning Glassworks manufactured Oz drinking glasses as a premium for Sealtest cottage cheese. Each was approximately five inches high; in addition to those pictured, there was also a Wizard glass. (far right) Theater employees in 1939 promoted the film by wearing this rayon tag made by Whitney Manufacturing. (courtesy Meinhardt Raabe) (right) The Wizard of Oz Carpet Sweeper was manufactured by Bissell and sold in both adult and children's sizes into the 1940's. (courtesy Mildred Martin) (bottom) "Ray Bolger—MGM's El Mago de Oz" was one of a reported set of eleven Spanish buttons advertising the foreign release.

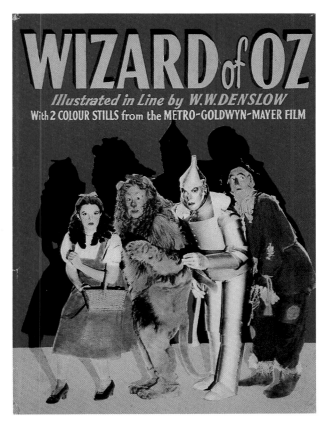

(left) Hutchinson & Co. issued the full-length Wizard of Oz in Great Britain in 1940. In addition to the MGM cover, the book was illustrated with eight hand-colored stills and portraits of the film cast. (courtesy Peter E. Hanff) (above left) This British paperback utilized outlines of the original Denslow plates as inspiration for its "colouring" pages. (1940) (above) This British abridgement was illustrated with line drawings after Denslow and included two hand-tinted stills. (1940)

(top left) O Magico de Oz *was one of the first foreign books to capitalize on the film. It was issued in December 1939 in São Paulo, Brazil, by Rotografica Limitada. (top right)* El Mago de Oz, *published the following year by Biblioteca Infantil/Empresa Editora Zig Zag in Santiago, Chile, also followed the film story with accompanying stills. (Both books courtesy Turner Entertainment Co.) (bottom) Front and back covers of* Trollkarlen från Oz, *published by Reuter & Reuter in Stockholm, Sweden, in 1940. (courtesy David L. and Douglas G. Greene)*

(top left) The Danish Troldmanden fra Oz *from Tempo in Copenhagen, 1940. (top right)* O Feiticeiro de Oz, *issued in 1940 by Editorial Progresso in Lisbon, Portugal. Six years later, Livraria Civilizacâo of Porto published a new edition (above). (at right) An Italian* Il Mago di Oz, *circa 1948, from Societa Apostolato Stampa in Rome. (All courtesy David L. and Douglas G. Greene)*

(On facing page) "The Wizard of Oz Card Game" consisted of forty-four playing cards, each illustrated with a hand-colored still photograph. (When aligned sequentially, the cards provided a visual recap of the film plot.) Although of British manufacture, circa 1940, the game carries no identification. A similar Snow White deck was issued in the late 1930s by Castell Bros., Ltd., of London.

(top left) Public response to the Oz songs led Decca to issue a 78-rpm four-record set of "the Musical Score from Metro-Goldwyn-Mayer's Motion Picture Triumph" in autumn 1939. The collection featured Judy Garland in studio recordings of "Over the Rainbow" and "The Jitterbug," while Victor Young and His Orchestra and the Ken Darby Singers offered other selections from the picture. (top right) In conjunction with the 1949 Oz reissue, Decca rereleased their original recordings in a newly designed package, available in both the 78-rpm format and as a ten-inch, long-play recording. (middle left) This two-record MGM package also appeared in 1949 and was available in both 78-rpm and 45-rpm. A studio orchestra and chorus presented seven songs from the film score (several with additional and/or alternate lyrics). (bottom left) The interior of the double-sleeve MGM jacket contained a particularly Ozzy illustration. (above) This 1949 78-rpm Capitol Records adaptation of Baum's fourth Oz book was not a direct tie-in but probably appeared to capitalize on the MGM rerelease. Both the title of the set and character illustrations on the cover seem aimed toward public identification and recognition.

(top) Two 78-rpm releases from Little Golden Records, 1950. (middle left) MGM's first Oz soundtrack album (1956) was also available in a boxed set of 45-rpm records. (bottom left) The elaborate, double-jacketed reissue of the soundtrack (circa 1963). (middle right) The Singer Sewing Company's discount edition of the soundtrack (1970). (bottom right) Meco's Oz disco album (1978) was brilliantly orchestrated by Harold Wheeler but ironically gave no credit anywhere to Arlen, Harburg, or Stothart.

Los Angeles Examiner (Louella O. Parsons, August 16): "*Oz* completely fascinated the sophisticated audience of first-nighters. Enthusiasm over the amazing achievement of MGM was heard on all sides. When a picture is as good as this, it means that another milestone in motion pictures has been achieved, and that is glory in which every studio may well share. MGM will realize a handsome profit. This is little Judy Garland's great triumph and the best thing she ever has done. I thought at first she would be far too robust and energetic for Dorothy, but Judy grows on you and before the end of the picture, you find yourself enthusiastic over her conception of the Baum heroine. You'll love Lahr, who is such a sissy that he has a permanent wave. Bolger is excellent, Haley is splendid, [and] the inimitable Frank Morgan gives his own original interpretation to the Wizard."

Los Angeles Illustrated Daily News (Harry Mines, August 16): "First and foremost a technician's triumph, *Oz* offers a constant series of surprises in fascinating sights...a lush and lovable production, told with laughter, song and pathos [and] acted with zest. Lahr has a field day...it is the hit performance of a hit picture. The best picture of the year...the perfect piece of entertainment."

Associated Press report (August 16): "*Oz* was unveiled to the public Tuesday night, bringing 'ohs' and 'ahs' from the colony's upper crust and an almost unheard-of outburst of raves from usually blasé critics. The best picture that Metro has turned out in many a day."

Los Angeles Evening News (Virginia Wright, August 16): "Baum's rich imagination could not have guessed what a fabulous budget and Hollywood showmanship would do with his fantasy. The imaginative splendor of the dream sequence on the screen actually is visually entrancing. The whole production is careful and affectionate but, unless you are one of the 'young in heart' to whom the film is dedicated, you may find *Oz* a little on the tedious side. The character most perfectly in tune with its theme is the Cowardly Lion. Lahr is uproariously timid, in a wonderfully effective makeup. Garland is sweet and sensitive, with an exceptionally good voice, and it is to her special credit that at the last she manages to touch the heart even in her unbelievable predicament. Hamilton is a triumph of villainy, enough to frighten young and old alike, and she does. The songs are ingeniously fitting, but the writers could have done better with the dialogue which, too often, is just commonplace. In the main, however, *Oz* is a glittering creation, and if the world is peopled by 'the young in heart,' a fabulous budget may prove a good investment. It is jampacked with entertainment for the whole family [and] should be required showgoing for every member of the industry. A good picture, handled so neatly as to make reviewing a pleasure."

Ed Sullivan syndicated column (August 19): "No picture ever has caused such a wholesale tossing of hats into the air...one of the most artistic achievements of the Hollywood decade."

Los Angeles Examiner (Sara Hamilton, August 20): "There is no better cure for a troubled heart or a troubled world than a journey back to a cherished childhood memory. And MGM's *Oz* is just that, a memory glorified on the screen. Not since *Snow White* has there been such a glad welcoming for any picture by men, women, and children."

Hollywood Spectator (September 2): "One of the greatest technical feats the screen has to its credit: a picture which would make LeRoy famous if it had been his sole contribution to the screen. Visually a cinematic masterpiece...but much more than a visual treat. It is really a human document, one with a lesson in it, one of the few to which grandfather can take grandchild and both of them find entertaining. To me, the outstanding feature of the production is the astonishingly clever performance of Judy Garland ...holding [the picture] together, being always its motivating feature, and so natural is she, so perfectly cast, one scarcely becomes conscious of her contribution to the whole. I have read all the other local reviews of the picture and have not found in one of them the praise which in my opinion is due this accomplished child.... Her performance strengthens my conviction that in a few years she will be recognized as one of the screen's foremost emotional actresses...Like *Snow White, [Oz]* is a piece of screen entertainment which can be shown every year from now on. The most imaginative exhibitor cannot promise to his patrons more than the picture will deliver."

After the Capitol premiere in New York on August 17:

New York Times (Frank Nugent, August 18): "A delightful piece of wonder-working which had the youngsters' eyes shining and brought a quietly amused gleam to the wiser ones of the oldsters. It is all so well-intentioned, so genial and so gay that any reviewer who would look down his nose at the fun-making should be spanked and sent off, supperless, to bed.... Judy Garland's Dorothy is a pert and fresh-faced miss with the wonder-lit eyes of a believer in fairy tales, but the Baum fantasy is at its best when the Scarecrow, the Woodman, and the Lion are on the move." (Nugent labeled Lahr "comicalest of all," noted the ingenious rhymes in the actor's material, and concluded, "Mr. Lahr's lion is fion." He listed scenes and effects he personally found most impressive and decided, "they are entertaining conceits...presented with a naive relish for their absurdity and out of an obvious— and thoroughly natural—desire on the part of their fabricators to show what they could do. It is clear enough that Mr. Dawn, the makeup wizard, Mr. Fleming, the director wizard, Arnold Gillespie, the special effects wizard, and Mervyn LeRoy, the producing wizard, were pleased as Punches with the tricks they played. They have every reason to be." In a follow-up piece on August 20, Nugent wonderingly defended the picture against the two or three unenthusiastic "chip on the shoulder critics" of New York.)

New York Daily News (Kate Cameron, August 18): Four-star [highest] rating—"Oh, to be at the Capitol now that *Oz* is here...a delightful fantasy. The satire of the fable is not as cleverly pointed as it was in *Snow White,* but the broad comedy touches of [Lahr, Bolger, Haley, and Morgan] makes up for those side-tickling subtle touches. Garland is perfectly cast as Dorothy. She is as clever a little actress as she is a singer, and her special style of vocalizing is ideally adapted to the music of the picture."

New York Post (Archer Winsten, August 18): "*Oz* is a brilliantly Technicolored, beautiful and humorous fantasy, the appeal of which is not limited to the juvenile trade. The picture brings Oz to life beyond one's happiest expectations...The performers, with heavy assist credited to miraculous makeup, are beyond cavil. Lahr's Lion is the top, a triumph of type-casting. The songs deserve mention for their tuneful and lilting quality. They are a distinctly superior bunch, doubly delightful because they add to the enjoyment of the picture with their appropriate sentiments. [LeRoy and Fleming] have something to be proud of and you have a picture to put on your things-to-do-today list."

New York Mirror (August 18): "Three million dollars worth of charm, stupendous in every detail...It is possible to go quite daft over the Lion. Were it the season for acting prizes, Mr. Lahr would get them all. [*Oz*] is unlike all movies, and it has a very potent enchantment for the very young. Borrow a child and see it. If the adults accompanying the small fry found it dragged a little, they are very naughty adults indeed and should be spanked and sent to bed without their caviar."

New York Journal American (August 18): "A spectacular show...an outstanding achievement. It's Mr. Lahr who romps off with the acting honors, and a good deal of the credit for the proceedings goes to Jack Dawn. Outstanding, too, is the musical score."

New York Herald Tribune (Howard Barnes, August 18): "Fantasy has never been treated more prodigally on the screen...a vastly entertaining and delightful offering. It is dangerous to try to approximate the grotesque figures and images of fantasy in concrete terms, but MGM has met the challenge with flying colors. Pictorially, *Oz* will not disappoint even the most imaginative reader of the book...Many of the scenes are the sort to stick in one's memory for a long time. At the same time, I feel that this stunning reproduction of a dreamed-up world is a bit too real to completely sustain the illusion of fantasy. While youngsters are likely to be utterly captivated by the mise-en-scene, older fairy tale enthusiasts are apt to find the film's mood of enchantment being rudely shattered by a too tricky rendering of trick effects. When the Wicked Witch goes scooting around on her broomstick or conjures up endless fields of poppies to put Dorothy to sleep, the imagery is exquisite, but when she starts doing skywriting.... the spell snaps rather badly. The saving grace...is that the production itself is always handsome and intriguing and that the principal characters are impersonated with feeling, humor, and charm. When Dorothy is on the Kansas farm or is meeting fantastic friends in Oz, the narrative is sustained and charming, and her final leave-taking of her three companions is genuinely moving. Where the fantasy falters, to my mind, is when the color backgrounds and colorful figures are involved in antics that have no place in Oz. I would have been much happier, for example, without [the Munchkins] doing song-and-dance numbers for [Dorothy]. I would have been content with a bit less conventional clowning on the part of the first-rate comedians in the company. An attempt to get contemporary overtones into a forty-year-old classic strikes me as being definitely ill-advised...Where *Oz* can't hold a candle to *Snow White* is in building up and conserving a mood of enchantment so powerful that one is transported briefly into a world of faery, [but] it has done very well indeed in blending sorcery and caricatures into a fantastic spectacle...It may make Oz more of a Hollywood than a Baum conception, but it has the capacity to hold your interest throughout. Thank the performers for much of this...Thanks to its pictorial splendor and engaging portrayals, *Oz* is first-rate entertainment, but I would not call it a great piece of screen fantasy." (Two days later, Barnes wrote a follow-up piece, in which he commented: "That perennially enchanting fairy tale...has been made into a resplendent motion picture...It is an entertaining photoplay and at times it is curiously moving, but it has a tendency to be definitely mundane when it might have been engagingly chimerical. Although it deals with the stuff that dreams are made of, it rarely has the power to bemuse us. [But] whatever the film may lack in sheer fantasy, it never fails to be an arresting spectacle.... The [cyclone] sequences are superb; there are magnificent background shots of Oz itself. The makeup jobs are nothing short of triumphant. [Victor Fleming] has kept the action fast-paced and

intriguing except when musical numbers are interpolated...the weakest elements in the film. They are neither catchy in a conventional sense nor are they any help in building up the fairy-world illusion of the production.")

New York Citizen: "An eye- and ear-filling thing of unmitigated delight. MGM, with wonted precision and its lavish striving after perfection, has produced a magnificent film, second to none in its class, including *Snow White.* The twister is one of the most fearsome things to reach the screen yet...and the ensuing scenes ...are marvels of the split screen and other Hollywood hocus pocus. [Haley is] excellent. His wistful quest after a heart is really well projected in a difficult setting. Bolger's rubbery legs suit the Straw Man to the last wisp...There is really nothing that can be criticized about the whole thing. It is Grade A, No. 1, off-the-top-shelf cinema fantasy."

New York World Telegram (William Boehnel, August 18), "[*Oz* is a] handsomely mounted, frequently delightful, and charming fantasy which cries out for the light, deft, humorous touch of a Disney...it always keeps one foot in Hollywood. Most of the players are excellent..."

New York Sun (Eileen Creelman, August 18): The picture is one about which almost anyone might have two minds...it does have a certain charm [and] the scenes all look startlingly like the book's illustrations brought to life. [But] the picture lacks that spontaneity which is the spirit of all great fantasy. It is surprisingly short on comedy...the makeup men are the real stars of the film. The songs are rather dull. *Oz* has a pleasant quality, the sense of rereading a childhood favorite. But its elaborateness smothers much of its charm."

The Daily Worker (Howard Rushmore, August 18): "One of the most expensive (and also the most beautiful) examples of film fantasy ever to grace the American screen.... The social angle of the picture is comparatively nil. But as pure entertainment (at the same time regretting that MGM neglected this opportunity to satirize dictators), we heartily recommend *Oz*...an outstanding film."

The New Yorker (Russel Maloney, August 19): "I sat cringing before MGM's... *Oz,* which displays no trace of imagination, good taste, or ingenuity. I will rest my case...on one line of dialogue. It occurs in a scene in which...the Wicked Witch snarls, 'You keep out of this!' Well, there it is. Either you believe witches talk like that, or you don't. I don't. Since *Oz* is full of stuff as bad as that, or worse, I say it's a stinkeroo. The vulgarity...all through the film is difficult to analyze. Part of it was the raw, eye-straining Technicolor, applied with a complete lack of restraint. And the gags!... Bert Lahr is funny but out of place. If Bert Lahr belongs in the Land of Oz, so does Mae West...I don't like the Singer Midgets under any circumstances, but I found them especially bothersome in Technicolor." (In his own follow-up comments on the film in the August 30 *New York Post,* Archer Winsten took Maloney to task and riposted: "[*Oz*] could give anyone a new lease on life, barring the substitute tyrant of movie criticism at *The New Yorker*...whose magnificent spleen is a joy forever. His insistence on archaic dialogue for witches indicates one possible source of dissatisfaction with *Oz.* But if you can be broadminded, which after all is a very nice distinction, you will be rewarded. It is just as easy to admire Margaret Hamilton for her colloquial witchery and to feel that she has added a persuasive, modern note to the sorority of the broomstick. As for the Lion who sings and quavers like our own Bert Lahr, that's pure gravy...In the case of Judy Garland, I found her infinitely more appealing than Snow White herself in respect to face, movement, and voice. Although a few crusty realists might not be able to stand so much and such colorful fantasy, *Oz* is one of the pictures everyone must try...The Capitol continues to be the best bet in town.")

Damon Runyon/King Features syndicated column (August 23): "One of the greatest motion pictures we have ever viewed ...[Compared to *Snow White*], *Oz* is far and away the more human of the two in every touch. There are several great performances...but we're inclined to think that the one who walks off with most of the honors is Lahr. [*Oz* is] a triumph for us cash customers seeking entertainment."

Commonweal (Philip T. Hartung, August 25): "Youngsters, oldsters, all the young in heart will go into raptures...LeRoy has added modern touches...but not too many to spoil the sentiment. Splendorous Technicolor, fantastic settings, makeups, staging, swell tunes and lyrics add a new vividness to the Baum story. The brightest spots are the meetings between Dorothy and her new friends. The cleverest are Bolger, whose gay dancing and song are delightful, and Lahr, whose impersonations of timidity and toughness are a masterpiece of travesty. Billie Burke's saccharine Good Witch hardly compensates for Margaret Hamilton's evil Bad Witch. A six-year-old sitting next to me loved the whole proceedings; he bit off all his nails, but was gleeful most of the time. I nearly roared when he asked his father if Grover Whalen built Emerald City."*

As the film opened across the country:

Pittsburgh Press (Kaspar Monahan, August 17): " 'We're off to see the Wizard—' The words suggest that you bestir yourself and go to see him yourself. Thousands of young and old converged on Loew's Penn yesterday for that delightful purpose...Through trial and error and month on month of toil and sweat, *Oz* finally emerged, and the results are a near-miracle for the movie industry.... definitely a picture to see."

Boston Transcript (John Gibbons, August 18): "There is warming fantasy in its conception, lovely color in its execution, and there should be an Academy Award, even if a special award has to be created, for its Bert Lahr...Mr. Lahr carries the illusion that Baum has in mind in the story to its most beguiling end."

Boxoffice (August 19); "A completely charming and wholly delightful film in a direction rarely attempted. Production boundaries have given way to new approaches in sets, costuming and conception which make *Oz* a beautiful thing to behold in gorgeous Technicolor."

Christian Science Monitor (August 19): "Two splendid hours of melody and magic. The technical trickery is perhaps even more impressive than the story itself. Witches and hobgoblins have been reproduced with realism which may be too terrifying for the very youngest."

Cue (Jesse Zunser, August 19): "Amusing, chuckleful, and quite

delightful...MGM, not content with leaving well enough alone, has seasoned and occasionally soured this lovely dish with two million dollars' worth (it all shows) of Technicolored, candy-sticked, Hollywood splendiferousness. I think we can agree that in *Oz* MGM [has] a solid hit—and you, a pleasant evening's entertainment."

Minneapolis Tribune (Merle Potter, August 20): "The cosmos is all lighted up, as cheerful as a rainbow:...*Oz* [is] one of the major blessings of this cinematic year, a privilege to be offered you next Thursday when this happy musical will glorify the State Theatre. It must deserve a five A rating or nothing at all. Of course, if sheer fantasy is likely to trouble you, no doubt you will not be able to share in the delight the great majority of us are going to find ...We'll just be sorry for you and pray for your spiritual rejuvenation."

St. Paul Pioneer Press (Hubbard Keavy/Associated Press, August 20; Keavy gives his column over to an eight-year-old's review of the picture): "I guess the best part of it was the Cowardly Lion... I liked everything about it except the tornado and the Witch. I didn't want to look at the picture...I didn't hear what she said because I shut my eyes and put my fingers in my ears. I was glad everything ended all right. I dried my eyes and a man at the studio said, 'Tim, how did you like it?' And I told him...that it was just like the book, only better, but that I didn't like the tornado part and the Witch part."

Newsweek (August 21): "[Baum's] whimsy has been broadened by antics after the musical-comedy manner and the interpolation of patter songs in Stothart's excellent score. Magnificent sets and costumes, vivid Technicolor, and every resource of trick photography bolster the competent cast that strikes a happy medium between humor and make-believe. The more fanatic Ozophiles may dispute MGM's remodeling of the story, but the average movie-goer—adult or adolescent—will find it novel and richly satisfying to the eye."

Time (August 21): "*Oz* should settle an old controversy: whether fantasy can be presented on the screen with human actors as with cartoons. It can. As long as *Oz* sticks to whimsy and magic, it floats in the same rare atmosphere of enchantment that distinguished *Snow White*. When it descends to earth, it collapses like a scarecrow in a cloudburst. No children's tale is MGM's *Oz*. Lavish in sets, adult in humor, it is a Broadway spectacle translated into make-believe. Most of its entertainment comes from the polished work (aided by Jack Dawn's expert make-up) of seasoned troupers Lahr, Bolger, and Haley. MGM...left out only the kitchen stove. [The] tornado rivals Sam Goldwyn's *The Hurricane*. Its final scene is as sentimental as *Little Women*. Its Singer Midgets...go through their paces with the bored sophisticated air of slightly evil children."

Chicago Daily News (Clark Rodenbach, August 25): "Never did we hope some day to have these delightful characters come to life in colors as bright and gay as those in our [Oz] book, and speak to us. Yet that's what they do in MGM's elegant production...How the effects were produced, don't ask us. Just sit and look back in wide-mouthed astonishment and admiration...If there's a stand-out figure in this delightful fantasy, let's give the call to Lahr..."

Minneapolis Morning Tribune (John Alden, August 25): "I am an expert on all matters pertaining to the wonderland of Oz...As an expert, then, I attended the State Theatre yesterday expecting to

---

*Grover Whalen was an extremely dapper New York City police commissioner in the 1920s. In the 1930s, he returned to the presidency of the John Wanamaker department store and served for a time as New York's "official greeter." He heartily promoted both the City and himself in pursuit of personal publicity.

be aggrieved over the film treatment. I beg to report I was anything but aggrieved. Sure, this wasn't strictly the Oz I knew. It was a new and wonderful oziological adventure of its own. Judy and Dorothy were identical. I took it for granted that Bolger was stuffed with straw and that Haley was made of tin. I expected to see Lahr's face on the Lion. I had heard that, for the purpose of making credible this film excursion, Dorothy dreams the whole thing. That saddened me. I had been brought up to believe that these things actually happened. I didn't want to be disillusioned...That was before I went to the State. Now I don't care if it was all a dream. I'm for it. It was a splendid adventure for me. I'm more of an Oz expert than before. I've found an Oz where L. Frank Baum satire has given way to MGM buffoonery. And I'm happy to report the discovery."

Film Bulletin (August 26): "*Oz* should find a ready-made audience practically everywhere. It is engrossing and amusing. Class houses will get the best returns. Parents will bring their children. It will fail to attract the young adults and action fans."

Chicago Daily Tribune (Mae Tinée [*sic*], August 26): "It is gorgeous, fantastic, radiant with Technicolor. It teems with midgets. It is alive with trick photography, is jeweled with hummable tunes, and features a Kansas tornado that makes you want to live anywhere but in Kansas...Judy Garland was a perfect choice for Dorothy. She portrays, without a false move, an honest-to-goodness little girl, genuinely flabbergasted, curious, terrified, game, lonely, ecstatic, as the case may call for—and you're just going to love her. The picture *is* too long...there's padding in the last reels that could easily have been dispensed with. But as I remember *Oz,* this does the old favorite pretty proud."

Chicago Sunday Tribune (Burns Mantle, August 27; Mantle had seen the 1902 *Oz* stage musical several times in its initial Chicago engagement and reminisced at length about its history and the more recent *Oz* film premiere and Garland/Rooney stage show in New York. He then opined): "...it seems to me it would have been a good business move to have given Fred Stone a chance at his old part of the Scarecrow. He can still negotiate the dances, his experience these last twenty years has made him a good actor and a resourceful comedian, and he still has a considerable following among older playgoers. But I suppose [producers] thought the picture should be kept in the tempo of the present. Bolger and Haley seemed to me to be a bit overwhelmed by their roles, but they get through creditably. I suspect that you are going to agree with me that Lahr is the best of the trio. Little Miss Garland [is] properly wide-eyed and appealing. Not many, I have a notion, will like *Oz* as well as they did *Snow White.* There is great pictorial beauty in the Technicolor shots...but there is little comedy to substitute for the antics of the Seven Dwarfs. There is a good deal of camera wizardry. You are fascinated and amused to see Billie Burke step out of an iridescent bubble. Of course, you expected Sally Rand, but Billie is better for the children. It is nice to discover, too, that ...Frank Morgan comes through as the same old whimsical clown."

Minneapolis Star Journal (August 27): "A grand transposition of the famous Oz story, with a wealth of color, fantasy, and humor. The cyclone sequence is one of the high spots of all-time motion picture magic. Good tunes and lavish production distinguish the Oz sequences. The appeal should be as much to adults as to children. Garland is a happy choice, and color enhances her beauty. Picture-stealer is Lahr."

Dallas Morning Star (John Rosenfield, August 27): "Disney's best cartoon technique could never duplicate the rubber-legged movement of Ray Bolger...Haley also is as effective as an artist might have drawn. While Disney might have sketched the Lion, he couldn't possibly get Lahr on his pencil point. Lahr's impersonation is among the acting triumphs and one of the singing high spots of the year. [The] songs are sprightly and, we demur, not as good in tunes or lyrics as they might be. The well-fed Miss Garland is surprisingly effective as Dorothy, bringing a wide-eyed naivety to the role and nothing of a dreaded simper, coo, and yodel. She plays seriously, earnestly, and without disturbing mannerisms. Billie Burke is as dainty and lovely as anybody has ever remembered her. For the young in heart and their tots, *Oz* is a continual delight. For the incorrigibly sophisticated, it is still a beautiful splash of color and a prodigy of advanced makeup and costuming. It is worth the full one hundred minutes of their condescending interest."

Minneapolis Star-Journal (Mary Diane Seibel, nine-year-old "daughter of a theater press agent," August 28): "I sure am glad I got to see *Oz. Snow White* was my favorite till now. *Oz* is wonderful... [it] just took my breath away. I think I liked the Lion best of all. I didn't like the Wicked Witch with the ugly green face, and it's a good thing she melted. Everybody but Dorothy and Toto thought it was a dream. I don't know what to think."

Kansas City Star (Jack Moffat): "Three generations will see their gayest dreams come true in *Oz*...Don't miss this movie. You may want to see it every day this week."

San Francisco News (Claude LaBelle): "I am one of those nuts that still reread occasionally children's stories and still like 'em, and so I toss bouquets at MGM for *Oz,* because it is the first one that ever came to one hundred per cent specification for me. Five gets you ten it will run close to *Snow White* in receipts."

Fort Worth Press (Jack Gordon): "Any fairy tale that can pull thousands from the war scareheads to pack theaters must have something. *Oz* has beautiful coloring, Hollywood's best technical wizardry, a rollicking musical score, and delightful performances."

Screen and Radio Weekly (Clark Wales): "A great adventure...a charming, exciting, and beautiful picture."

A number of national organizations also included *Oz* reviews in their August newsletters or publications: "A most refreshing entertainment...a super-delightful fantasy with superlative treatment throughout" (*California Federation of Music Clubs*). "The producer and director, with every artist and artisan...merit a medal for their distinguished service. Highest form of entertainment for all ages, worthy to be seen many times" (*General Federation of Women's Clubs*). "An artistic masterpiece...the cast is unbeatable. Perhaps, as Dorothy learned, 'there's no place like home'; but if you are going to the movies, there is no picture like *Oz*" (*National Council of Jewish Women*). "Tops in entertainment for all ages...a cinema triumph which will delight all audiences" (*National Society of New England Women*). "Fascinating and beautiful as a lovely jewel...everyone will enjoy this visit to make-believe land and regret their compulsory return to an everyday world" (*Southern California Council of Federal Church Women*).

Young America (September 15): "This is a film we recommend highly to you. Not only because it follows the story closely and captures the mood of delight that has made *Oz* such a favorite, but also because of the technical tricks."

Scholastic (September 18): "The magic never weaves its spell over the characters except Dorothy... Lahr's particular brand of comedy may be hilariously funny on a vaudeville program, over the radio, or in a straight comedy, but it completely spoils the illusion here. Garland is really the only one who could begin to make us believe in this Land of Oz. It's too bad, because the production is colorful and entertaining, and there are several catchy tunes..."

The New Republic (Otis Ferguson, September 20): "*Oz* has dwarfs, music, Technicolor, freak characters, and Judy Garland. It can't be expected to have a sense of humor as well—and as for the light touch of fantasy, it weighs like a pound of fruitcake soaking wet. It will be delightful for children mostly to their mothers, and any kid tall enough to reach up to a ticket window will be found at the Tarzan film down the street. The story... has some lovely and wild ideas... but the picture doesn't know what to do with them. [Garland's] thumping, overgrown gambols are characteristic of [the story's] treatment here. When she is merry, the house shakes, and everybody gets wet when she is forlorn."

Liberty (Beverly Hills, September 23): Four-star ("extraordinary") rating—"Pinning elusive fantasy down to literal camera shots is one of the ultra-precarious jobs. Disaster is just around the first close-up. That this expensive, streamlined version of Baum's fantasy is entertaining, sometimes quite lovely, and frequently amusing is, in itself, a triumph. There are innumerable amazing camera tricks and... lavish hues, perhaps in too garish color. Music enlivens every foot of the film, and there are some mildly tinkling tunes. You will find Judy Garland a pleasant and wholesome Dorothy. Of the rest, I liked best Bert Lahr [whose] Lion is a richly amusing character, right after Androcles' own heart."

McCalls (Pare Lorentz, September): "It was fairly courageous on the part of MGM to try to put Baum's story on film. But 'put' is hardly the word. 'Hurled' is more accurate. *Oz* has the most awe-inspiring sets ever put on the screen and the most colorful and successful Technicolor work I have seen to date. But the picture seems tiresome for the most part, simply because you do not believe you are in a Never-Never Land. Garland is simple and fresh enough. [But] *Oz* should have been kept simple. Instead, we have Lahr in a burlesque song, which—if he were singing at the Winter Garden with Beatrice Lillie—would have been funny. In a fairy kingdom, it's not only unfunny but slightly embarrassing to find him a sophisticated songster. Almost a third of *Oz* is given over to the evil witch chasing the little girl from Kansas all around the castle—a business that is produced as though the girl were a gangster and the witch and her cohorts a band of G-men. It is a film you should see as an example of the extraordinary mechanical possibilities of the motion picture [but it is] powered by the production office."

Sociology and Social Research (Journal of the University of Southern California, November 1939): "Imaginative, fantastic, and whimsical... but behind the colorful effects is social satire [the way people allow themselves to be humbugged] and personality analysis."

Screenland (Delight Evans, November 1939): [*Oz* has] dazzling scenes in color... songs with just the proper lilt and tinkle you have every right to expect and, for once, get; a hair-raising cyclone... to blow you back into childhood. Producer LeRoy is Public Benefactor No. 1."

Script (Richard Sheridan Ames): "MGM... [has] elevated the artistic standards of musical extravaganza to a point unequaled in screen history. My capitulation was so complete that I neglected to bring out the critical yardstick and admired the Baum fantasy as extravagantly as a child. The film has been so felicitously contrived, the actors are so uniformly appealing, atmosphere and illusion so persuasive that the story and its characters ought to amaze and delight all of those Young in Heart to whom the production has been dedicated. Ballyhoo is the business of the publicity department, but I don't envy it the task of equaling in words the visual splendors of *Oz*. Go to it, boys, but I doubt whether you can extol this remarkable attraction too extravagantly. Not when it's a cinemasterpiece."

CHAPTER 13

The Twelfth Annual Academy Awards

The competition was especially strong for motion-picture awards and recognition when the "best" lists for 1939 were assembled. Film releases during the twelve months of the year included *Gone With the Wind*, *Mr. Smith Goes to Washington*, *Goodbye, Mr. Chips*, *Wuthering Heights*, *Ninotchka*, *The Women*, *Gunga Din*, *Beau Geste*, *Stagecoach*, *Young Mr. Lincoln*, *Babes in Arms*, *Juarez*, *Love Affair*, *The Private Lives of Elizabeth and Essex*, *Of Mice and Men*, *The Hunchback of Notre Dame*, *Intermezzo*, *Dark Victory*, *Destry Rides Again*, *Golden Boy*, *Drums Along the Mohawk*—and *The Wizard of Oz*.

The industry's most coveted accolade was, then as now, the "Oscar" award, presented by the Academy of Motion Picture Arts and Sciences. Their nominees in twenty categories were announced in January 1940. *Oz* was cited in five areas:

Best Picture (in competition with *Dark Victory*, *Gone With the Wind*, *Goodbye, Mr. Chips*, *Love Affair*, *Mr. Smith Goes to Washington*, *Ninotchka*, *Of Mice and Men*, *Stagecoach*, *Wuthering Heights*)

Art Direction—Cedric Gibbons, William A. Horning (in competition with *Beau Geste*, *Captain Fury*, *First Love*, *Gone With the Wind*, *Love Affair*, *Man of Conquest*, *Mr. Smith Goes to Washington*, *The Private Lives of Elizabeth and Essex*, *The Rains Came*, *Stagecoach*, *Wuthering Heights*)

Song—"Over the Rainbow" by Harold Arlen, E. Y. Harburg (in competition with "Faithful Forever" from *Gulliver's Travels*, "I Poured My Heart into a Song" from *Second Fiddle*, and "Wishing [Will Make It So]" from *Love Affair*)

Original Score—Herbert Stothart (in competi-

tion with *Dark Victory*, *Eternally Yours*, *Golden Boy*, *Gone With the Wind*, *Gulliver's Travels*, *The Man in the Iron Mask*, *Man of Conquest*, *Nurse Edith Cavell*, *Of Mice and Men*, *The Rains Came*, *Wuthering Heights*)

Special Effects—A. Arnold Gillespie, Douglas Shearer (in competition with *Gone With the Wind*, *Only Angels Have Wings*, *The Private Lives of Elizabeth and Essex*, *The Rains Came*, *Topper Takes a Trip*, *Union Pacific*)

(Victor Fleming probably would have received a nomination as Best Director for *Oz* but was competing instead as director of *Gone With the Wind*.)

The Academy Awards were presented on Thursday evening, February 29, at the Ambassador Hotel. Bob Hope, in what was the first of many stints as Oscar master-of-ceremonies, played host to twelve hundred representatives of the film industry. It would be the final year in which the Academy released the names of the award-winners to the press prior to the proceedings. Although newspaper editors were pledged to hold the results until their late-night editions, the *Los Angeles Times* broke the news midevening on February 29. As a result, celebrants on their way to the awards ceremony were able to read all about the outcome. (Beginning with the 1941 presentations, the Academy instituted a "sealed envelope" policy and no one but Price Waterhouse knew the results of the balloting until the announcements were made on stage.)

Gone With the Wind won in the majority of its nominated categories, achieving a record eight awards by evening's end, plus two honorary plaques and a special citation for producer David O. Selznick. As expected, it captured the Best Picture and Art Direction prizes over *The Wizard of Oz*. In what was a new category for the Academy, the Special Effects citation honored *The Rains Came* rather than *Oz*.

But *Oz* got its accolades when announcer Gene Buck was called to present the music awards. Herbert Stothart was saluted in the Original Score division for his overall supervision of the underscoring and adaptation of the Arlen/Harburg songs. According to the *Hollywood Reporter* on March 1, Buck "was especially enthusiastic" when announcing the Best Song presentation and delighted to be able to give the Oscar to Arlen and Harburg for "Over the Rainbow." Arlen accepted for both of them as the lyricist was in New York.

The two music awards won by *Oz* were supplemented by one other that evening. The Academy had established a tradition in 1935 of presenting a miniature statuette (when warranted) for exceptional work by a juvenile performer. Only three had been given in the past (to Shirley Temple, Deanna Durbin, and Mickey Rooney), but the Academy added to that list in selecting Judy Garland for the honor in recognition of her "outstanding performance" as a screen juvenile in 1939.

It was Garland's first participation of any kind in an Academy Awards ceremony. She wore a floor-length blue gown, topped with a short fur jacket and orchids, and sat at one of the MGM tables with her mother, Mr. and Mrs. Spencer Tracy, Greer Garson, Norma Shearer, George Raft, Mr. and Mrs. Victor Saville, and studio executives Eddie Mannix, Ben Thau, Arthur Loew, and Hunt Stromberg (the latter two also with their wives).

A magazine reporter who later described the entire evening for his readers felt that there were three highlights at the 1940 Oscar ceremony. These included:

- the special presentation by Academy President Walter Wanger to Douglas Fairbanks, Jr., in honor of his father, film pioneer Douglas Fairbanks, Sr. (who had died the preceding December);

- the Best Supporting Actress award to Hattie McDaniel for her performance as Mammy in *Gone With the Wind*—the first black person ever to win an Oscar; and

- "Mickey Rooney handing Judy Garland her statuette for the best performance of a juvenile during the past year."

The writer continued, "It was charming to watch Mickey, with his new-found dignity upon him, presenting Judy with her Oscar, and then forgetting himself and kissing her with kid enthusiasm . . . and Judy was never more persuasive than when she crooned 'Over the Rainbow' . . . into the mikes, with a suspi-

Harold Arlen (right) poses with Gene Buck as they recreate the Best Song presentation for photographers. (© copyright Academy of Motion Picture Arts and Sciences)

A glowing Garland poses with Rooney after receiving her award. Though later nominated as Best Actress for A Star Is Born *(1954) and Best Supporting Actress for* Judgment at Nuremberg *(1961), Judy Garland's only Oscar came for* The Wizard of Oz. *She later affectionately—if wryly—dubbed the miniature statuette "the Munchkin award."*

cious little quaver in her voice."

The Garland/Rooney exchange was termed "a bright touch of sentiment" by the *Hollywood Reporter* and, after her ovation for her rendition of "Rainbow," she and Rooney were once again surrounded by the press. He was asked to kiss Judy again and again for the photographers, and *Daily Variety* chortled that Rooney "looked very happy . . . but had a hard time removing the lipstick after-effects."

Mervyn LeRoy had, by February 1940, given up producing pictures and returned to directing, his first love. Despite all the acclaim for *The Wizard of Oz* over the preceding seven months, he won no Academy Award that night. But, as one columnist pointed out, LeRoy "did get a souvenir that he'll treasure. After Judy Garland received the special award for her performance . . . she scribbled a note on a napkin and sent it to Mervyn.

" 'I owe you everything, Mr. LeRoy,' she wrote."

PART FOUR
Oz and Ends

CHAPTER 14

Original Ozzy Merchandising

In touting *The Wizard of Oz* (figuratively, anyway) as "*Snow White* with living actors," MGM obviously hoped its characters would immediately endear themselves to the public as had Disney's animated cartoons. There had been many earlier movie tie-in products—celebrating Mickey Mouse, Shirley Temple, et al.—but the release of *Snow White* ushered in an unprecedented flood of merchandise derived from a single film. It's safe to assume Metro aspired to a similar mass reaction from manufacturers primed for an *Oz* bandwagon.

Yet a September 1940 listing of *Oz* licensees shows that relatively few companies paid Loew's, Inc., for the rights to produce *Oz* material, and fewer still actually marketed *Oz* items. Indeed, some of the companies who announced their products during the late summer of 1939 failed to follow through as scheduled. The well-known Louis Marx Co., for example, was to have produced tin wind-up figures. Regrettably, this never came to pass.

Viable corporate cooperation between Loew's and the various manufacturers might have been somewhat deterred by the fact that MGM's parent company was totally inexperienced in the field of commercial licensing; *Oz* was their first foray into such activity. It is also likely that many potential licensees decided there was more financial security in merchandise tied to a cartoon feature rather than a live action film. So they set their sights not on *Oz* but on the immediate future: Max Fleischer's animated *Gulliver's Travels* and Disney's *Pinocchio*. Consequently, some of the *Oz* items were cheaply made and poorly marketed in limited production. These factors contribute to their present-day rarity, but examples survive of much of the 1939–40 MGM *Oz* merchandise, and these are presented here (and in color on pages 151–158 and 175–181).

A toy rubber figure identified as "Jack Haley—Wizard of Oz" was issued by the A. A. Burnstein Sales Organization in 1939. "The Tinwoodman" (sic) was the first of the small figures to be manufactured, according to Playthings *magazine. Figures of (at least) Dorothy, the Scarecrow, and the Cowardly Lion were also marketed. (courtesy Hake's Americana & Collectibles, York, Pennsylvania)*

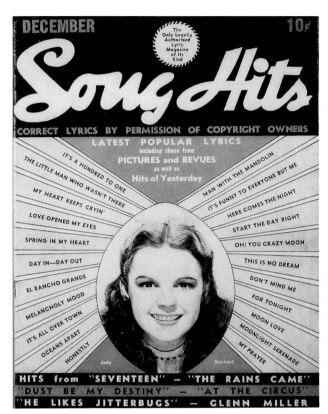

Once it was decided to delete "The Jitterbug" from the release print of The Wizard of Oz, *production of this song-sheet was halted. (Its title was also eliminated from the list of songs on the folio cover.)*

Due to the immediate success of the Oz *score, especially "Over the Rainbow," the voice of Judy Garland became even more popular in the months following the release of the film. Her picture was thus not a surprising choice for the cover of* Song Hits *in December 1939.*

THE WIZARD OF OZ DART GAME

↓

ORDER A SAMPLE DOZEN TODAY

NOW ready—just in time to cash in on the biggest publicity tie-up of the year. Made by America's largest Dart Board Manufacturers, the WIZARD OF OZ Dart Game is an ace value to retail for $1.00. For immediate profits, *promote it now!*

Safe for both children and adults. (Played with rubber cupped darts.)

DART BOARD EQUIPMENT CO.

306-08 CHERRY STREET   PHILADELPHIA, PENNA.

New York Office: Room 321 200 Fifth Avenue

"The Wizard of Oz Dart Game" was displayed in Playthings *(August 1939), a trade journal for the toy industry. It is possible that this unusual tie-in was never commercially marketed.*

(below right and right)
In their 1939
Christmas catalogue,
Sears advertised a
Dorothy-style "Judy
Garland dress" and the
Ideal character doll
modeled after the star.

(below) Two four-inch painted-wood composition figures of the
Scarecrow and Tin Woodman (circa 1939). Marked only
"Artisans Studio/Nashua N.H.", they were probably
unauthorized as they did not bear the customary Loew's
copyright. (courtesy Hake's Americana & Collectibles, York,
Pennsylvania)

CHAPTER 15

Oz Abroad

The Wizard of Oz was first shown outside the United States in Canada, where it was released on September 14, 1939. It became the first film to topple the eight-year-old Quebec provincial law barring minors under the age of sixteen from admission to a theater unless accompanied by an adult. The Honorable Gilbert Layton, minister without portfolio in the Quebec government, lobbied for "general accessibility" to *Oz*, and Canadian Premier Duplessis granted the film special dispensation—something even *Snow White* had not achieved. As a result, hundreds of children crammed the Montreal theater for the *Oz* engagement, and *Variety* commented that such business was "in a class by itself . . . [*Oz*] will top everything."

In November, *Oz* opened south of the border. MGM and the General Electric Company put together two thirty-minute shortwave radio shows (one in Portuguese and one in Spanish) to promote the Latin versions of the film in Rio de Janeiro and Buenos Aires. The programs went out on November 16, the day prior to both premieres. Special editions of *The Wizard of Oz* book were also issued in Portuguese and Spanish, among the first of many foreign-language versions of the story published in connection with (or because of) the film. In February 1940, the Mexican motion picture magazine *Illustrado* awarded a "special degree of merit" to *Oz* as the best picture released in Latin America in 1939.

The film hit one snag when it reached Great Britain in December. The London Board of Film Censors, concerned that some scenes would frighten juveniles, decreed *Oz* could be seen by children only when they were accompanied to the theater by an adult. In spite of that, the picture was an immediate favorite, providing not only relief but inspiration for the populace in the midst of the war blitzkrieg. Reviewers found the film a "spectacular fantasy . . . magnificently produced . . . a feast of beauty for eye and ear. It has tuneful songs, graceful dances, and the rich pageantry of its settings lingers in the memory . . . The acting is admirable . . . one and all outstandingly good . . . The ap-

peal will be quite definitely more to adults than to children. For the latter, its outlook is too sophisticated and its humour too mature . . . " The London *Daily Mirror* printed several columns of praise, calling *Oz* "a brilliant colour film of irresistible charm with a delicious sense of humour . . . The young-in-heart . . . will indeed love it. It will take a very crabbed heart to resist it." Writing in *The Spectator*, formidable critic Graham Greene was not completely taken by the somewhat "crude" American morality or Baum's "dry goods" characters and plot devices. But he found "the

With the British release of Oz *following that in America by several months, this ad in their* Picturegoer *film magazine hails 1940 as the year for which the film will be remembered.*

(above) This two-page spread ran in sepia-tone in the November 12 Sunday Manila Tribune *magazine in the Philippine Islands. Similar layouts, which told the story of the film in sequential photos and captions, were incorporated as part of the publicity material in the 1939 campaign book and thus included in several newspaper rotogravure sections. (right) Although made up of several of the same illustrative elements, the overall appearance of the British Oz sheet music was quite different from its American counterpart.*

songs . . . charming, the Technicolor no more dreadful than the illustrations to most children's books, and the sepia prologue on the Kansas plain . . . very fine indeed. Miss Judy Garland, with her delectable long-legged stride, would have won one's heart for a whole winter season 20 years ago, and Miss Margaret Hamilton . . . can compete successfully with a Disney drawing." Greene also bemoaned the "adults only" status of the picture ("in many places, parents will be forbidden by the by-laws to take their own children"); he was joined in his complaint by the reviewer for *The New Statesman and Nation* who, in the case of *Oz*, described the ruling as "wanton cruelty." Among the only dissenters were *Picturegoer* columnists Ralph and Jane Denton. They found the picture unsuitable for children, uninteresting for adults, and thought Glinda was "alarmingly played"(!) by Billie Burke.

De Grote Tovenaar van Oz *was issued by L. J. Veen of Amsterdam in 1940. Drawings by Van Looij followed the MGM characterizations. (For other foreign MGM-style Oz books, see pages 177–179).*

In spite of the Dentons, *Oz* triumphed in Great Britain—to the extent that "Over the Rainbow" became a wartime anthem of hope and fortitude. The picture was equally popular when it reached Australia, and some of their fighting forces carried the film songs with them to African war camps. A contemporary newspaper clipping stated, "Their favorite . . . was 'We're Off to See the Wizard.' You could hear them singing this song even after the Italian artillery opened up against them." A parody to the same tune, "We're Off to See Herr Hitler," was later one of the songs sung by some Allied troops during the D-Day invasion.

The film continued to promote publication of foreign *Wizard of Oz* books. A raft of British editions proliferated in 1940, as did translations in Dutch, Hungarian, Danish, Swedish, Rumanian, and German (the latter issued in Switzerland). Some of these were strict translations or adaptations of the Baum original; a few were actual retellings of the film plot. The illustrations varied from Denslow reproductions to film stills, frame blowups, or drawings of the film characters. After World War II, an edition of *The Wizard* influenced by the MGM movie appeared in Italy; in subsequent years, the story was translated into Hebrew, Turkish, Persian, Japanese, Chinese, Serbo-Croatian, Czechoslovakian, Russian, and other languages. Many of these versions were a direct result of the appearance or popularity of the film.

Great Britain enjoyed a full rerelease of the picture

The front and back covers of an Austrian pressbook (circa 1946) offered unusual concepts for advertising and promotional artwork.

An illustration by Harry Hartz from the Danish Troldmanden fra Oz, *published by Tempo in Copenhagen in 1940.*

One of the most beautiful of all Oz posters was the French one-sheet, circa 1940.

The British lobby cards for the initial release of Oz were quite different from those used in America the year before. They still, however, consisted of eight black-and-white scenes from the film, hand-colored for display purposes. (The card at top was probably derived from a picture taken during rehearsal, as Judy Garland wears fur-lined booties rather than the famous ruby slippers.)

(above) This Spanish Oz poster (circa 1940) was designed in connection with the first showings of the film south-of-the-border. (courtesy Rob Roy MacVeigh) (left) The British quad movie poster (circa 1980) served the dual purpose of promoting both The Wizard of Oz and Tom Thumb. The illustration of Oz characters at the bottom is very similar to artwork in the original American advertising and merchandising (i.e., the Sunday full-page comic-section layouts and the cover of the 1939 Whitman board game).

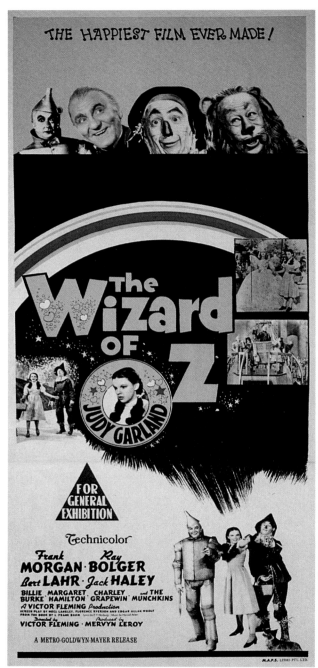

(above) An Australian day-bill poster hailing "the happiest film ever made!" This undated piece is most likely from the late 1970s, although the artwork resembles that in promotion for earlier American reissues. (above right) O Magico de Oz: a Portuguese one-sheet for a Brazilian engagement. Like most of the American reissue material, the poster placed much emphasis on Judy Garland. (right) A Spanish reissue poster for El Mago de Oz, circa 1983. Unlike most American promotional material through the years (which called little attention to Margaret Hamilton), this display shows a fairly large portrait of the Wicked Witch, dressed colorfully (if inaccurately) in purple and red.

"A Metro-Goldwyn-Mayer Masterpiece Reprint": The 1949 American reissue was accompanied by a new publicity campaign, and Judy Garland's billing increased commensurate with the international stardom she'd achieved in the intervening decade. (bottom left) The title card from the 1949 lobby set. (bottom right) This scene card was, like the rest of the set, a "colorization" of an original black-and-white still and shows (with unabashed inaccuracy) the famous Red Brick Road.

On facing page: (left) The 1949 insert poster. (top right) The 1949 one-sheet poster featured a large portrait of Garland from Meet Me in St. Louis. (bottom right) The top third of this 1949 window card is missing; it was a blank area in which the theater owner could print his name and playdates.

On this page: (top) "Let's Go 'Over the Rainbow' with Judy in her Greatest Hit!" This was the slogan for the second American reissue in 1955. Garland's portraits were those of the adult Judy rather than Dorothy. (bottom) Two lobby cards for the reissue. The scene card is a hand-colored conception of a sequence that only appears in black-and-white in the film.

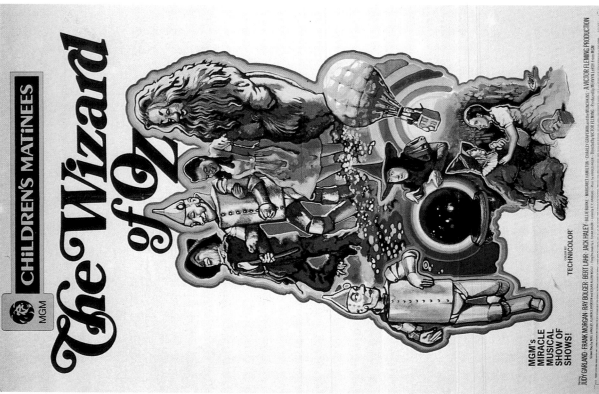

These one-sheet posters promoted the "children's matinee" reissues of Oz in 1970 and 1972.

Mundo Cinematográfico

Año X. Núm. CVII.

Síntesis estimativa profesional del cinema en México

Se publica dos veces por mes

JUDY GARLAND • FRANK MORGAN
EL MAGO de OZ
UN CUENTO DE MARAVILLA
NARRADO EN TECNICOLOR
ALTO ORGULLO DE M·G·M

aparece el hombre de paja

El Mago de Oz

Maravilloso sueño
que JUDY GARLAND y
FRANK MORGAN y
M·G·M
nos cuentan en
TECNICOLOR

ESTRELLAS
POR RUBI GUTIERREZ MARVIN

JUDY GARLAND
protagonista de
EL MAGO DE OZ

No podemos menos de recordar a Judy Garland como la encantadora personificación de los cuentos de la Cenicienta tierra de Oz, aquel país encantado que sólo existe en la geografía de los sueños infantiles.

Vimos como Judy supo caracterizar tan acabadamente a Dorothy, la chiquilla a quien suceden las más extraordinarias aventuras en la pintoresca ciudad, corazón de la imaginación de Frank Baum.

Los personajes que en su compañía aparecen, son: el hombre de hojalata, el espantapájaros y el león cobarde. Allí los vemos en el más perfecto ambiente de cuento infantiles, o más bien diríamos, como los hemos soñado y sun visto en nuestros primeros años. Judy Garland con su bella interpretación se ha puesta de un salto entre las estrellas de Hollywood.

Les merveilles du pays d'Oz

Rêve fantaisiste d'un charme irrésistible

"THE WIZARD OF OZ"

Production en technicolor, coûtant $2.500.000.

Film de Mervyn LeRoy

Jack Haley, le bûcheron en fer-blanc, n'a pas plaisir de peur de rouiller ses articulations.

CHINA

作藝文的奇傳怪神

綠野仙蹤

A four-page German film flyer (circa 1961) promoted Der Hexer von Oz.

in December 1945 as *Oz* continued its international circuit. In some countries, the film was issued with subtitles in the language native to the locale. In others, the dialogue was redubbed although, in those cases, the songs were usually heard in English, as sung by the original cast. The film remained in periodic reissue throughout the 1950s and 1960s. Another Great Britain appearance came in 1964, complete with press showing, and the critic of *The Scotsman* found the screening "very valuable . . . I had forgotten that [*Oz*] was such a glorious entertainment for the young." The reviewer in the *Brighton Gazette* offered similar enthusiasm: "I had forgotten what a delightful film it woz! How well this classic wears!"

Oz found its way around the world again via home video in the 1980s. It was dubbed into such languages as German, French, Italian, Spanish, and Portuguese; with an English soundtrack and appropriate subtitles, it appeared in such locales as Japan, Israel, South Africa, Mexico, Germany, and France. Reviews of the tape were published as far away as Saudi Arabia when Haroon Sugich wrote in the *Arab News*:

Even with the hi-tech wonders developed by [George] Lucas and company, there has yet to be a film that can match the glorious adaptation of Baum's homely allegory . . . The greatness of any classic children's entertainment really lies in the maturity of its intellectual content. *The Grim's* [*sic*] *Fairy Tales, The 1001 Nights, Alice in Wonderland* and *Aesop's Fables* have all made indelible impressions upon the imaginations of generations of children not because of their childishness, but because of their underlying profundity. *Star Wars* had so much appeal because Lucas imbued it with a kind of mythic philosophical symbolism. But the cinema of the 1930s and 40s was a less profound, if more wholesome, medium than it is today. The Disney classics and *Oz* did not really contain literary messages of a universal nature. Their messages were simple messages of home and happiness. What they did contain was a visual sophistication that remained unequalled for two generations. And therein lies their enormous pleasures. *Oz*, like the early Disney cartoons, is a visual feast of movement and color. It is also a celebration of . . . songs [that have become] so imbedded into American consciousness that it is almost impossible to appreciate their virtues with any sense of perspective . . . This film has given me so much pleasure over the years. All that need be said is that [it] is now available in the market for your pleasure and the delight of your children.

CHAPTER 16

Theatrical Reissue

Perhaps asserting its original claim that *The Wizard of Oz* would endure for ten years, MGM first reissued the film late in April 1949. They "tested" it over Easter at New York's Mayfair Theatre where *Oz* enjoyed a rousing five-week engagement and achieved a box-office gross of more than one hundred thirty thousand dollars. Given that success, Metro went on to launch an official rerelease in June.

The studio gave the film the benefit of a new press and exploitation campaign, if not the coast-to-coast saturation booking of a decade earlier. Understandably, there was little of the national press or notoriety that attended the *Oz* debut, but several magazines happily reviewed the picture all over again. *Rotarian* dubbed it "delightful entertainment," and *Time* improved on its positive 1939 comments by stating, "*Oz* . . . proves that true wizardry, whether in books or on the screen, is ageless." In the *New York Times*, critic Bosley Crowther editorialized on the "happy experience [of] escape" offered in the film's revival and labeled it "one of the nicest attractions to be seen . . . a pristine excursion into realms of enrapturing gold."

The initial national audience for *Oz*, beginning in mid-June, was astonishing, and *Variety* once again told the story in its weekly film section. In Chicago, the picture did the "best biz in months" at its theater,

This mammoth display graced a theater lobby in conjunction with the 1949 reissue of The Wizard of Oz. *The large portrait of Judy Garland was derived from a publicity still taken during her 1945 work in* The Harvey Girls.

bringing in thirty thousand dollars in two weeks. *Oz* was "really outstanding" in Cincinnati, and went on to be "nifty" in Philadelphia, "fast" in Detroit, and "hardy" in Cleveland.

By early July, *Variety* observed that *Oz* had "shaped up nicely" in its first dates. Even MGM was surprised. They were celebrating their twenty-fifth anniversary season in 1949 and had filled the trades with ads extolling their new output. By mid-July, *Oz* was sandwiched into that promotional list of "summer hits," the only vintage picture on the roster. *Variety* cited *Oz* on July 20 as doing "real business"; a week later, they termed the reissue "outstanding."

The film went on to rack up nearly thirty-five thousand dollars in its three weeks in Cleveland. A July sojourn in Los Angeles came to almost sixty thousand, and a one-week gross of twenty-seven thousand in Washington, D.C., was termed "better than the first time." *Oz* was "socko" in San Francisco, "very strong" in Minneapolis, "tall" in Louisville, "big" in Buffalo, and "terrific" in Portland. By the end of August, *Variety* reiterated its earlier estimation: *Oz* was an "outstanding" reissue, and they predicted its success would spur the rerelease of other classic motion pictures.

The film went on to play the neighborhood theater circuit during autumn 1949 and, when the box-office totals were posted, *Oz* had added more than $1,500,000 to its total gross. The production was, after ten years, not only a much-loved and revered "prestige picture," it was also in the black and turning a profit for MGM.

Six years later, television had made great inroads in the entertainment business. Weekly attendance at movie theaters was at its lowest ebb in more than three decades, the audience diminished by the pull of free, at-home diversion. The public had also become somewhat more discriminating over the years, and a film had to offer something special (or at least be publicized as offering something special) to make the impact of earlier successes.

However, in winter and spring 1955, Judy Garland was once again much in the consciousness of the movie-going public, by virtue of her much-heralded 1954 screen return in *A Star Is Born* and subsequent Academy Award nomination as Best Actress. Feeling that *Oz* might well benefit from her personal publicity, and the fact that a new generation of youngsters had not seen the picture, MGM decided to reissue it once again.

(top) Newspaper ad for the first theatrical reissue. (left and above) Just as it had done in 1939 and 1949, MGM provided theater owners with a pressbook/publicity guide for the 1955 theatrical reissue of Oz. Although not nearly as lavish as the earlier layouts, the 1955 edition also included newspaper advertisements and copy, and samples of posters and insert cards (as shown on the front and back covers pictured here).

On June 22, *Variety* noted that Metro was "giving the picture the new film treatment, bolstering the release with publicity and advertising efforts equal to a first-time-around property. Pic is clicking in test engagements . . . [and] kicked off with a nation-wide publicity break via the airing of several scenes on the NBC-TV spectacular Sunday titled 'Remember?— 1938.'"

MGM took a full-page ad in *Variety* a week later to offer promotional ideas to exhibitors and trumpet the film's early returns. *Oz* did "almost three times average rerelease business" in Salt Lake City, "twice the average" in Columbus, and topped "many new attractions" in Indianapolis. The film had officially reopened June 17 in New York and gave the Normandie Theatre its second biggest opening week in history. *Oz* was, according to *Variety*, "going great guns . . . [and] looms terrific"; its extended six-week engagement did close to fifty thousand dollars' worth of business. *Daily Variety* stated the film was "magical at the box office, with the night trade [for probably the first time] topping the matinees."

Such success continued through the summer in Philadelphia, Cleveland, St. Louis, Baltimore, Portland, San Francisco, Washington, Seattle, and in extended engagements in Chicago and Detroit. *Variety* praised the reissue as "another box office winner . . . continues to rack up nice biz" and commented that, "on the basis of the early returns, M-G is hopeful of topping" the income achieved by the 1949 release.

This was, however, not to be the case. In spite of "neat-to-sturdy" business, *Oz* was relegated to second-run houses in some cities and often saddled with a variety of inferior pictures in double-bill programs. This almost always resulted in less business than the film was doing elsewhere on its own. The lack of special showcasing and promotion led to some grosses that were only "mild" or "fair" or "okay." As a result, the revenue generated in 1955 didn't approach that from 1949, although *Oz* added another four hundred sixty-five thousand dollars to its grand box-office total.

The Wizard of Oz would begin its legendary television career in 1956, but there were two other "official" theatrical reissues as well. In both 1970 and 1972, the film was used to successfully launch an MGM Children's Matinee series of family pictures; these bookings were specifically geared to weekend afternoon audiences. In addition—and in spite of the increasing familiarity of the film due to its nearly annual television appearances—*Oz* became a 1970s' staple for college film societies and, ultimately, for revival houses across the country. The latter showings marked the first extended theatrical engagements for *The Wizard of Oz* in over twenty years, and notable among the bookings was its first "test reappearance" in Los Angeles. The Vagabond Theatre drew capacity houses with *Oz* in 1976, and entrepreneur Tom Cooper turned away hundreds of potential customers. Audiences jammed the auditorium and often their anticipatory cheers lasted the entire length of the film's opening credits.

(left) "Judy and Joy!" exclaimed this two-color flyer, designed as part of the second rerelease publicity campaign. The 1955 pressbook included a sample of the flyer, which theater owners could then purchase by the thousands and imprint on the back with their Oz *playdates, cofeature, and address.*

(on facing page) Bert Lahr and Liza Minnelli were seen "live" in an introduction to the November 1956 television debut of The Wizard of Oz, *and no publicity pictures were taken. The preceding Saturday, however, CBS arranged a special screening of the film in their nineteenth-floor Madison Avenue viewing room. That afternoon provided an opportunity to photograph Liza and her almost four-year-old half-sister Lorna Luft as they watched their mother in* Oz. *(CBS photograph by Emile Romano)*

PART FIVE
Television Perennial

CHAPTER 17

Guest Hosts on CBS

By 1956, MGM was ready to consider new suggestions for the future of *The Wizard of Oz*. Its second theatrical reissue the year before hadn't done the business they'd hoped but, at the same time, they recognized the picture was still an important property.

The studio was then in the process of leasing to individual television stations its library of 770 films made prior to 1949. Several major MGM features were held back from these "packages"; *Gone With the Wind* and *The Wizard of Oz* were among them.

Acknowledging the appeal of the "holdout" films, CBS approached MGM about a possible nationwide telecast of *Gone With the Wind*. The studio's response was an immediate no, so the network countered with an offer for *The Wizard of Oz*. The announcement of the deal was made on July 25, 1956, and contracts were signed on August 2. *Oz* would have the distinction of being the first motion picture MGM sold to network television, and CBS agreed to pay what was regarded as a premium price: two hundred twenty-five thousand dollars for each of two broadcasts. (The contract also included "safety" options for several additional showings, but it's doubtful that anyone thought they would be necessary or implemented.)

CBS scheduled the first performance of *Oz* as the finale of its "Ford Star Jubilee," an uneven monthly

★ Tonight 8:00 to 10:00 P.M. ch. ②③⑥⑦⑲

FORD STAR JUBILEE

Presents in color and black and white— a television first

The Wizard of Oz

Starring
JUDY GARLAND

Two full hours of classic entertainment
for all the family-the original performance in
which Judy first enchanted millions!

Also starring

Ray Bolger   Bert Lahr   Jack Haley
Frank Morgan   Billie Burke

Presented by FORD and its DEALERS

8:00 ②③⑥⑦⑲ FORD STAR JUBILEE — Movie

Judy Garland in

"*The Wizard of Oz*"

[COLOR] In 1900 L. Frank Baum wrote his fantasy for children "The Wonderful Wizard of Oz," and it proved so popular that he wrote a whole series of Oz books. In 1939 the Judy Garland movie was made, and it is seen in its entirety in a two-hour presentation tonight.

This is the story of Dorothy, the Kansas farm girl, who is whirled away by a cyclone and finds herself in the magic land of Oz. There she and her dog Toto try to make their way to the castle of the great Wizard, who has the power to grant all kinds of wishes. In their search they have the company of the Scarecrow, who'd like to have the Wizard give him a brain; the Tin Woodman, who wants a heart; and the Cowardly Lion, who needs some courage. The group is menaced by the Wicked Witch.

Harold Arlen and E. Y. Harburg wrote the songs, which include "Over the Rainbow," "We're Off to See the Wizard," "Ding Dong, the Witch Is Dead," "If I Only Had a Brain," "Munchkinland," "The Merry Old Land of Oz" and "Follow the Yellow Brick Road."

Cast

Dorothy . . . . .Judy Garland
Scarecrow .Ray Bolger
Tin Woodman . . . . .Jack Haley
Cowardly Lion . . . . .Bert Lahr
Wizard .Frank Morgan
Glinda, the Good Witch. . . . . .Billie Burke
Wicked Witch . . . . .Margaret Hamilton
Uncle Hem . . . . .Charley Grapewin
Aunt Lem .Clara Blandish

(above) The premiere of The Wizard of Oz *on network television drew a special "close-up" from* TV Guide. *The magazine also added two "new" characters to the cast: "Uncle Hem" and "Aunt Lem," the latter played by Clara Blandish, not Blandick. (left) An ad for the debut.*

WIZARD OF OZ
(Ford Star Jubilee)
With Judy Garland, Ray Bolger, Jack Haley, Bert Lahr, Frank Morgan, Billie Burke, Margaret Hamilton, Charlie Grapewin, Clara Blandish, others
Producer: Mervyn LeRoy (MGM)
Director: Victor Fleming
Writers: Noel Langley, Florence Ryerson, Edgar Allan Woolf (from L. Frank Baum novel)
Score: Harold Arlen, E. Y. Harburg
120 Mins., Sat. (3), 9 p.m.
FORD MOTORS
CBS-TV (film)
(J. Walter Thompson)

If Saturday's (3) "Ford Star Jubilee" was the last in the monthly spec series—and from all indications Ford and CBS-TV are through with "Jubilee"—then they couldn't have picked a grander swansong than "Over the Rainbow" or "If I Only Had a Brain" or "We're Off to See the Wizard" or a half-dozen other great songs in the Harold Arlen-E. Y. Harburg score to Metro's classic "Wizard of Oz."

In fact, they couldn't have picked a grander show than "Oz," which defies both time and the diminution to homescreen size. Every-thing in this 1939 production stands up, from the songs to the story to the individual routines by such show biz stalwarts as Judy Garland, Ray Bolger, Jack Haley and Bert Lahr. The pic is great in any medium, and though of course the color was a key factor in its greatness, even the black & white signal held up beautifully on tv.

CBS-TV paid $225,000 for the privilege of the one-time showing—it's also committed to a second showing next year at the same price, with additional options for years to come. Just how much Ford paid CBS for the privilege of using it on "Jubilee" isn't known, but bookkeeping aside, it's not too important. Even if Ford paid nothing, CBS could chalk that 225G off to goodwill and still come out the winner. It was tops in entertainment, and the network should make provisions for making an annual out of it, preferably at an earlier time period and closer to the holiday season in the future.

Ford was also kind to it in the matter of cuts, keeping the commercial breaks down to a minimum and thus leaving the maximum enjoyment in the pic. As to color, there's no question that one missed a lot viewing it in black-and-white, but the b&w compatible signal was excellent. The reduction to homescreen size was only mildly bothersome in such big scenes as the Munchkinland number and "The Merry Old Land of Oz," but otherwise the pic played as if it had been shot for video, with lots of medium and closeup shots were they counted, in the individual scenes with Lahr, Haley & Bolger. As for Judy, one can't long for the old days after seeing her at the Palace, but she sure was great then too.

There's only one possibility that CBS will have cause for regret. That's the fact that while for all practical "Jubilee" is dead and buried, it can be resuscitated at the drop of a Ford exec's hat. It's been an on-and-off-again hassle between Ford and CBS on the series, and while both parties have finally agreed to call it quits, the door is still open. CBS at this point would rather forget about the entire thing. So what if the "Oz" showings make Ford change its mind again?
Chan.

Variety (November 7, 1956) reviewed the telecast almost as if it were a brand-new program.

series of "television spectaculars." The first "Jubilee," on September 24, 1955, had offered the TV debut of Judy Garland in a modified reprise of her 1951 Palace Theatre act. Though traumatized by the idea of live television and burdened with laryngitis for the show, Judy attracted the largest audience ever to watch a "special" program. Subsequent episodes of "Jubilee" were not always as successful, and the series was beset by segments best described by *Variety* as "missouts." (A remarkable dual concert by Mary Martin and Noël Coward, for example, won plaudits from the critics but comparatively few viewers according to the ratings services.)

So Ford decided to discontinue the series after 1956. The running time of their final "Jubilee," however, was extended from its usual ninety minutes to one hundred twenty minutes to accommodate the full-length *Wizard of Oz*, and an air date near the Christmas holiday was envisioned. Both network and sponsor then decided to move the telecast up to Saturday evening, November 3, in order to benefit from the favorable national publicity Judy Garland received for her second Palace Theatre engagement, which had opened on Broadway on September 26.

Oz, of course, was barely 101 minutes long and, in those early days of television, it was considered excessive to incorporate twenty minutes of commercials in a two-hour program. So CBS approached Bert Lahr to fill in a few of those moments by hosting the show, and he was joined in his live introductory comments by Garland's ten-year-old daughter, Liza Minnelli. (Appearing with them was thirteen-year old Justin G. Schiller, who had garnered publicity in the New York area the preceding spring when his interest in Oz and L. Frank Baum led to participation in the Columbia Library Baum centennial exhibition. The same Justin Schiller would, two months later, found the International Wizard of Oz Club.)

Lahr and Minnelli were introduced on the air after an announcer heralded *Oz* as "a motion picture classic . . . a masterpiece of literature which has fascinated children and adults for years [and] ranks with the great works of all times." The actor then exchanged some scripted patter with the girl, reminiscing about the making of the picture and the fact that he had only seen it once before, "at the premiere, seventeen years ago." He also advised her to be aware that "when your Mommy . . . is in Kansas, all the scenes are in black and white. But when she opens her eyes in the wonderful Land of Oz, everything is in beautiful color, just like a fairyland should be."

"Mommy," meanwhile, was backstage at the Palace, viewing the proceedings on her dressing-room TV set. She wasn't alone; the first telecast of *Oz* won an (right) To coincide with the first *Oz* telecast in November 1956, *Screen Stories* reprinted a novelization of the film screenplay in its January 1957 issue. (The text was originally published in August 1939 in the magazine's forerunner, *Screen Romances; see cover illustration on page 94.)* (below) *Red Skelton and his twelve-year-old daughter Valentina hosted the second* Oz *telecast in 1959. (CBS photograph)*

JUDY GARLAND in

THE WIZARD OF OZ

BY POPULAR REQUEST!

Once upon a dream a little girl blew off to a land somewhere over the rainbow...

... on the road she met a Scarecrow without a brain ...

a Tin Man without a heart. They begged her to go along...

astounding rating. Nearly thirteen million sets tuned into the film, which meant an estimated audience of more than forty-five million people. Dorothy and Company were seen by 53 percent of those watching television between nine and eleven o'clock (EST) that evening and, as the *Hollywood Reporter* pointed out on November 6, "had the picture gotten an earlier showing to catch children who were bedded at the late hour, the audience probably would have jumped another 5,000,000 to 8,000,000."

CBS held *Oz* for three seasons before scheduling a second telecast, this time both closer to the holidays and at an earlier hour. On October 16, 1959, CBS comedian Red Skelton and his twelve-year old daughter, Valentina, prerecorded their host comments for the show, which aired on Sunday, December 13 from 6–8 P.M. (EST). *TV Guide,* in commenting on the introductory statements, publicly verbalized the reasons for a "guest" segment: "CBS wanted a major star as host for two reasons. Since the movie runs only one hour and 40 minutes, there was time to be filled— entertainingly. Without a major personality to introduce the movie, it might seem somewhat like a routine airing of an 'early show.' " By using Skelton, CBS also established the precedent of spotlighting one of its own series' stars as the movie host; the comic first appeared (à la Baum) as a Victorian storyteller and then later as himself.

The earlier hour of the 1959 telecast did indeed attract millions more viewers than the *Oz* premiere three years earlier, and critic John Crosby rhapsodized in the *New York Herald Tribune,* "*The Wizard of Oz* is pure magic . . . it gains luster with each passing year. What a lot of marvelous touches! . . . The trouble is, there aren't many movies quite in that class, or quite that ageless. It's a lucky thing for television that there aren't. Television—any television—looks awfully prosaic, awfully ordinary after *The Wizard of Oz.*" (December 16, 1959)

With an audience attraction like that, the network happily scheduled a third airing the following year and thus began the pattern of annual *Oz* appearances. For its next four telecasts (1960–1964), CBS would pay

MGM two hundred thousand dollars per showing.

In 1960, the *Oz* cohosts were Richard Boone and his seven-year-old son, Peter. Boone was on location in Apache Junction, Arizona, playing the role of "Paladin" for CBS in "Have Gun, Will Travel"; father and son did their *Oz* "wraparound" on November 13 for a December 11 telecast. The next two years, Dick Van Dyke and three of his children were utilized for the show, prerecording their segments on November 12, 1961 (for a December 10 airing) and November 11, 1962 (for a December 9 airing). The second presentation by the Van Dykes marked the final time *Oz* appeared as a pre-Christmas holiday treat; instead of a December 1963 telecast, CBS opted instead to wait until January 26, 1964. Danny Kaye was one of the network's big new variety stars that season (Judy Garland was the other), and he taped his introduction on January 13. Kaye also served as host for the next three CBS broadcasts (through 1967), and the network simply replayed the same tape to preface and conclude the showing of the film. In 1965, CBS paid Metro one hundred fifty thousand dollars for *Oz*; in 1966 and 1967, the fee was one hundred sixty-two thousand five hundred dollars.

The ratings for all nine CBS telecasts were phenomenal; the picture inevitably placed in the top four programs for its week and always won at least 49 percent of the viewing audience in its time period. The annual showing of *The Wizard* also gradually boosted its

(above) A news clipping photograph of Dick Van Dyke, who twice hosted Oz. Each time, he was assisted by three of his four children. (When they made their first appearance in 1961, Christian, Barry, and Stacey were eleven, ten, and six years old respectively.) The actor, a fine caricaturist, did a sketch of the Oz principal cast as "title art" for the 1962 introductory segments.

(top) The TV Guide "close up" for the 1960 Oz telecast. *(above)* An ad for the 1961 showing.

217

Many television magazines carried this photograph of Danny Kaye, taken as he taped his Oz *wraparound in 1964; his segments were reused for the next three seasons.*

status from fondly remembered movie to happily hallowed Family Television Event in millions of American homes during the 1960s. As early as 1961 and 1962, it caused a genuine (albeit local) contretemps when the Milwaukee, Wisconsin, CBS affiliate decided to carry football instead of the network *Oz* programming. So many and so vehement were the outraged public objections that the station—both years—had to get special permission to show *Oz* locally a couple of weeks later.

That same era saw increasing press comment on the appeal and quality of the film. *Look* for April 10, 1962, published a two-page picture story of a little girl's reactions to a first televiewing of her favorite tale. On January 15, 1965, *Time* kicked-off its "Show Business" page with a feature headlined, "The Oz Bowl Game." In addition to an appreciation of Margaret Hamilton's memorable Wicked Witch, the article also reflected on the standing *Oz* had achieved as a television perennial: "Parents are again preparing for the occasion. It will occur this coming Sunday for the seventh straight year, and the children, with a special restlessness, will collect around the television set in much the way that their fathers do for the professional football championships. The children know the names and styles of the players they are going to see, for the program has become a modern institution and a red-letter event in the calendar of childhood. It is the Oz Bowl Game . . . "

Eventually, comment on the film found its way from the entertainment sections of newspapers to editorial pages as well. The writings were always highly complimentary to the picture, although in 1967 the telecast sponsors were taken to task for their specially produced commercials which utilized actors costumed like the *Oz* principals to sell deodorant soap and household cleaner. "To say [this] violated the mood of the movie is being milder than Ivory soap," chastised the Orange Coast *Daily Pilot* of Costa Mesa, California. "The plain fact is that the sponsors deliberately used children's imaginative involvement in a story for the purpose of hard-core commercialism. And while that may not seem *too* unexpected, one might have supposed there would be a slight residual respect for the children's classic, if not for the children themselves." (February 25, 1967)

Perhaps the most compassionate testimonial of the time came from Dr. Max Rafferty in the *Los Angeles Times* on March 21, 1966. He paid lengthy tribute to L. Frank Baum as "the greatest writer of children's books" and continued

I was sharply reminded of . . . Mr. Baum recently when, for the umpteenth time, I watched his classic *Wizard of Oz,* this time on color television . . . what an evergreen, joyous combination of adventure and spectacle and fun it is, to be sure. Its colors are as fresh, its songs as lilting, its cast as winning as when it was made almost three decades ago. Hollywood has had much to answer for since those halcyon days but, when it put together the best of its talents and its techniques to make *Wizard*, it laid up compensating crowns in heaven for itself. If only it would use its genius today to keep us young at heart instead of pandering to the oldest, the shabbiest, the shoddiest parts of each of us!

One final thought. *Wizard*'s little star, Judy Garland, has grown older and graver, like all of us who watched her skipping down the yellow brick road with those three amiable companions so long ago. She may have long since wearied of that simple, sad little song about the rainbow, though she still sings it as graciously and beautifully as ever. It's not easy to be the center of a classic, to become in a very real sense immortal when one is still a child. It haunts you down the years. Everything you try to do is measured against that one supreme and magic moment when all the stars were right and nothing you could do was wrong. Moments like that come seldom, if ever, to us ordinary mortals. When they come to a child and then pass on, never to return, they may create such problems for that child grown to womanhood as few of us have ever had to face. And yet all of us are seen through a glass darkly, never as we really are. I think there may be harder fates than skipping down the winding road of time, arm in arm with Love and Wisdom and Kindness, forever young, forever welcomed by the laughing hearts and the bright eyes of childhood. Only one of all our millions, Judy, could bring our greatest fairy tale to everlasting life. There are far worse things than being Dorothy.

Perhaps the most humorous bit of *Oz* reportage during its first decade on TV appeared in the Toronto *Globe and Mail* for January 18, 1965:

> Judy Garland is fifteen times as popular as Ed Sullivan. And the Metropolitan Toronto Works Department has graphs to prove it.
>
> A television showing of Miss Garland's vintage film, *The Wizard of Oz*, ended last night at 8:30. All over Toronto, toilets flushed furiously, children's bath water was turned on, and kitchen taps began to flow as thousands of viewers rose from their seats after two spellbound hours.
>
> At one transfer station, the water level in the reserve tank dropped 30 feet at 8:30, but only two feet at 9 p.m. when the Ed Sullivan show ended on another channel. "It's the first time I've ever been caught," said one works department operator. Another reported a drop from 70 pounds pressure to 35 at his station. He described it as the largest pressure drop due to television he's seen after seven years on the job.
>
> "The only thing we can think of is the end of that children's program, *The Wizard of Oz*," said shift engineer Thomas Walker . . .

THE CROWD TRAVELING to Oz today on CBS includes Judy Garland, Jack Haley (left), Bert Lahr and Ray Bolger in the ninth TV run of "The Wizard of Oz."

A contemporary Oz *cartoon provided newspaper art for one of the 1960s CBS telecasts.*

CHAPTER 18

NBC Interlude/CBS Comeback

*T*he Wizard of Oz was a television institution by 1967 and, when the CBS/MGM contract expired after that year's telecast, Metro felt justified in more than tripling its asking price for the annual performance. (To open negotiations, the studio purportedly suggested a fee of one million dollars per showing.) CBS refused to consider such an increase, but NBC willingly leaped into the breach, outbidding ABC, who also attempted to acquire *The Wizard*. Although press sources stated that NBC agreed to pay eight hundred thousand dollars for each of five *Oz* screenings, the annual price was actually six hundred fifty thousand dollars for the first three years and five hundred thousand for each of the next five. (If all options were exercised, *Oz* would remain on the network through its 1975 telecast.)

The film justified NBC's investment and continued its triumphal television reign. Only once did *Oz* slip out of the top twenty programs of its week and, in

eight years on the network, it attracted a better-than-44-percent average of TV viewers during its time period.

The most notable of the NBC telecasts came after Judy Garland's death on June 22, 1969. The *Oz* broadcast of March 15, 1970, was sponsored by the Singer Company as a tribute to her, and the *Hollywood Reporter* estimated that—between the royalty fee to MGM and Singer's own special merchandising program, publicity, and ad campaign—the sponsor would spend two million dollars on the *Oz* show. To promote the telecast, Singer took full-page magazine and newspaper ads throughout the country, gave away Oz posters in its sewing-center outlet stores, and arranged for a series of publicity pictures and media interviews with the film's surviving principal players, Margaret Hamilton, Jack Haley, and Ray Bolger.[*] Singer also issued a discount edition of the film soundtrack record album with a new jacket and illustrated brochure.

Most important, the company arranged a tie-in with the Motion Picture and Television Relief Fund. They donated twenty-five thousand dollars for a Judy Garland Medical Library at the Motion Picture Country House and Hospital, a Los Angeles retirement and nursing facility for aged and ailing members of the industry. Singer then commissioned a Norman Rockwell portrait of Garland as Dorothy, which was used in promotion for the telecast and later given to the Country House. Alfred di Scipio, group vice-president of the Singer Company, flew to Hollywood from New York to present the painting and donation to George L. Bagnall, president of the Fund.

Finally, Singer provided a prerecorded speech by

Norman Rockwell's portrait of Judy Garland as Dorothy is displayed by Mervyn LeRoy and Alfred di Scipio of the Singer Company. (1970)

---

[*]Frank Morgan had died on September 18, 1949, Bert Lahr on December 4, 1967. Billie Burke was in failing health during the winter of 1969–70 and would die on May 14, 1970.

Somewhere over the rainbow there may be a more captivating movie —but don't bet on it.

THE WIZARD OF OZ

Just sit back and enjoy **Judy Garland** and co-stars Ray Bolger, Bert Lahr and Jack Haley as they transform the yellow-brick road into a super-highway of fun, color and song!

6:30PM NBC 4

(above, right, and on following page) Some of the more recent Oz television print ads.

Gregory Peck to open the 1970 *Oz* broadcast—the only time after 1967 that a host was present to introduce the movie. Mervyn LeRoy did his first television work by directing Peck in the spot, and the actor's quiet tribute stated:

Judy Garland left behind her a legacy of performances perhaps unequaled by any star of our time. Judy was only seventeen [*sic*] when she made *The Wizard of Oz*, one of those rare films which became an instant and unquestioned classic—which has for years appealed to family audiences at every age level—and which boosted Judy herself to a plateau of stardom unique in entertainment annals—and which, through theater engagements and telecasts may well have been enjoyed by more people than any other entertainment production in the history of the world.

That's something to think about.

Judy always displayed a deep and generous concern for the welfare of others, particularly those within the motion picture industry with whom she worked so closely for so many years. It is thus fitting that, through tonight's telecast, there has been established at the Motion Picture Country House and Hospital here in Hollywood, the Judy Garland Memorial Cottage.

The single regrettable aspect of the NBC *Oz* telecasts was the fact that, for the first time on television, a minute of the film was deleted to make room for more commercial time. The footage in question—a long tracking shot of Munchkinland after Dorothy's arrival in Oz—remained on the cutting-room floor throughout the film's career on the network.

WEDNESDAY ⊙ EVENING

Tonight, there's no place like home...

THE WIZARD of OZ

8PM ⊙2WCBS-TV

A CBS Special Movie Presentation

Nevertheless, the picture continued to be a television sensation. Thanks to the ratings achieved by *Oz* and other, newer films, the use of movies as major broadcast fare remained an important aspect of network programming during the 1960s and 1970s. Most pictures, however, were good for but two or three national showings, and there was generally a decrease in the price a studio could command for a second or third telecast. *Oz* was the exception to the rule. In 1975, it enjoyed its seventeenth network appearance, and when MGM drew up new contracts for its future use, they were once again able to demand a higher fee. CBS, primed to reclaim from NBC what they felt was their prize motion picture, met Metro's request and paid four million dollars for the rights to five telecasts (1976–80). A CBS source said, simply, "That picture is better than a gushing oil well," and he could have been speaking for either MGM or the success that seemed certain for the network in again leasing the film. The accuracy of his statement was further underscored when, in 1981, CBS renewed its contract for another five years. From 1981–85, MGM received one million dollars for each annual showing.

Unfortunately, once the film was back on CBS, the only way the network felt it was possible to absorb that kind of expenditure was to sell more commercial time—and cut more of the picture. By the early 1980s they had deleted: the film's dedicatory preface during the opening credits; the continuity shots of Dorothy and Toto running away from the Kansas farm; most of the initial scenes of the tornado sequence; the aforementioned minute of Munchkinland; the establishing shot of the poppy field; and several bits of the triumverate trip to the Witch's castle to rescue Dorothy. Such indiscriminate editing also tore up the background scoring in several places.*

Even in a truncated edition, however, viewers tuned in to *The Wizard of Oz* year after year. It became as well a semiregular television favorite in some foreign countries, and its debut in Great Britain on December 25, 1975, drew an overwhelming audience of twenty million. *Oz* did similarly well on Australian television.

The complete film was released on MGM video cassette in 1980, and the use of home recorders also meant that viewers could easily tape the picture while watching the annual telecast. But the movie continued to win outstanding ratings, placing in the Nielsen top ten for its week in 1983, 1984, and 1985. In 1988, *Oz* tallied its lowest rating when CBS misguidedly scheduled it on a weeknight instead of a weekend; the network was further forced to delay the film by forty minutes in order to cover a presidential news conference. But, with all that, *Oz* still managed to rank as seventh-highest-rated theatrical film of the season.

CBS did finally restore all of the film to the home screen beginning in 1985 by using a method of video time compression. This, in effect, removed fragments of seconds from portions of the film and made it less than one hundred minutes in length. The network then had the amount of commercial time it desired, and viewers were not deprived of any scenes from the picture.

In August 1987, CBS renewed its claim on *Oz* yet again in a deal whereby Ted Turner acquired the television rights to *Gone With the Wind.* Turner had purchased the MGM film library outright several years earlier for use on his own cable stations, but CBS controlled *Oz* and had also leased *Wind* from Metro for teleshowings in the 1970s and 1980s. The network willingly let Turner take over *Wind,* as long as he allowed them to extend their television license for *Oz.*

*Another local irritation plagued *Oz* in 1978 when its Chicago audience was deprived of the final minute of the film by a computer malfunction. *Oz* was inexplicably interrupted by forty-two seconds of commercials, and the station switchboard was swamped for hours by irate calls from viewers. Those who couldn't get through to the station lodged protests with Chicago newspapers.

OLD FRIENDS are coming your way tonight. (see Color Cover, Page 2)

Judy Garland
The Wizard of Oz's 8th CBS Visit
Sunday 7 PM
(See Cover Close-up, Page 9)

(above) The Milwaukee Journal "TV Screen" magazine paid tribute to the third Oz telecast on December 11, 1960, by assigning staff artist Einar V. Quist to sketch the cast and actor Richard Boone. The latter was cohost that year with his seven-year-old son, Peter. (above right) This drawing contrasts the mature Judy Garland with Dorothy of Oz and was originally done for the January 26, 1964, cover of the Los Angeles Herald Examiner TV magazine. "It's Judy Garland Night" read the explanatory caption, with reference to the sixth showing of Oz and the regular weekly installment of "The Judy Garland Show," both on CBS that evening. The artwork was picked up by the Hollywood Citizen-News two years later for the 1966 Oz telecast. (right) The first lengthy examination of the making of MGM's Oz appeared in the Autumn 1969 issue of The Baum Bugle, journal of the International Wizard of Oz Club, Inc. Ten years later, for the fortieth anniversary of the film, the Club again published a special tribute Bugle. The 1969 covers reproduced the 1939 title lobby card and an enlargement of Al Hirschfeld caricatures from the same year. The 1979 covers utilized frame enlargements; those on the rear were from the French Oz trailer.

One of two thousand limited-edition prints produced in 1977 by the Art Merchant. Not only did this striking collage offer portraits and scenes from MGM's Oz, but each print was personally signed by Ray Bolger and Jack Haley, individually numbered, and accompanied by a certificate of authenticity.

In 1977, The Wizard of Oz *became the first motion picture to be honored by a commemorative plate collection. This series, produced by the Edwin M. Knowles China Company, included eight limited-edition plates featuring the Oz characters as rendered by artist James Auckland. Highly successful, the plates continue to be actively sought by Oz enthusiasts and plate collectors alike. (Top row, from left: "Over the Rainbow," "If I Only Had a Brain" copyright 1977 MGM, "If I Only Had a Heart" copyright 1978 MGM; second row, from left: "If I Were King of the Forest" copyright 1978 MGM, "Wicked Witch of the West" copyright 1979 MGM; bottom row, from left: "Follow the Yellow Brick Road," "Wonderful Wizard of Oz," "The Grand Finale" copyright 1979 MGM; courtesy The Bradford Exchange.)*

(top left) This multihued Wizard of Oz trash can, marked "Cheinco, made in U. S. A.," was produced during the mid-1970s. (top right) Plastic Wizard of Oz Christmas ornaments were produced by the Bradford Novelty Company in 1977. There were several different sets, featuring both round and bell-shaped ornaments, all decorated with various scenes from the film. (middle) This unusual set of hand-painted ceramic banks was sculpted by Eurich Stauffer and distributed in the late 1960s by Arnart Imports, Inc. Licensed by MGM, each bank carried a tag listing the names of Garland, Bolger, Lahr, and Haley and their respective characters. (left) Sharon Marketing distributed this 1977 Ottenheimer Publishers, Inc., storybook. Its very brief (and sometimes highly original) retelling of the Oz plot was accompanied by bright drawings extremely faithful to the concept of the movie characters.

(top) Although they bore slight resemblance to their movie counterparts, the animated characters of ABC-TV's prime time "Off to See the Wizard" program were licensed by MGM. The show lasted just one season (1967–68), but dozens of tie-in dolls, toys, and games were marketed. (above) The Wizard of Oz acrylic paint-by-number set (Craft House, circa 1979). (right) This set of porcelain sculptures was made by Seymour Mann, Inc., in 1974. Although less than exact likenesses of the movie characters, each was accompanied by a tag showing the MGM copyright, as well as the name and a photograph of the representative actor.

In 1974, Mego introduced its successful Oz line. The eight-inch vinyl dolls were fine likenesses of the film actors in authentic costumes. Mego also produced an Emerald City playset (below) and followed it with a Witch's castle and Munchkinland. (right) In 1984, Effanbee manufactured a beautiful, all-vinyl sixteen-inch Garland Doll.

(On facing page, bottom) Allegedly only fifteen-hundred sets were manufactured of these fourteen-inch, cloth-bodied Mego dolls. They were either never marketed commercially or distributed only in limited quantities. (This page, top left) One of four Oz frame-tray puzzles issued by Jaymar in the 1960s. (top right) "Judy Garland as Dorothy" was a hand-painted, five-and-one-half-inch porcelain figure, produced in 1985 as fifth in the Avon Products' "Images of Hollywood Series." In 1987-88, the Franklin Mint was one of the first manufacturers to introduce merchandise commemorating the fiftieth anniversary of MGM's Oz. They produced a series of large porcelain dolls, a set of twenty miniature sculptures (right), and a tiny ruby-slipper pendant of 22-karat gold. (courtesy The Franklin Mint)

Video Posters:
(top left) In 1985, MGM/UA Home Video reissued the videocassette of Oz in a new case and at a reduced price. (above) The 1988 video design emphasized the Wicked Witch. (left) One of five known pairs of ruby slippers designed for Oz, these shoes belonged to Roberta Jeffries Bauman for forty-eight years and were then sold for one hundred sixty-five thousand dollars at Christie's East in 1988. It was the highest price paid to that time for an item of movie memorabilia. (courtesy Christie's New York.)

PART SIX
The Legend

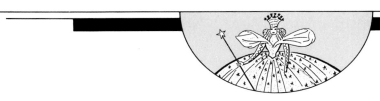

CHAPTER 19

Reunions and Reminiscences

The new plateau of fame first reached by *The Wizard of Oz* in the 1960s owed much to the power of television. But the film's legend had grown quietly long before that, beginning with the initial success of the picture itself. In late 1940, there were even rumors that MGM would follow *Oz* with a film sequel, the project to be produced the next year as a vehicle for Shirley Temple. (She was briefly under contract to Metro in 1941.) Such conjecture was subtle indication of *The Wizard*'s popularity, especially in an era when motion picture entertainment rapidly came and went. More substantial proof of the (perhaps subconscious) hold the film had established on the public was manifested when Judy Garland found "Over the Rainbow" her most requested song at benefits, on Armed Forces Radio and in service camp performances during World War II. Even then, people were warmed by memories of MGM's *Oz*.*

When MGM first began to issue commercial recordings in 1946, one of their first considerations was a series of *Oz* soundtrack songs with Frank Morgan providing new, connective narration as the voice of the Wizard. The project didn't get beyond the planning stage; it took until 1956 for MGM Records to compile and release its best-selling recording of musical and dramatic extracts from the *Oz* tracks.

The continuing popularity of the *Oz* score stemmed, at least in part, from its use in stage adaptations with Baum's story. MGM originally made the film orchestrations available at the request of the St.

Louis Municipal Opera in 1942. Although the script for the stage show was an original one and not that of the picture, the songs more than compensated, and the Muny enjoyed a great success. They periodically revived their production of *Oz*, and news of its popularity soon led other professional companies to seek performance rights to the Arlen/Harburg score. In spite of the non-MGM script, the songs and story made it possible for *The Wizard of Oz* to become a staple of the light-opera and stock circuits well into the 1980s. Frequently film and television stars would topline the stage casts. Margaret Hamilton re-created her Wicked Witch in several of these shows; Buddy Ebsen finally appeared in *Oz* in another. Stage Dorothys ran the gamut from Dorothy Collins to Connie Stevens and Andrea McArdle, and one could also expect to see the likes of Stubby Kaye as the Cowardly Lion or Nancy Kulp (better known as "Miss Jane" on "The Beverly Hillbillies") as "Miss Gulch." Puppeteer Bil Baird used the film songs in a marionette *Oz* off-Broadway in 1968; brief adaptations with film songs became a fixture in ice shows and even the circus in the 1950s and 1960s.

What was perhaps the first genuine adaptation of both film script and score was prepared for the CBS "Lux Radio Theatre" on Christmas Day, 1950. The coast-to-coast broadcast was probably prompted by the success of the 1949 theatrical reissue of the film. Judy Garland re-created the role of Dorothy for Lux; she had made more than twenty films since *The Wizard of Oz*, but that picture had remained one of her greatest hits and affected her career more than that of anyone else who had been involved. Eleven years after the fact, the public still held her in the emotional and spiritual image of Dorothy Gale. When Garland returned to stage work in 1951, her concerts always hit their peak with a rendition of "Over the Rainbow." The song became her unquestioned theme and, over

---

*The Oz series itself was too firmly established to be much influenced by the MGM film, but "Over the Rainbow" was used as a chapter title in John R. Neill's *Lucky Bucky in Oz* (1942), and *The Shaggy Man of Oz* was published in 1949 to capitalize on the film reissue. Jack Snow broached the idea of an Oz book to be titled *Over the Rainbow to Oz* in 1956, but he died before the story could be realized.

(on preceding page) Dress rehearsal for "The Judy Garland Show," October 11, 1963, at CBS Television City in Hollywood.

Miss Gulch and Toto reunited! Margaret Hamilton worked again with terrier Terry three years after their Ozian conflict. This publicity still was posed on one of the sets of Twin Beds, a 1942 United Artists film. (courtesy Michael Patrick Hearn)

the ensuing eighteen years, the media seldom missed the opportunity to refer to Dorothy when reviewing a Garland triumph or trauma. And whatever career heights she was later to hit, the *Oz* connection was invariably revived.

In 1961, tentative negotiations were begun by Garland's agent to use her voice in an Oz cartoon series, though the idea never came to fruition.* Garland enjoyed a brief reunion with Ray Bolger in MGM's *The Harvey Girls* (1945), and they got together again for an episode of her weekly CBS-TV variety show in 1963. The two reminisced informally about *Oz*, showed some film stills, and sang impromptu choruses of "If I Only Had a Brain" and "We're Off to See the Wizard." With guest Jane Powell, they offered "The Jitterbug," although its presentation that night had no Oz overtones.

When Bert Lahr died in December 1967, Garland was so distraught that she canceled a Las Vegas performance at Caesars Palace. She returned to work the next evening and, at the finale of the show, prefaced "Over the Rainbow" by saying, "This I am singing to my dear Cowardly Lion. God bless him." In Decem-

ber 1968, six months prior to her own death, Garland guest-hosted the Merv Griffin TV show and was happily surprised on camera by Margaret Hamilton. "Laugh! Just do that wicked, mean laugh!" implored Garland. Hamilton complied—and brought the house down.

Garland often expressed her gratitude for the fame she won in *Oz* and her delight at having been Dorothy. She also marveled at the money MGM was still making from the film via television and good-naturedly wished she "owned a piece of it." Perhaps the best example of her attitude toward the picture came when the writers of her TV series suggested she build "a funny bit" around "Over the Rainbow." She evenly but immovably refused, referring to the song as "kind of sacred" and concluding, "I don't want anybody, *anywhere* to lose the thing they have about Dorothy and that song."

Most of the *Oz* principal cast enjoyed solid acclaim for their subsequent stage, screen, and television work. Jack Haley semiretired from show business in the 1950s and successfully pursued real-estate and other business ventures. His occasional TV work included a 1970 appearance with Mike Douglas and Terry-Thomas on the former's daily talk show. He sang a bit of "If I Only Had a Heart" that day, perhaps remembering the response the song had won during an earlier appearance he'd made on Jackie Gleason's program. To Haley's surprise, it "went over very well.

*The next year, producer Norman Prescott signed Judy's sixteen-year-old daughter Liza Minnelli to sing and speak the role of Dorothy in his feature cartoon, *Return to the Land of Oz*. Among others in the all-star cast was Margaret Hamilton as Aunt Em. The soundtrack was completed in 1962, but it took Prescott another ten years to finance all the animation and achieve a limited release. The cartoon, retitled *Journey Back to Oz*, was a quick failure.

The audience loved it and applauded like crazy. It touched me, I must admit." Ray Bolger had a Broadway smash in *Where's Charley?* (1948), made several more movies, and became a major supper-club and television attraction. Bert Lahr also got raves on stage in everything from musical revue to Samuel Beckett's *Waiting for Godot* (1956), Feydeau's *Hotel Paradiso* (1957), and S. J. Perelman's *The Beauty Part* (1962). He won the Best Shakespearean Actor of the Year award from the American Shakespeare Festival in 1960 for his performance in *A Midsummer Night's Dream.*

Some of those involved with *Oz* passed away before the picture became a family and familiar television favorite. Victor Fleming died in 1949, Charley Grapewin in 1956, and Clara Blandick in 1962. Billie Burke made her last film in 1960 and then spent her final decade in quiet retirement.

Margaret Hamilton had played perhaps the film's most memorable character—especially to children. She maintained a steady schedule of acting work for more than four decades after *The Wizard of Oz* and successfully sold Maxwell House Coffee as TV's Cora for several seasons (much as Lahr became a cherished spokesman for Frito-Lay potato chips). Hamilton was increasingly interviewed about *Oz* in the 1960s, and she once confessed that she thought the Witch was too frightening for children ("there were some shots that even I was appalled at"). She also made two appearances on the syndicated children's television show "Discovery." The first of these, in 1963, was titled "A Trip to the Land of Oz"; it featured the Wicked Witch in full costume and a fine discussion of Baum's life and career. The second edition (1965) offered Hamilton, again in Witch regalia, in explanations about some of the film's special effects. In 1969, she and Bolger were reunited in an unsuccessful Broadway musical, *Come Summer.*

The television success of MGM's *Oz* led to other Ozzy broadcast ventures. Most were original, if unimaginative, treatments of those Oz characters then in public domain. The programs included "Tales of the Wizard of Oz," a series of cartoon shorts (1961); "Return to Oz," an hour special from the same animators (1964); and Shirley Temple's adaptation of the second Oz book, "The Land of Oz" (1960). MGM produced a weekly series for ABC-TV in 1967–68; "Off to See the Wizard" featured brief animations of the Oz characters as an introduction to suitable family movie fare.

In Summer 1969, an amusement park largely built around the MGM concept of Oz opened on Beech Mountain in Banner Elk, North Carolina. "The Land of Oz" was designed to lead visitors through a park-long re-creation of Dorothy's adventures and included displays of Oz memorabilia along with the usual souvenir and concession stands. It was successful for several years, but public interest dwindled, and it closed in 1980 after its twelfth season.

But the park's opening was another indication that *The Wizard of Oz* had reached a new level of public familiarity. Similar proof came in the references to the film, paraphrases of its dialogue, and parodies of its characters and situations that were turning up in TV situation comedies, comic strips, editorial cartoons, and even adult magazines. *Oz* had, at that point, been on network television eleven times; that fact remained central to the new surge of notoriety.

As the film entered its fourth decade, however, public awareness of *The Wizard of Oz* was extended yet again by two other events: the death of Judy Garland in June 1969 and the auction of MGM costumes and props in May 1970. Both incidents helped punctuate the end of an era. By 1970, the country was deep in a new kind of social unrest and change; the turmoil would continue, but *The Wizard of Oz* remained a vivid annual reminder of a recent, at least outwardly peaceful, past for millions of all ages.

The MGM auction also opened the door for a new level of Oz appreciation: the idea of pop culture as history and investment. On May 17, a pair of the ruby slippers sold for fifteen thousand dollars, the highest price paid for any item at the auction. (A Dorothy dress, the Witch's hat and cloak, the Cowardly Lion skins, and the Wizard's suit also went on the block.) The "unidentified millionaire" who purchased the shoes has, ever since, retained his anonymity, but among those bidding against him that night were actress Debbie Reynolds (who wanted the shoes for a possible Hollywood museum), the Carolina Caribbean Corp. (who wanted display items for the "Land of Oz" park) and, most notably, Culver City Mayor Martin A. Lotz. The latter represented not only the interests of his town—the home of MGM—but also those of a "Save the Ruby Red Slippers" committee. According to the *Los Angeles Times,* Lotz had been "inundated with pledges from civic service groups and the nickels and dimes of children. Hundreds of schoolchildren . . . supported the campaign . . . and thousands signed petitions" to try to keep the ruby slippers in Culver City.

The furor over the slippers not only represented the appreciation level achieved by MGM's *The Wizard of Oz* but, although no one realized it at the time, provided an indication of greater Oz legend to come.

CHAPTER 20

Merchandising

The majority of the original *Wizard of Oz* tie-in products disappeared by the time the film played out the last of its second- and third-run movie-house engagements in 1940. Little additional Oz merchandise appeared during the following decade. Leo Feist reissued the film song sheets in plain white wrappers in the mid-1940s and, a little later, their souvenir songbook was also reprinted in a slightly less elaborate format. (It was kept available until the mid-1960s when an expanded and revised edition appeared.) In the late 1940s, Decca reissued its *Oz* recordings in a new jacket as part of the "Judy Garland Personality Series"; the 78 rpm set was shortly made available as well on a ten-inch long-play album.

Though the 1949 reissue of the film was most successful, Oz merchandise released in the 1950s saw a trend toward more literal adaptations of Baum's original characters. This intensified when *The Wizard of Oz* book entered the public domain in 1956. By the 1960s, however, the annual *Oz* telecast made the MGM concepts more and more familiar to millions of Americans, and the demand began to increase for Oz movie-related collectibles.

In the early 1970s, more than three decades after the original release of *The Wizard of Oz*, a wide variety of toy and novelty items was suddenly made available. Many appeared as a direct result of the successful line of dolls and playsets issued by the Mego Toy Corporation. New products for young Oz enthusiasts ranged from Christmas ornaments to party goods and toiletries and, although the marketing activity diminished only a few years after it began, the fortieth anniversary of the film soon renewed it and brought about yet another level of Oz merchandising.

By the late 1970s, MGM's *The Wizard of Oz* had achieved its legendary status, and collectibles and collector's items were specifically designed to reflect or exploit such fame. The Knowles China Company was among the first to acknowledge this when, beginning in 1977, they offered a series of eight limited edition collector's plates featuring accurate depictions of the

movie characters. Similarly designated collectibles appeared soon after, including posters, figurines, music boxes, calendars, and several sets of dolls. The rush of new Oz merchandise hardly faltered before becoming almost supercharged in anticipation of the film's fiftieth anniversary in 1989.

By then, MGM's *Oz* reached the point where it was being marketed and sought after on at least three different levels: as a branch of the greater Oz legend;

MGM Munchkin Parnell St. Aubin was the happy recipient of one of the Knowles Oz collector's plates on August 17, 1979 (the fortieth anniversary of the film's New York premiere). Tom Foster, director of development for the Bradford Exchange, made the presentation at the Midget Club, a tavern owned and operated at that time by St. Aubin in Chicago.

(right) Durham Industries, Inc., offered wind-up toys that included a walking Scarecrow, Tin Man, and Cowardly Lion, as well as a pair of spinning ruby slippers (1975). (far right) A complete line of MGM Oz children's toiletries was manufactured in 1976 by the Ansehl Company of St. Louis. In addition to this set (which included soap, talc, and moisturizing cream), there were those that featured compacts, lipsticks, perfumes, bubble bath, and foaming bath beads.

(above) In 1975, Marvel and DC Comics joined forces to present an oversize adaptation of the MGM film. Though popular with fans for its fidelity to the plot and look of the 1939 movie, the publication was not successful in the comic marketplace due to its awkward size. It was, however, followed by a similar version of Baum's second Oz book and, due to a contractual agreement with MGM, the illustrated portrayals of the Scarecrow and Tin Woodman were those of the film characters.

as an almost astoundingly famous motion picture classic; and as a focal point in the career of Judy Garland (around whose life and times there was centered a similar archival passion). That *The Wizard of Oz* film became "desirable" in three such major collectible forums may well be an accomplishment unique in American popular culture.

[Latter-day MGM collectibles are also pictured in color on pages 224—229.]

(above) These Oz collector's glasses are unique in that they were available only at Kentucky Fried Chicken restaurants in Kansas in the early 1980s.

CHAPTER 21

Icon

In its fourth and fifth decades, *The Wizard of Oz* quietly, if inevitably, reached another unique plateau of preeminence. There were other films as much enjoyed, other films more respected and critically revered, other films that certainly reflected life on a more adult or intellectual level, other films the equal or superior of *Oz* in cinematic art. *The Wizard of Oz*, however, had become the best-known, most familiar picture of all time. MGM's version of the Oz story had passed into public awareness as had no other popular entertainment. To list the resultant uses of Oz characters, situations, and references would fill a volume of its own.

Stage versions of *The Wizard of Oz* flourished and included two landmark interpretations. Broadway's all-black *The Wiz* (1975) was an original, pop-music retelling of the Baum story, but one reason for its success was the public's familiarity with the plot and characters, thanks to the MGM film. A quality peak was reached with the first official adaptation of both MGM

script and songs when the Royal Shakespeare Company presented *The Wizard of Oz* in London in 1987. (The earlier version had been a favorite in Great Britain and Australia for decades, much in the tradition of holiday pantomime presentations.) The United States first saw this adaptation at the Long Beach (California) Civic Light Opera in July 1988. In October 1988, plans were announced for an expanded $7,500,000 production of *The Wizard of Oz* to tour arenas in the United States and Canada in 1989. (Similar plans for an arena tour had been announced but abandoned in 1973, 1976, and 1982.)*

Throughout the 1970s and 1980s, the MGM concepts of the Oz characters appeared (authorized or not) on greeting cards, postcards, posters, and T-shirts. The treatments were sometimes stunning, sometimes (at best) irreverent. Similar Oz renderings

---

*As early as 1952, Arthur Freed wanted to present MGM's version of *Oz* on Broadway, using the film score and an adaptation of the film script by Yip Harburg and his *Finian's Rainbow* coauthor, Fred Saidy.

Oz cast members from the Long Beach Civic Light Opera pose with their counterparts, July 1988. Cathy Rigby played Dorothy, Carl Packard was the Tin Man, Timothy Smith the Scarecrow, and Michael Tucci the Lion. The Oz statues have been traced back to the MGM auction of 1970. They were later part of a touring truckload of film memorabilia; their earlier history remains a mystery. (courtesy Chip Baldoni)

advertised such products or services as Weight Watchers, Minolta cameras, Reebok shoes, Dunkin' "Munchkin" Donuts, and the National Bowling Council. AT&T used "Over the Rainbow" for background music in 1988–89 television commercials; another TV plug, for the United States Air Force, showed the black-and-white scene of a young man and dog walking through the doorway of a clapboard house onto a full-color airfield.

Editorial cartoons and (especially) newspaper comic strips thrived on Oz parodies or adaptations, whether the statements being made were those of "Doonesbury," "Mother Goose and Grimm," "Marvin," "Bloom Country," "The Family Circus," or "The Wizard of Id." The same influence was even more obvious on television and in films. By the mid-1980s, it would be a rare week of TV viewing that did not provide several direct or indirect references drawn from MGM's *Oz*. The MGM-TV show, "Fame" devoted its February 14, 1983, episode to an affectionate takeoff on the Oz story, tailored to its regular cast and with the High School for the Performing Arts as background.

From the late 1960s, film producers and directors frequently borrowed from the 1939 film to make a point, garner a laugh, or just pay homage—whether in *The Boy Friend, Alice Doesn't Live Here Anymore, Flash Gordon, Volunteers, Gremlins, Poltergeist, Good Morning, Vietnam, Spaceballs,* or *Who Framed Roger Rabbit?* When Margaret Hamilton's character was killed off in Robert Altman's *Brewster McCloud* (1970), the director did a pan shot to her feet and, without explanation, showed the actress wearing a pair of ruby slippers. An entire lackluster film, *Under the Rainbow* (1981), was built around a fictitious story and the fact that one hundred midgets were imported to Hollywood to make a fantasy film in 1938. In the case of the mammothly successful George Lucas *Star Wars* (1977), many critics drew parallels between his characters and scenes with those in MGM's *Wizard of Oz*. The same comparisons were even more pointedly proffered with the release of Steven Spielberg's *E.T.* (1982). The affecting story was frequently described as "Oz in reverse": someone from an unusual country finds himself stranded in a normal country, and his quest throughout is to return home. His newly acquired friends help him along the way and, after a sentimental farewell, watch him depart for his own planet; the spaceship leaves behind it a brief rainbow trail.

Unfortunately, the major Oz motion picture of the era failed as popular entertainment. Walt Disney's *Return to Oz* was a loose retelling of episodes from the second and third Baum books. The Disney picture echoed the MGM version when its Kansas characters doubled for those Dorothy would meet in Oz, and the studio had to negotiate with MGM for the rights to include the concept of the ruby slippers.

Musically, the Arlen/Harburg *Oz* songs withstood rock, country-western, and disco interpretations in the late 1960s and 1970s. More meaningful were the original references to the film in the pop song lyrics of singers like Don McLean, the tribute paid by Elton John with his album title, *Good-Bye, Yellow Brick Road,* or the album cover for the Electric Light Orchestra *Eldorado,* which showed a frame blowup of Margaret Hamilton's green hands setting off sparks from Judy Garland's ruby slippers. *Oz* parodies even found their way into MTV pop song videos.

Writing in a more appropriate show-music form, cabaret entertainer/composer Fred Barton built a highly successful 1980s nightclub turn around the *Oz* film character Almira Gulch. His tongue-in-cheek interpretation musically told her life story before, during, and after her *Wizard of Oz* experience. A number of comedy club performers also came to capitalize on the film's renown; Oz routines became a standard portion of many acts.

Surviving *Oz* cast and crew members were more and more called upon for interviews and participation in *Oz*-related events. Hamilton, Bolger, Haley, LeRoy, and several of the Munchkins were among those occasionally gathered in connection with the annual tele-showing, or to publicize new Oz products, or to appear at Oz festivals or conventions. Bolger and Haley were interviewed on the NBC "Tomorrow" program in December 1977, the former waxing rhapsodic about the *Oz* experience, and Haley grumbling delightedly about the murderous work schedule and makeup problems. Margaret Hamilton appeared as the Witch on a 1976 episode of the PBS-TV "Sesame Street" and later paid a visit to "Mister Rogers' Neighborhood" to talk about the film.

After the success of *The Making of The Wizard of Oz,* Aljean Harmetz adapted her knowledge and contacts with the film's survivors into a thirty-minute PBS documentary (1980). This was in some ways an extension of the "Wizardry of Oz" day, sponsored by the University of Southern California the preceding May. Harmetz also moderated a symposium on the film at the Academy of Motion Picture Arts and Sciences in May 1983. The evening included reminiscences from Hamilton, Bolger, LeRoy, Jerry Maren, Ken Darby, William Tuttle, and John Lee Mahin.

The public's affection for the *Oz* movie was stimulated by such events, as was their curiosity about the

On March 3, 1976, the Center of Films for Children in Los Angeles presented awards to MGM Oz participants. Pictured honorees here include (from left) Jack Haley (with son, Jack, Jr.), Liza Minnelli (who accepted the "Ruby Slipper" trophy for her mother), Mervyn LeRoy, "Munchkin" Billy Curtis, and Ray Bolger. Also cited: Margaret Hamilton, Noel Langley, Harold Arlen, "Yip" Harburg, Harold Rosson, Buddy Gillespie, Jack Dawn, and George Stoll. (CBS photograph by Tony Esparza)

The surviving Oz stars were reunited for publicity pictures in 1970; they would meet again several times in the ensuing years for Oz-related events.

film's deleted footage. Jack Haley, Jr., garnered press space and fan gratitude when he presented Arlen's home movies of "The Jitterbug" dress rehearsal on a 1983 episode of the ABC-TV "Ripley's Believe It or Not!" (The scenes had been shown in part on the CBS "Twentieth Century" profile of the composer in 1964.) Haley also unveiled the cut Ray Bolger dance to "If I Only Had a Brain" as a highlight of *That's Dancing!*, a 1985 theatrical release.

Oz festivals began popping up all over the country. There were already long-established conventions held each year by the International Wizard of Oz Club that celebrated every aspect of Oz lore, including the MGM film. Then, in the 1980s, a regular "Oz Day" was presented by citizens of Chittenango, New York, birthplace of L. Frank Baum. Although conceived as a tribute to the Oz author, the activities were more geared toward those who knew Oz from its MGM incarnation. An original Oz play and parade became a standard part of the Mount Holyoke College Summer Theatre program in South Hadley, Massachusetts, and the Yellow Brick Road Gift Shop and Museum in Chesterton, Indiana, found itself the centerpiece of an annual, lavish "Wizard of Oz Days" weekend. "Dorothy's House," a re-creation of the MGM farm dwelling, was constructed in Liberal, Kansas, to honor the legendary little American girl who first discovered Oz; in Grand Rapids, Minnesota, another legendary American girl was celebrated in her hometown with the foundation of the Judy Garland Museum.

The myriad Oz gatherings were well covered by the media, as were the passings of the remaining members of the film's production staff and principal cast. Telecast announcements and newspaper headlines always linked the actors with their Oz characters when noting the deaths of Jack Haley on June 6, 1979, Margaret Hamilton on May 16, 1985, and Ray Bolger on January 15, 1987. Oz producer Mervyn LeRoy died on September 13, 1987; Arthur Freed had passed away fourteen years earlier on April 12, 1973. Oz lyricist E. Y. Harburg died on March 5, 1981, and composer Harold Arlen on April 23, 1986.

Through all this, mania for collecting Oz MGMemorabilia reached new heights. This was especially apparent when several more pairs of the ruby slippers came up for auction. The first of these, made available through Christie's East in New York in October 1981, brought twelve thousand dollars. Five years later, one of the Judy Garland Dorothy dresses sold for twenty thousand dollars at New York's Sotheby's.* But ruby-slipper fanaticism really hit its stride after the *Los Angeles Times* published a lengthy two-part feature on the history and collectibility of the shoes on March 13 and 20, 1988. Journalist Rhys Thomas traced the origins of all known pairs of ruby slippers preparatory to the June 21 Christie's auction of those belonging to Roberta Jeffries Bauman. She had won them in a 1940 "best movie" competition through her high school. After forty-eight years in Mrs. Bauman's possession, the shoes were sold by Christie's for one hundred sixty-five thousand dollars, the highest price ever paid to that time for an item of movie memorabilia. When asked by Christie's Julie Collier what he would do with the shoes, the anonymous buyer said, simply, "Treasure them." (On December 16, 1988, Sotheby's in New York auctioned the Oz Witch's hat for thirty-three thousand dollars.)

In 1979, the general public was given the opportunity to see a pair of ruby slippers when they were donated to the Smithsonian Institution in Washington, D.C. (The shoes were thought to be those purchased at the MGM auction in 1970.) The Smithsonian estimates that more than five million people see the shoes annually; they are the single most popular item in their field. The Smithsonian also has a draft of one of Noel Langley's early Oz scripts, and Ray Bolger's Scarecrow costume, donated by the actor himself.

The Wizard of Oz continued to gain other kinds of

*There are a number of Dorothy dresses in existence. (Several duplicates were made for Judy Garland in 1938–39.) One of them was donated to the Catholic University of America in Washington, D.C. in 1973. The presentation was made by the University's artist-in-residence, Mercedes McCambridge.

The Mt. Holyoke College Summer Theatre Festival first did an Oz play in 1983. With its success, their adaptations of both traditional and original Oz stories became an annual event in South Hadley, Massachusetts, and the celebration grew to include an Oz costume parade of hundreds of children. Grand Marshall of the parade in 1986 was Margaret Pellegrini (above), one of the original "sleepyhead" Munchkins in the 1939 film; she poses here with three local representatives of the Lollipop Guild. "Coroner" Meinhardt Raabe and his wife Marie participated in the Festival in 1987. (photograph by Fred Moore)

acclaim as well. On November 17, 1977, thousands of members of the American Film Institute named it one of America's ten greatest movies. It made a similar "ten best" listing in 1987 when the Centennial Committee of the Hollywood Chamber of Commerce polled one hundred critics, film experts, and historians. On June 30, 1987, the *Los Angeles Times* ranked Oz as one of their readers' eighteen favorite films, and it was shown on one of the eighteen theater screens of the new Cineplex Odeon Cinerama at Universal City.

Mass Oz enthusiasm grew again to herald the film's fiftieth anniversary in 1989, and a new 1980s achievement was posted as well: the picture began its sixth decade with the estimate that world-wide sales of *The Wizard of Oz* on video cassette were approaching two million units.

On its fiftieth anniversary, *The Wizard of Oz* is not only the most widely seen and most familiar film in history but, arguably, the most beloved motion picture of all time. It has defied changing tastes in music, entertainers, and entertainment to become a cornerstone of American popular folklore, and its unique status may never be equaled, if only because the elements that produced its achievements no longer exist.

The environment that created *The Wizard of Oz* is gone now. But Hollywood's "studio system"—probably best exemplified by the MGM of the 1930s and 1940s—not only brought together an unparalleled group of talented people, it then provided those people with the opportunity, the encouragement, and the financial backing to do their professional best. There were certainly flaws in the procedure and, by today's

Doug Sneyd

Editorial cartoons underscored the loss felt at the passing of principal members of the Oz cast and provided an indication of the place won by the film in the nation's consciousness and heart: (above) for Judy Garland in the Toronto Daily Star *(June 23, 1969) by Doug Sneyd; (above right) for Jack Haley in the* Dayton Journal Herald *(June 8, 1979) by Bob Englehart; (right) for Margaret Hamilton in the* Milwaukee Sentinel *(May 18, 1985) by Stuart Carlson.*

This memorial cartoon for Ray Bolger was drawn by Dick Locher and appeared in the Chicago Tribune (January 19, 1987).

auteur theories, *The Wizard of Oz* succeeded in spite of its creative process. But *Oz* seems instead to have blossomed and succeeded *because* of the participation of so many, the fates having somehow brought together those who cared about the project, those who were more than capable at their jobs, those who were inordinately proud of their work. *The Wizard of Oz* was the happy result of their efforts.

There were, of course, other equally successful products of the studio system. But of them all, only *Oz* fell heir to more than thirty national telecasts. That environment, responsible for the burgeoning Oz legend, is gone, too. Cable television and home video have eliminated much of the mass-scale anticipation and sharing of an annual network TV event "for the whole family." *Oz* was its prime beneficiary, and the film's theme, "there's no place like home," made the picture especially meaningful for the audience that grew to love it on television. It was at home that the vast majority of them first saw *The Wizard of Oz*. And as Margaret Hamilton once noted, it didn't matter whether the home was happy or not because, in the words of Ray Bolger, "a home isn't just a place or an abode—it's people, people you love and who love

you. That's a home." *The Wizard of Oz*, shared year after year, came to mean that kind of "home." To children, the film was an extraordinarily special family friend, seen once a year. When they grew up, it was for millions of them a happy, emotional memory.

Obviously, *Oz* was provided with special opportunities to succeed. But in turn it had to be equal to those opportunities, and the talent, the emotions, the associations of *Oz* were all built on the foundation of a solid, simple story. Both book and movie were envisioned, then designed, then realized as an intermingling of pure popular entertainment and a quiet philosophy about the need for sharing and caring, for bravery and intelligence, for family, friends, and love.

All analysis aside, *Oz* is loved because the millions subject to its magic can enjoy it in so many ways. It offers a rare opportunity for involvement and participation, a joyous, restorative, warming entrée to a place where—however briefly—"there isn't any trouble."

MGM was seemingly (if unintentionally) more prophetic than promotional when their 1939 dedication to *The Wizard of Oz* noted, "Time has been powerless to put its kindly philosophy out of fashion."

Many of the following books were of help in the preparation of this pictorial history, and they are recommended to anyone who would like to further explore MGM's *Wizard,* the people who created it, or the marvelous lands of Oz or Show Business:

Harmetz, Aljean, *The Making of The Wizard of Oz* (New York, Alfred A. Knopf, 1977). A detailed examination of the film-making process at the height of the studio system. The Golden Age of MGM and Hollywood are scrutinized through historically important interviews with the *Oz* cast, staff, and crew, material from the MGM files, and behind-the-scenes photographs. (Paperback version from Limelight Editions, New York, 1984; reprinted by Delta Books, New York, in 1989 as a trade paperback—updated, revised, and with a new introduction by Harmetz. The Delta version also restored the color plates from the original Knopf editions.)

Langley, Noel; Ryerson, Florence; and Woolf, Edgar Allan, *The Wizard of Oz: The Screenplay* (New York: Delta, 1989). A facile introduction by Michael Patrick Hearn segues into the first publication of the *Oz* screenplay, including some scenes deleted from the shooting script and finished picture. Illustrated with film stills and other photographs.

Thomas, Rhys, *The Ruby Slippers of Oz: The Power, Passion, and Pursuit of the World's Most Famous Shoes* (Los Angeles: Tale Weaver Publishing, 1989). The history of Dorothy's cinema slippers, from creation to collectibility. A much-expanded trade paperback version of the author's 1988 Los Angeles *Times* articles.

Cox, Stephen, *The Munchkins Remember/The Wizard of Oz and Beyond* (New York: E. P. Dutton, 1989). An illustrated trade paperback that focuses on the little people of *Oz*, their memories of the picture, and their careers before and after MGM.

McClelland, Doug, *Down the Yellow Brick Road* (New York: Pyramid Press, 1976). A journalistic retelling of legends behind the MGM classic in trade paperback format, notable for its assortment of well-reproduced *Oz* film stills. (Scheduled for reissue by Ottenheimer in 1989.)

Also:

Baum, Frank Joslyn and MacFall, Russell P., *To Please A Child* (Chicago: Reilly & Lee Co., 1961). The first full-length biography of L. Frank Baum, Royal Historian of Oz.

Eyles, Allen, *The World of Oz* (Tucson, Arizona: HPBooks, Inc., 1985). A colorful pictorial summation of Oz: books, characters, films, shows, and legends.

Finch, Christopher, *Rainbow* (New York: Grosset & Dunlap, 1975). Probably the definitive biography of Judy Garland to date, both well-researched and objective.

Fordin, Hugh, *The World of Entertainment* (Garden City, New York: Doubleday and Company, Inc., 1975). A fascinating and richly detailed history of MGM's Arthur Freed "Unit," which began with *The Wizard of Oz.* A paperback reprint was issued as *The Movies' Greatest Musicals* by Frederick Ungar Publishing Co., New York, 1984.

Frank, Gerold, *Judy* (New York: Harper & Row, 1975). A highly detailed account of the life and times of Judy Garland, if with less perspective than the Finch book.

Greene, David L. and Martin, Dick, *The Oz Scrapbook* (New York: Random House, 1977). A lavish, intelligent, and beautifully illustrated overview of Oz in all its facets. The two authors are among the most knowledgeable and warmly respected of all Oz historians.

Hearn, Michael Patrick, *The Annotated Wizard of Oz* (New York: Clarkson N. Potter, 1973). The leading Baum authority provides biography, bibliography, and many textual notes to accompany a colorful facsimile of the first edition of *The Wonderful Wizard of Oz.*

Jablonski, Edward, *Happy With the Blues* (Garden City, New York: Doubleday and Company, Inc., 1961). A discerning biography of the *Oz* composer. Reprinted as a trade paperback, *Harold Arlen/Happy With the Blues* by the Da Capo Press, New York, 1986.

Lahr, John, *Notes on a Cowardly Lion* (New York: Alfred A. Knopf, 1969). Bert Lahr's life, from burlesque to Broadway, in an affecting portrait by his son. Reprinted as a trade paperback by Limelight Editions, New York, 1981.

LeRoy, Mervyn (as told to Alyce Canfield), *It Takes More Than Talent* (New York: Alfred A. Knopf, 1953). The *Oz* producer examines the film-making process.

LeRoy, Mervyn (as told to Dick Kleiner), *Take One* (New York: Hawthorn Books, 1974). An autobiography.

Morella, Joe and Epstein, Edward, *Judy/The Films and Career of Judy Garland* (New York: The Citadel Press, 1969). A pleasant, well-illustrated survey of the Garland motion pictures with a brief biography and examination of her other performing activities.

Watson, Thomas J. and Chapman, Bill, *Judy/Portrait of an American Legend* (New York: McGraw-Hill Book Company, 1986). The best of the Garland books from the point of view of glowing photographs and the most complete, concise recap of her extraordinary career.

These books provided additional background on Oz, on Hollywood or Broadway, on specific performers or craftspeople—or all of the above:

Astor, Mary, *A Life on Film* (New York: Delacourte Press, 1967)
Barnes, Clive (introduction), *The New York Times Directory of the Theatre* (New York: An Arno Press Book published in cooperation with Quadrangle/The New York Times Book Co., 1973)
Behlmer, Rudy (editor), *Memo from David O. Selznick* (New York: The Viking Press, 1972)
Bordman, Gerald, *American Musical Theatre/A Chronicle* (New York: Oxford University Press, 1978)
Brownlow, Kevin, *The Parade's Gone By...* (New York: Alfred A. Knopf, 1969)
Burke, Billie (with Cameron Shipp), *With a Feather on My Nose* (New York: Appleton-Century-Crofts, Inc., 1949)
Dahl, David and Kehoe, Barry, *Young Judy* (New York: Mason/Charter, 1975)
Denton, Clive (and Kingsley Canham), *The Hollywood Professionals: King Vidor, John Cromwell, Mervyn LeRoy* (New York: A. S. Barnes & Co., 1976)
Eames, John Douglas, *The MGM Story* (New York: Crown Publishers Inc., 1975)
Green, Stanley, *Ring Bells! Sing Songs!/Broadway Musicals of the 1930's* (New Rochelle, New York: Arlington House, 1971)
Halliwell, Leslie, *The Filmgoer's Companion,* Fourth Edition (New York: Hill and Wang, 1974)
Haver, Ronald, *David O. Selznick's Hollywood* (New York: Alfred A. Knopf, 1980)
Henderson, Mary C., *The City and the Theatre/New York Playhouses from Bowling Green to Times Square* (Clifton, New Jersey: James T. White & Company, 1973)
Hemming, Roy, *The Melody Lingers On/The Great Songwriters and Their Movie Musicals* (New York: Newmarket Press, 1986)
Hirschhorn, Clive, *The Hollywood Musical* (New York: Crown Publishing Inc., 1981)
Michael, Paul (editor-in-chief), *The American Movies Reference Book/The Sound Era* (Englewood Cliffs, New Jersey: Prentice-Hall, Inc., 1969)
Osborne, Robert, *Academy Awards Illustrated* (Hollywood: Marvin Miller Enterprises, 1965)
Parish, James Robert and Bowers, Ronald L., *The MGM Stock Company* (New Rochelle, New York: Arlington House, 1973)
Shipman, David, *The Great Movie Stars/The Golden Years* (New York: Crown Publishers, Inc., 1970)
Thomas, Lawrence B., *The MGM Years* (New York: Columbia House, 1972)
Thomas, Tony and Terry, Jim, *The Busby Berkeley Book* (New York: New York Graphic Society Ltd., 1973)
Tormé, Mel, *The Other Side of the Rainbow/with Judy Garland on the Dawn Patrol* (New York: William Morrow and Company, Inc., 1970)
Wilk, Max, *They're Playing Our Song* (New York: Atheneum, 1973)

[Note: It would be impossible to list all of the newspaper, magazine, television, and radio features that enabled us to assemble portions of this history. Over the years (and especially in the last two decades), there has been a proliferation of interviews and articles quoting the film's major and minor participants on their memories of its creation and their reactions to its fame. We extend our gratitude to the literally hundreds of media journalists who—sometimes intentionally, sometimes inadvertently—spurred their subjects on to big and little revelations about *The Wizard of Oz* and thus provided many disparate elements that, when brought together, helped to tell different aspects of the story.]

ACKNOWLEDGMENTS

This celebration of *The Wizard of Oz* has been a collaborative effort far beyond the names of the three principal authors, and these acknowledgments are testimony to the genuine love felt for the film by so many. Whether the following names are those of long-standing friends or newer, "book-vintage" acquaintances, they have contributed to this project in many ways and made possible much of the special material presented here.

The first thank you must go to Jack Haley, Jr., for his friendship and evocative introduction. It was also Jack's enthusiasm and faith that, two years ago, led us to Roger L. Mayer, president and chief executive officer of the Turner Entertainment Company. With Jack as intermediary, Mr. Mayer not only kindly approved our proposal but sent us to Carole Orgel (then manager of licensing for MGM/UA Telecommunications, Inc., and now director of licensing for Turner Home Entertainment). Her energies and spirit for *Oz* matched our own, and it was she who arranged the remaining, all-important corporate cooperation. Among many other Turner employees, Diana R. Brown of the legal department, Lois N. Sloane, Richard May, Ben Presser, Esther Blanchard, and Sharon Inamoto were instrumental in research, help, and hospitality.

Since 1957, the International Wizard of Oz Club has been responsible for much of the continuing interest in Oz, its authors and illustrators, dramatic adaptations. and collectibles. Their comprehensive magazine, *The Baum Bugle*, maintains a record of Oz events past and present and provided invaluable material for this book. Anyone interested in any facet of Oz could find no finer organization; for further information, please send a long, self-addressed stamped envelope to The International Wizard of Oz Club, Inc., P. O. Box 95, Kinderhook, Illinois, 62345.

The international Judy Garland Club began as a branch of an American organization in 1957 but has been run independently since 1963. Their *Rainbow Review* was also an excellent reference tool, and admirers of the legendary "Miss Show Business" are encouraged to contact the Club membership secretary, Peter Gannaway, 1 Bicester Court, Bicester Road, Kidlington, Oxford OX5 2NJ, England.

For many years, anyone interested in entertainment has turned to the *Hollywood Reporter, Daily Variety,* or *Variety* for a thorough account of the industry and its workings. Their past reporting helped supply much information on both the day-to-day activities at MGM fifty years ago and during the *Oz*-related periods since then. We especially acknowledge *Variety* for permission to reprint their reviews of the Capitol Theatre stage show and the "Ford Star Jubilee" telecast; *Daily Variety* for permission to reprint the clipping on page 19; and Steve Sanders and John Ginelli for providing access to the files at the *Hollywood Reporter.* (Steve then continued to champion any and all work done on behalf of the book both in California and elsewhere.)

Specific photo and archival credits appear separately, but if any single organization can be said to have "made" this book, it would be the Academy of Motion Picture Arts and Sciences. The Academy houses an unparalleled collection of source material, and they disseminate it with knowledgeability and pride. Their possessions and professionalism made the many hours spent at the Margaret Herrick Library among the happiest and most exciting of any concerned with the project, and special appreciation is extended to Robert Cushman, Sam Gill, Douglas Edwards, Susan Sheehan, and Richard Stermer. A large percentage of credit for previously unpublished pictures and information goes to them, their associates, and the Academy.

Similar intelligence and assistance was provided by the University of Southern California Cinema-Television Library and Archives of Performing Arts. Anne G. Schlosser, head of the Archives, and Carolyn Harrison were particularly helpful, but specific recognition is due Ned Comstock, whose scholarship and proficiency led to the extraordinary *Oz* items in the Arthur Freed, Roger Edens, and King Vidor Collections.

Miles Kreuger, president of the Institute of the American Musical, was generosity itself in sharing his time, personal knowledge, and the rare production records possessed by the Institute. Other research was undertaken at the New York Public Library for the Performing Arts at Lincoln Center and the Milwaukee Public Library.

Among our personal associates, we especially want to thank:

Meinhardt Raabe and Wallace Worsley for their professional consideration and warm reminiscences;
Michael Patrick Hearn for his invaluable, seemingly limitless knowledge about Oz and L. Frank Baum, and for his friendship and counsel in innumerable situations;
John Graham, who enthusiastically and with great generosity offered advice and material from his own exhaustive research about the life and times of Judy Garland and the film-making process;
Bill Chapman, who opened his Garland collection and provided a number of extraordinary "centerpiece" elements for this book, including the transparencies for pages 31 and 34–37;
Joseph S. Simms for his beneficence in loaning the Adrian costume sketches;
Sarah Fleming and William Tomkin for their assistance and kind efforts in making available the requested and admired elements from the Victor Fleming scrapbook;
Woolsey Ackerman, who provided reference guides and photographs and who, through the Directors' Guild of America, arranged for the Wallace Worsley interview;
Robert A. Baum, Jr., and his family for their warmth and courtesy in sharing prized family memorabilia.

For arranging accommodations in West Hollywood, special thanks go to L'Hermitage Hotels and Cézanne (Kathleen Blazer and Vera and Bud Davidson). Transportation in the Los Angeles area was genially provided by the indefatigable Chip Baldoni and Betty Boop's Used Cars of Bellflower, California.

There were many others who made substantial contributions to the contents of this book. They selflessly opened doors, took time, made telephone calls, paved the way, and/or provided information and material from their own investigations, collections, or family archives—sharing, sending, delivering, entrusting, and enthusing. (In some instances, they have already been credited in the text or captions; in others, they have preferred a certain amount of specific anonymity but can certainly be acknowledged here:) James Auer, Margaret Augustine, Brenda Baum, The Baum Trust, Ruth Berman, the Bradford Exchange (Ginny Sexton), CBS Television (Krystina Slavik and Martin Silverstein), Christie's New York (Bethe T. Goldberg and the late Julie Collier), Contemporary Books, Stephen Cox, Gail and Bruce Crockett, Given Eaton, Buddy Ebsen, Hugh Fordin, the Franklin Mint (Jack Wilke), Michael Gessel, David L. Greene, Douglas G. Greene, Peter E. Hanff, Ted Hake (Hake's Americana & Collectibles, P. O. Box 1444, York, Pennsylvania, 17405), Randy Henderson, Edward Jablonski, Linda LeRoy Janklow, the Kobal Collection (Superstock International, Inc./Bob Cosenza), Barbara S. Koelle, Jane Lahr, Allen Lawson, Marc Lewis, Sid, Lorna, and Joseph Luft, Tod Machin, Rob Roy MacVeigh, Victor Mangum, Ozma Baum Mantele, Dick Martin, Mildred Martin, Dorothy Curtiss Maryott, Christian Matzanke, Pat McMath, Fred M. Meyer, MGM/UA Telecommunications, Inc. (Sue Procko, George Feltenstein, Ralph Tribbey, Kris Larson, Wanda Rachel Glinert, Susan Isaacs, Paul Rich), Fred Moore, NBC Records Administration (Catherine Lim, Marilyn C. Dean), Colonel James and Dorothy Tuttle Nitch, Robert Osborne, Marvin Paige, Les Perkins, Bronson Pinchot, Max Preeo, Brad Saiontz, Justin G. Schiller, Larry Schlick, Stephen Sisters, Robert Sixsmith, Lynne and Dan Smith, James H. Spearo, Charlotte Stevenson, Anne Suter, Rhys Thomas, Ion Trewin (Hodder & Stoughton Publishers, London), Lou Valentino, Bill Van Camp, John Van Camp, and Richard L. Wall.

For their active help, support, encouragement, advice, and friendship, we would like to thank: Michael Adams, Russell Adams, Barbara Arnstein, Michael Barham, Herman Bieber, Judy Bieber, Sherry Biggart, Tom Bonawitz, Jo Moeller Bostedt, the Bramson Entertainment Bureau, Langley Brandt, Richard Brock, Jean Brockway, Ed Brody, Tom Brook (British Broadcasting Corporation), Ann Dorszynski Caird, Ron Cohen, Carlos Colón, Martha Coolidge, Chuck Cowherd, Michael Cruz, Scott Cummings, the staff and especially the "bureau girls" of the Cunard Princess, Arlene Del Fava, the late Judy-Lynn del Rey, Dana Correll Dial, Lucinda Ballard Dietz, John F. Dion, Albert DiOrio, Eric Donlan, Michael Fastert, Michael Feinstein, Jan Fischer, Shula Fischer, Helen Fisher, Irene Fisher, Harry Forbes, Virginia Fowler, the late Dore Freeman, Dorothy and Walter Fricke, Erin, Linda, and Michael Fricke, Sonny Gallagher, Peter Gannaway, Kurt Gardner, Eric Gjovaag, Geoffrey Gould, Gregg Gourley, John Grant, the late James E. Haff, Pat Hammond, the Reverend Dale D. Hansen and St. Luke's Lutheran Church (New York City), Ronald Haver, Susan Heath, David Heeley, Ray and Marguerite Heiden, Martha Henard, Ted Heyck, Joe Hoffman, Liese Jacobson, James Jensen, Tom Jones, Marge Karney, Joan Kramer, Kim Kuhlmann, Wayne Lawless, Erik Liberman, Martha Liehe, Tom Lynch, Frank Mannino, Fred Martin, Patrick Maund, Deanna Mayer, Tom and Mary McCabe, Fred McFadden, Robin McMaster, Richard Mills, Barry Monush, Jean Nelson and the Yellow Brick Road Gift Shop and Museum (Chesterton, Indiana), Pastor E. H. and Juanita Neuenschwander and the West Hollywood Community Church, Mrs. Gerald F. O'Brien, Robin Olderman, John R. Olson, Fred Orlanski, Lynn Webster and Rod Oram, Charlotte Oshe, Frederick E. Otto, Joseph W. Page, Sue LeBeau Parry, Mr. and Mrs. John Pattrick, Boots and Fran Pedersen, Shelley Pedersen, the Reverend David Peters, Judy Pike, Roslyn Portnoy, Gwen Potter, Ned Price, David Rambo, Dorothy Raye, David Rebella, Rachel Reckford, Scott Rokosny, Robert Rosterman, Wendy Roth, Sam Rush, Tom and Hal and Jane Sando, Kathy Hawkins Sanford, Hollene Scarfone, Jul Scarfone, Tony Scarfone, Mike Scarfone, Nick Scarfone, Scott Schecter, Michael Schurr, Dorothy Scott, Ken Sephton, Eric Shanower, Erickson Skye, Donald F. Smith, Lee Speth, Donald Stannard, Chris Sterling, Beulah H. Stillman, William L. H. Stillman and sons, Larry Stouch, Eric Tasker, Bob Tetirick, Bev, Johna, and Amy Tiedke, Patty Tobias, Judy Tucker, Drew Vaupen, Emily, Nick, Vince, Joe and Christine Schimenz Vitrano, Michael Vodde, Peter Vogt, John Walther, Tom Watson, Betty Welch, Nancy West, Elaine Willingham, the Reverend Raymond Wood, Jeffrey Woodman, and Robert Jon Yudysky.

Over and above the other credits, we acknowledge those who saw to it that all the components were brought together and realized in what to us has been the best possible manner:

Mitchell Rose, our agent, who provided first belief, quiet encouragement, and—in the face of many obstacles—"meritorious conduct, extraordinary valor, and conspicuous bravery";

Michaelis/Carpelis Design Associates, Inc., who produced a distinctive, sparkling pictorial concept and instinctively created the book we'd envisioned: Sylvain Michaelis, Irene Carpelis, and their staff (Rachel Geswaldo, Marianne Palladino, Amy Theiss-Kravatz);

James Frost, our editor, who offered unrelenting faith, knowledge, compassion, patience, and perfectly tempered jubilance; and all of those at (or associated with) Warner Books, for exemplary service in their Oz-associated duties, especially Christine Barba, Blanche Bayless, Olivia Blumer, Michele Brinson, Nick Caputo, Charles Conrad, Tom Dupree, Susan Edelman, Jeffrey Gorney, Ellen Herrick, Jenny Keenan, Harvey Jane Kowal, Fred Marcellino, Rachel Mendez, Jackie Meyer, Anne Douglas Milburn, Robert Miller (now at Dell), Charles Morea, Harry Nolan, Paul O'Halloran (now at G. P. Putnam's Sons), Katharine Phillips, Laurie Pittelli, Laura-Ann Robb, Denise Schultheis, Ann Schwartz, Karen Torres, Kate Wheble, and Margaret Wolf.

Special, additional photography for the book was done by the Tim McGowan Studios in Lebanon, Pennsylvania, and by Michael Chan in New York City. We thank them for their time, professional expertise, and cooperation.

The final expressions of gratitude go to Patty Fricke for her journalistic input, editorial suggestions, and unwavering, invaluable sisterly belief and support; and to Christopher O'Brien, who lived with (and surrounded by) the project every day from its inception and—despite that—loved it, guided it, and helped to see it through.

The following photographs are reproduced through the courtesy of the Academy of Motion Picture Arts and Sciences:

from the Metro-Goldwyn-Mayer Collection: the frontispiece and pictures on pages 51 (top left), 64, 70 (right center), 80, 85 (top center), 95, 99 (top), 101 (center), 103 (top), 106 (top), 114, 117 (top), 141–144, 148, 159, 160 (top), 163, 164, 189, 209

from the John Truwe Collection: pictures on pages 46, 47, 48 (top center and right, bottom right and left), 49, 50, 51 (top right, bottom right), 52, 53, 54 (right top and bottom), 55, 56, 57, 58, 59, 61, 72, 73, 74 (bottom left and right), 75 (top left), 79 (bottom left), 103 (bottom)

from the Tom Tarr Technicolor Collection: the frame enlargements on the rear dust jacket and on pages 11–14, 87

from the A. Arnold Gillespie Collection: special effects sheets on page 105 (bottom); special effects sheets and frame enlargement on page 113

The Academy also provided much-appreciated access to materials in the Hedda Hopper, Louella O. Parsons, and Sidney Skolsky collections.

Illustrations on the following pages are reprinted courtesy of the University of Southern California Cinema-Television Library and Archives of Performing Arts:

from the Arthur Freed Collection: pages 19 (bottom), 27, 29, 40, 116 (bottom), 117 (bottom), 119 (top), 120 (bottom)

from the Roger Edens Collection: page 41

from the King Vidor Collection: page 107

Illustrations on the following pages are reprinted by permission of the Turner Entertainment Company: pages 21, 24, 44, 78 (top), 81, 100 (bottom), 101 (top).

We gratefully acknowledge the permission of The Baum Trust to reprint materials to which they retain the rights.

Illustration on page 19 (top), copyright 1938 *Daily Variety* Ltd. Reprinted by permission.

Song lyrics from "The Jitterbug" (page 116), "If I Only Had a Brain" (page 117), and "Ding! Dong! The Witch Is Dead" (page 120): composers E. Y. Harburg, Harold Arlen, © 1938, 1939 (renewed 1966, 1967), Metro-Goldwyn-Mayer, Inc. Rights assigned SBK Catalogue Partnership. All rights controlled and administered by SBK Feist Catalog, Inc. All rights reserved. International Copyright secured. Used by permission.

Song lyric from "Over the Rainbow" (page 119): composers E. Y. Harburg, Harold Arlen, © 1938, 1939 (renewed 1966, 1967), Metro-Goldwyn-Mayer, Inc. Assigned to Leo Feist, Inc. Rights of Leo Feist, Inc. assigned by SBK Catalogue Partnership. All rights controlled and administered by SBK Feist Catalog, Inc. International Copyright secured. Made in U.S.A. Used by permission.

Illustration on pages 128–29, courtesy *Life* Picture Service; reprinted with permission, © *Life* Magazine, Time, Inc.

Illustration on page 138 (top) copyright 1939 *Baltimore Sun Times.* Reprinted by permission of the *Baltimore Sun.*

Illustrations on page 139 (top) copyright 1939 *Family Circle.* Reprinted courtesy *Family Circle.*

Illustration on page 157 (top) copyright 1939 Bobbs Merrill Company; (right center) copyright 1939 by Grosset & Dunlap; copyright renewed, reprinted by permission.

Illustration on page 158 reprinted courtesy Checkerboard Press.

Illustrations on page 162 and 215 copyright 1939 and 1956, respectively, by *Variety.* Reprinted by permission.

Illustration on page 170 (top left), copyright 1939 by Newspaper Enterprise Association.

Illustrations on page 181 (top left and right) reproduced courtesy MCA Records; (middle right) copyright Capitol Records.

Illustration on page 182 (bottom right) used by permission of Jimmy Ienner.

Illustrations on page 214 (bottom right) and 217 (top right) reprinted with permission from *TV Guide®* Magazine. Copyright © 1956, 1960 by Triangle Publications, Inc., Radnor, Pennsylvania.

Illustration on page 223 (left column) reprinted courtesy the *Milwaukee Journal;* (top right) reprinted courtesy the *Los Angeles Herald Examiner* and the *Hollywood Citizen-News.*

Illustration on page 236 (bottom left) © 1975 by Marvel Comics Group and National Periodical Publications, Inc.

Illustration on page 241 (top left) reproduced courtesy Doug Sneyd; (top right) reproduced courtesy the *Dayton Journal Herald* and Bob Englehart; (bottom) reproduced courtesy Stuart Carlson, © 1985 the *Milwaukee Sentinel.*

Illustration on page 242 reprinted by permission of Tribune Media Services.

"Academy Award®" (or "Oscar®") is the registered trademark and service mark of the Academy of Motion Picture Arts and Sciences.

Photograph of John Fricke by Michael Chan. Photographs of Jay Scarfone and William Stillman by Tim McGowan.

Entertainer JOHN FRICKE serves on the board of directors of the International Wizard of Oz Club and is past editor-in-chief of their magazine. While a teenager in 1969, he researched and wrote for the Club the first historical account of the making of MGM's *The Wizard of Oz.* He was creative consultant for the award-winning PBS television program, "Judy Garland: The Concert Years" and has provided editorial guidance for several books on the singer/actress. A graduate of Northwestern University's Medill School of Journalism, Fricke has written for newspapers in his native Milwaukee and worked in theatrical publicity both there and in New York City, where he now makes his home. His work as a singer has included performances at the Rainbow Room and Town Hall in New York, the MGM Grand Hotel in Las Vegas, and on cruise ships for Cunard (including the Queen Elizabeth II), Sitmar, and the Mississippi Queen line.

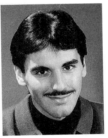

JAY SCARFONE is an honors graduate of his hometown Rochester Institute of Technology. He has collected MGM *Oz* memorabilia since childhood, and his articles on that topic have appeared in several collector's magazines. Scarfone is a public accountant in Pennsylvania and—like his coauthors—a member of the International Wizard of Oz Club.

WILLIAM STILLMAN is a Pennsylvania freelance illustrator whose drawings have appeared in the magazine *Oziana.* He has also taught art on the elementary school level and worked with developmentally disabled adults. An expert on the original 1939 *Oz* film collectibles, he has written for such publications as *Collector's Showcase.* Stillman is a graduate of Millersville University in Pennsylvania.

OZ the Magnificent has granted your wish!

**THE 50TH ANNIVERSARY, LIMITED EDITION VIDEOCASSETTE!
COMPLETELY RESTORED TO ORIGINAL THEATRICAL LUSTRE!
RARE FILM CLIPS NEVER BEFORE AVAILABLE ON VIDEO!**

No matter how many times you've enjoyed this MGM classic, you've never seen it like this! The technical wizards at MGM/UA Home Video have uncovered rare, original Technicolor materials from the Emerald City archives to provide you with the ultimate OZ.

Specially packaged, this Limited Collector's Edition includes an illustrated 24-page booklet about the production!

The cassette also features rare film clips of Ray Bolger's "Scarecrow Dance" outtake ... Judy Garland accepting her 1939 Oscar®...OZ "home movies" of the cast on the set ... the theatrical release trailer and more!

ONLY
$24.95*

FOR A
LIMITED TIME ONLY
wherever video is sold.
Also available on
Laser Videodisc!

MGM/UA HOME VIDEO   **Turner**

"Oscar®" is the registered trademark and service mark of the Academy of Motion Picture Arts & Sciences.
Design © 1989 Turner Entertainment Co. All Rights Reserved. *Suggested videocassette list price. Price slightly higher in Canada.